FROM THE MAKER OF THE TEST

The Official SAT Subject Test Study Guide

Mathematics 2

The College Board
New York, N.Y.

About the College Board

The College Board is a mission-driven not-for-profit organization that connects students to college success and opportunity. Founded in 1900, the College Board was created to expand access to higher education. Today, the membership association is made up of over 6,000 of the world's leading educational institutions and is dedicated to promoting excellence and equity in education. Each year, the College Board helps more than seven million students prepare for a successful transition to college through programs and services in college readiness and college success—including the SAT® and the Advanced Placement Program®. The organization also serves the education community through research and advocacy on behalf of students, educators, and schools.

For further information, visit collegeboard.org

Copies of this book are available from your bookseller or may be ordered from College Board Publications at store.collegeboard.org or by calling 800-323-7155.

Editorial inquiries concerning this book should be addressed to the College Board, SAT Program, 250 Vesey Street, New York, New York 10281.

ISBN 13: 978-1-4573-0932-8

Printed in the United States of America

3 4 5 6 7 8 9   23 22 21 20 19 18

Distributed by Macmillan

Contents

The SAT Subject Tests

About SAT Subject Tests

SAT Subject Tests™ are a valuable way to help you show colleges a more complete picture of your academic background and interests. Each year, nearly one million Subject Tests are taken by students throughout the country and around the world to gain admission to the leading colleges and universities in the U.S.

SAT Subject Tests are one-hour exams that give you the opportunity to demonstrate knowledge and showcase achievement in specific subjects. They provide a fair and reliable measure of your achievement in high school—information that can help enhance your college admission portfolio. The Mathematics Level 2 Subject Test is a great way to highlight your understanding, skills, and strengths in mathematics.

This book provides information and guidance to help you study for and familiarize yourself with the Mathematics Level 2 Subject Test. It contains actual, previously administered tests and official answer sheets that will help you get comfortable with the tests' format, so you feel better prepared on test day.

The Benefits of SAT Subject Tests

SAT Subject Tests let you put your best foot forward, allowing you to focus on subjects that you know well and enjoy. They can help you differentiate yourself in a competitive admission environment by providing additional information about your skills and knowledge of particular subjects. Many colleges also use Subject Tests for course placement and selection; some schools allow you to place out of introductory courses by taking certain Subject Tests.

Subject Tests are flexible and can be tailored to your strengths and areas of interest. These are the **only** national admission tests where **you** choose the tests that best showcase your achievements and interests. You select the Subject Test(s) and can take up to three tests in one sitting. With the exception of listening tests, you can even decide to change the subject or number of tests you want to take on the day of the test. This flexibility can help you be more relaxed on test day.

REMEMBER

Subject Tests are a valuable way to help you show colleges a more complete picture of your academic achievements.

Who Should Consider Subject Tests?

Anyone can take an SAT Subject Test to highlight their knowledge of a specific subject. SAT Subject Tests may be especially beneficial for certain students:

- Students applying to colleges that require or recommend Subject Tests—be aware that some schools have additional Subject Test requirements for certain students, majors, or programs of study

- Students who wish to demonstrate strength in specific subject areas

- Students who wish to demonstrate knowledge obtained outside a traditional classroom environment (e.g., summer enrichment, distance learning, weekend study, etc.)

- Students looking to place out of certain classes in college

- Students enrolled in dual-enrollment programs

- Homeschooled students or students taking courses online

- Students who feel that their course grade may not be a true reflection of their knowledge of the subject matter

The SAT Subject Tests in Mathematics are particularly useful for students interested in majors with a quantitative focus, including Economics and STEM (Science, Technology, Engineering and Math) majors.

Who Requires the SAT Subject Tests?

Most college websites and catalogs include information about admission requirements, including which Subject Tests are needed or recommended for admission. Schools have varying policies regarding Subject Tests, but they generally fall into one or more of the following categories:

- Required for admission

- Recommended for admission

- Required or recommended for certain majors or programs of study (e.g., engineering, honors, etc.)

- Required or recommended for certain groups of students (e.g., homeschooled students)

- Required, recommended, or accepted for course placement

- Accepted for course credit

- Accepted as an alternative to fulfill certain college admission requirements

- Accepted as an alternative to fulfill certain high school subject competencies

- Accepted and considered, especially if Subject Tests improve or enhance a student's application

In addition, the College Board provides a number of resources where you can search for information about Subject Test requirements at specific colleges.

- Visit the websites of the colleges and universities that interest you.
- Visit College Search at www.collegeboard.org.
- Purchase a copy of *The College Board College Handbook*.

Some colleges require specific tests, such as mathematics or science, so it's important to make sure you understand the policies prior to choosing which Subject Test(s) to take. If you have questions or concerns about admission policies, contact college admission officers at individual schools. They are usually pleased to meet with students interested in their schools.

Subject Tests Offered

SAT Subject Tests measure how well you know a particular subject area and your ability to apply that knowledge. SAT Subject Tests aren't connected to specific textbooks or teaching methods. The content of each test evolves to reflect the latest trends in what is taught in typical high school courses in the corresponding subject.

The tests fall into five general subject areas:

English	History	Mathematics	Science	Languages	
				Reading Only	**with Listening**
Literature	United States History	Mathematics Level 1	Biology E/M	French	Chinese
	World History	Mathematics Level 2	Chemistry	German	French
			Physics	Italian	German
				Latin	Japanese
				Modern Hebrew	Korean
				Spanish	Spanish

Who Develops the Tests

The SAT Subject Tests are part of the SAT® Program of the College Board, a not-for-profit membership association of over 6,000 schools, colleges, universities, and other educational associations. Every year, the College Board serves seven million students and their parents, 24,000 high schools, and 3,800 colleges through major programs and services in college readiness, college admission, guidance, assessment, financial aid, and enrollment.

Each subject has its own test development committee, typically composed of teachers and college professors appointed for the different Subject Tests. The test questions are written and reviewed by each Subject Test Committee, under the guidance of professional test developers. The tests are rigorously developed, highly reliable assessments of knowledge and skills taught in high school classrooms.

Deciding to Take an SAT Subject Test

Which Tests Should You Take?

The SAT Subject Test(s) that you take should be based on your interests and academic strengths. The tests are a great way to indicate interest in specific majors or programs of study (e.g., engineering, pre-med, cultural studies).

You should also consider whether the colleges that you're interested in require or recommend Subject Tests. Some colleges will grant an exemption from or credit for a freshman course requirement if a student does well on a particular SAT Subject Test. Below are some things for you to consider as you decide which test(s) to take.

Think through your strengths and interests

- List the subjects in which you do well and that truly interest you.

- Think through what you might like to study in college.

- Consider whether your current admission credentials (high school grades, SAT scores, etc.) highlight your strengths.

Consider the colleges that you're interested in

- Make a list of the colleges you're considering.

- Take some time to look into what these colleges require or what may help you stand out in the admission process.

- Use College Search to look up colleges' test requirements.

- If the colleges you're interested in require or recommend SAT Subject Tests, find out how many tests are required or recommended and in which subjects.

Take a look at your current and recent course load

- Have you completed the required coursework? The best time to take SAT Subject Tests is at the end of the course, when the material is still fresh in your mind.

- Check the recommended preparation guidelines for the Subject Tests that interest you to see if you've completed the recommended coursework.

- Try your hand at some SAT Subject Test practice questions on collegeboard.org or in this book.

Don't forget, regardless of admission requirements, you can enhance your college portfolio by taking Subject Tests in subject areas that you know very well.

If you're still unsure about which SAT Subject Test(s) to take, talk to your teacher or counselor about your specific situation. You can also find more information about SAT Subject Tests on collegeboard.org.

When to Take the Tests

We generally recommend that you take the Mathematics Level 2 Subject Test after you complete three years of college-preparatory mathematics, prior to your senior year of high school, if possible. This way, you will already have your Subject Test credentials complete, allowing you to focus on your college applications in the fall of your senior year. Try to take the test soon after your courses end, when the content is still fresh in your mind.

Since not all Subject Tests are offered on every test date, be sure to check when the Subject Tests that you're interested in are offered and plan accordingly.

You should also balance this with college application deadlines. If you're interested in applying early decision or early action to any college, many colleges advise that you take the SAT Subject Tests by October or November of your senior year. For regular decision applications, some colleges will accept SAT Subject Test scores through the December administration. Use College Search to look up policies for specific colleges.

This book suggests ways you can prepare for the Subject Test in Mathematics Level 2. Before taking a test in a subject you haven't studied recently, ask your teacher for advice about the best time to take the test. Then review the course material thoroughly over several weeks.

How to Register for the Tests

There are several ways to register for the SAT Subject Tests.

- Visit the College Board's website at collegeboard.org. Most students choose to register for Subject Tests on the College Board website.

- Register by telephone (for a fee) if you have registered previously for the SAT or an SAT Subject Test. Call, toll free from anywhere in the United States, 866-756-7346. From outside the United States, call 212-713-7789.

- If you do not have access to the internet, find registration forms in *The Paper Registration Guide for the SAT and SAT Subject Tests*. You can find the booklet in a guidance office at any high school or by writing to:

    The College Board
    SAT Program
    P.O. Box 025505
    Miami, FL 33102

When you register for the SAT Subject Tests, you will have to indicate the specific Subject Tests you plan to take on the test date you select. You may take one, two, or three tests on any given test date; your testing fee will vary accordingly. Except for the Language Tests with Listening, you may change your mind on the day of the test and instead select from any of the other Subject Tests offered that day.

Student Search Service

The Student Search Service® helps colleges find prospective students. If you take the PSAT/NMSQT®, the SAT, an SAT Subject Test, or any AP® Exam, you can be included in this free service.

Here's how it works: During SAT or SAT Subject Test registration, indicate that you want to be part of the Student Search. Your name is put in a database along with other information such as your address, high school grade point average, date of birth, grade level, high school, email address, intended college major, and extracurricular activities.

Colleges and scholarship programs then use the Student Search to help them locate and recruit students with characteristics that might be a good match with their schools.

Here are some points to keep in mind about the Student Search Service:

- Being part of Student Search is voluntary. You may take the test even if you don't join Student Search.

- Colleges participating in Student Search do not receive your exam scores. Colleges can ask for the names of students within certain score ranges, but your exact score is not reported.

- Being contacted by a college doesn't mean you have been admitted. You can be admitted only after you apply. The Student Search Service is simply a way for colleges to reach prospective students.

- Student Search Service will share your contact information only with approved colleges and scholarship programs that are recruiting students like you. Your name will never be sold to a private company or mailing list.

Keep the Tests in Perspective

Colleges that require Subject Test scores do so because the scores are useful in making admission or placement decisions. Schools that don't have specific Subject Test policies generally review them during the application process because the scores can give a fuller picture of your academic achievement. The Subject Tests are a particularly helpful tool for admission and placement programs because the tests aren't tied to specific textbooks, grading procedures, or instruction methods but are still tied to curricula. The tests provide level ground on which colleges can compare your scores with those of students who come from schools and backgrounds that may be far different from yours.

It's important to remember that test scores are just one of several factors that colleges consider in the admission process. Admission officers also look at your high school grades, letters of recommendation, extracurricular activities, essays, and other criteria. Try to keep this in mind when you're preparing for and taking Subject Tests.

Fee Waivers

Students who face financial barriers to taking the SAT Subject Tests can be granted College Board fee waivers through schools and authorized community-based organizations to cover the cost of testing. Seniors who use a fee waiver to take the SAT will automatically receive four college application fee waivers to use in applying to colleges and universities that accept the waivers. You can learn about eligibility and other benefits offered to help you in the college application process at sat.org/fee-waivers.

Score Choice

In March 2009, the College Board introduced Score Choice™, a feature that gives you the option to choose the scores you send to colleges by test date for the SAT and by individual test for the SAT Subject Tests—at no additional cost. Designed to reduce your test day stress, Score Choice gives you an opportunity to show colleges the scores you feel best represent your abilities. Score Choice is optional, so if you don't actively choose to use it, all of your scores will be sent automatically with your score report. Since most colleges only consider your best scores, you should still feel comfortable reporting scores from all of your tests.

REMEMBER

Score Choice gives you an opportunity to show colleges the scores you feel best represent your abilities.

About collegeboard.org

The College Board website collegeboard.org is a comprehensive tool that can help you be prepared, connected, and informed throughout the college planning and admission process. In addition to registering for the SAT and SAT Subject Tests, you can find information about other tests and services, browse the College Board Store (where you can order *The Official Study Guide for all SAT Subject Tests* and other guides specific to mathematics, science and history), and send emails with your questions and concerns. You can also find free practice questions for each of the 20 SAT Subject Tests. These are an excellent supplement to this Study Guide and can help you be even more prepared on test day.

Once you create a free online account, you can print your SAT admission ticket, see your scores, and send them to schools.

More college planning resources The College Board offers free, comprehensive resources at Big Future™ to help you with your college planing. Visit **bigfuture.org** to put together a step-by-step plan for the entire process, from finding the right college, exploring majors and careers, and calculating costs, to applying for scholarships and financial aid.

How to Do Your Best on the SAT Subject Test

Get Ready

Give yourself plenty of time to review the material in this book before test day. The rules for the SAT Subject Tests may be different than the rules for most of the tests you've taken in high school. You're probably used to answering questions in order, spending more time answering the hard questions and, in the hopes of getting at least partial credit, showing all your work.

When you take the SAT Subject Tests, it's OK to move around within the test section and to answer questions in any order you wish. Keep in mind that the questions go from easier to harder. You receive one point for each question answered correctly. No partial credit is given, and only those answers entered on the answer sheet are scored. For each question that you try, but answer incorrectly, a fraction of a point is subtracted from the total number of correct answers. No points are added or subtracted for unanswered questions. If your final raw score includes a fraction, the score is rounded to the nearest whole number.

Avoid Surprises

Know what to expect. Become familiar with the test and test day procedures. You'll boost your confidence and feel a lot more relaxed.

- **Know how the tests are set up.** All SAT Subject Tests are one-hour multiple-choice tests. The first page of each Subject Test includes a background questionnaire. You will be asked to fill it out before taking the test. The information is for statistical purposes only. It will not influence your test score. Your answers to the questionnaire will assist us in developing future versions of the test. You can see a sample of the background questionnaire at the start of each test in this book.

- **Learn the test directions.** The directions for answering the questions in this book are the same as those on the actual test. If you become familiar with the directions now, you'll leave yourself more time to answer the questions when you take the test.

- **Study the sample questions.** The more familiar you are with question formats, the more comfortable you'll feel when you see similar questions on the actual test.

- **Get to know the answer sheet.** At the back of this book, you'll find a set of sample answer sheets. The appearance of the answer sheets in this book may differ from the answer sheets you see on test day.

- **Understand how the tests are scored.** You get one point for each right answer and lose a fraction of a point for each wrong answer. You neither gain nor lose points for omitting an answer. Hard questions count the same amount as easier questions.

A Practice Test Can Help

Find out where your strengths lie and which areas you need to work on. Do a run-through of a Subject Test under conditions that are close to what they will be on test day.

- **Set aside an hour so you can take the test without interruption.** You will be given one hour to take each SAT Subject Test.

- **Prepare a desk or table that has no books or papers on it.** No books, including dictionaries, are allowed in the test room.

- **Read the instructions that precede the practice test.** On test day, you will be asked to do this before you answer the questions.

- **Remove and fill in an answer sheet from the back of this book.** You can use one answer sheet for up to three Subject Tests.

- **For the mathematics tests,** use the calculator that you plan to use on test day.

- **Use a clock or kitchen timer to time yourself.** This will help you to pace yourself and to get used to taking a test in 60 minutes.

The Day Before the Test

It's natural to be nervous. A bit of a nervous edge can keep you sharp and focused. Below are a few suggestions to help you be more relaxed as the test approaches.

Do a brief review on the day before the test. Look through the sample questions, answer explanations, and test directions in this book, or on the College Board website. Keep the review brief; cramming the night before the test is unlikely to help your performance and might even make you more anxious.

The night before test day, prepare everything you need to take with you. You will need:

- Your admission ticket.

- An acceptable photo ID. (see page 10)

- Two No. 2 pencils with soft erasers. Do not bring pens or mechanical pencils.

- A watch without an audible alarm.

- An approved calculator with fresh batteries.

- A snack.

Know the route to the test center and any instructions for finding the entrance.

Check the time your admission ticket specifies for arrival. Arrive a little early to give yourself time to settle in.

REMEMBER
You are in control.
Come prepared.
Pace yourself.
Guess wisely.

Get a good night's sleep.

Acceptable Photo IDs

- Driver's license (with your photo)

- State-issued ID

- Valid passport

- School ID card

- Student ID form that has been prepared by your school on school stationery and includes a recognizable photo and the school seal, which overlaps the photo (go to www.collegeboard.org for more information)

The most up-to-date information about acceptable photo IDs can be found on collegeboard.org.

REMINDER   What I Need on Test Day

Make a copy of this box and post it somewhere noticeable.

I Need   **I Have**

Appropriate photo ID   _____

Admission ticket   _____

Two No. 2 pencils with clean soft erasers   _____

Watch (without an audible alarm)   _____

Calculator with fresh batteries   _____

Snack   _____

Bottled water   _____

Directions to the test center   _____

Instructions for finding the entrance on weekends   _____

I am leaving the house at _____ a.m.

Be on time or you can't take the test.

On Test Day

You have good reason to feel confident. You're thoroughly prepared. You're familiar with what this day will bring. You are in control.

Keep in Mind

You must be on time or you can't take the test. Leave yourself plenty of time for mishaps and emergencies.

Think positively. If you are worrying about not doing well, then your mind isn't on the test. Be as positive as possible.

Stay focused. Think only about the question in front of you. Letting your mind wander will cost you time.

Concentrate on your own test. The first thing some students do when they get stuck on a question is to look around to see how everyone else is doing. What they usually see is that others seem busy filling in their answer sheets. Instead of being concerned that you are not doing as well as everyone else, keep in mind that everyone works at a different pace. Your neighbors may not be working on the question that puzzled you. They may not even be taking the same test. Thinking about what others are doing takes you away from working on your own test.

Making an Educated Guess

Educated guesses are helpful when it comes to taking tests with multiple-choice questions; however, making random guesses is not a good idea. To correct for random guessing, a fraction of a point is subtracted for each incorrect answer. That means random guessing—guessing with no idea of an answer that might be correct—could lower your score. The best approach is to eliminate all the choices that you know are wrong. Make an educated guess from the remaining choices. If you can't eliminate any choice, move on.

REMEMBER

All correct answers are worth one point, regardless of the question's difficulty level.

IMPORTANT

Cell phones are not allowed to be used in the test center or the testing room. If your cell phone is on, your scores will be canceled.

10 Tips FOR TAKING THE TEST

1. **Read carefully.** Consider all the choices in each question. Avoid careless mistakes that will cause you to lose points.

2. **Answer the easier questions first.** Work on less time-consuming questions before moving on to the more difficult ones.

3. **Eliminate choices that you know are wrong.** Cross them out in your test book so that you can clearly see which choices are left.

4. **Make educated guesses or skip the question.** If you have eliminated the choices that you know are wrong, guessing is your best strategy. However, if you cannot eliminate any of the answer choices, it is best to skip the question.

5. **Keep your answer sheet neat.** The answer sheet is scored by a machine, which can't tell the difference between an answer and a doodle. If the machine mistakenly reads two answers for one question, it will consider the question unanswered.

6. **Use your test booklet as scrap paper.** Use it to make notes or write down ideas. No one else will look at what you write.

7. **Check off questions as you work on them.** This will save time and help you to know which questions you've skipped.

8. **Check your answer sheet regularly.** Make sure you are in the right place. Check the number of the question and the number on the answer sheet every few questions. This is especially important when you skip a question. Losing your place on the answer sheet will cost you time and may cost you points.

9. **Work at an even, steady pace and keep moving.** Each question on the test takes a certain amount of time to read and answer. Good test-takers develop a sense of timing to help them complete the test. Your goal is to spend time on the questions that you are most likely to answer correctly.

10. **Keep track of time.** During the hour that each Subject Test takes, check your progress occasionally so that you know how much of the test you have completed and how much time is left. Leave a few minutes for review toward the end of the testing period.

IMPORTANT

If you erase all your answers to a Subject Test, that's the same as a request to cancel the test. All Subject Tests taken with the erased test will also be canceled.

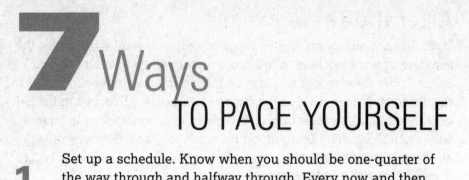

7 Ways TO PACE YOURSELF

1. Set up a schedule. Know when you should be one-quarter of the way through and halfway through. Every now and then, check your progress against your schedule.

2. Begin to work as soon as the testing time begins. Reading the instructions and getting to know the test directions in this book ahead of time will allow you to do that.

3. Work at an even, steady pace. After you answer the questions you are sure of, move on to those for which you'll need more time.

4. Skip questions you can't answer. You might have time to return to them. Remember to mark them in your test booklet, so you'll be able to find them later.

5. As you work on a question, cross out the answers you can eliminate in your test book.

6. Go back to the questions you skipped. If you can, eliminate some of the answer choices, then make an educated guess.

7. Leave time in the last few minutes to check your answers to avoid mistakes.

After the Tests

Most, but not all, scores will be reported online several weeks after the test date. A few days later, a full score report will be available to you online. Your score report will also be mailed to your high school, and to the colleges, universities, and scholarship programs that you indicated on your registration form or on the correction form attached to your admission ticket. The score report includes your scores, percentiles, and interpretive information. You will only receive a paper score report if you indicate that you would like one.

What's Your Score?

Scores are available for free at www.collegeboard.org several weeks after each SAT is given. You can also get your scores—for a fee— by telephone. Call Customer Service at 866 756-7346 in the U.S. From outside the U.S., dial 212 713-7789.

Some scores may take longer to report. If your score report is not available online when expected, check back the following week. If you have not received your mailed score report by eight weeks after the test date (by five weeks for online reports), contact Customer Service by phone at 866 756-7346 or by e-mail at sat@info.collegeboard.org.

Should You Take the Tests Again?

Before you decide whether or not to retest, you need to evaluate your scores. The best way to evaluate how you really did on a Subject Test is to compare your scores to the admissions or placement requirements, or average scores, of the colleges to which you are applying. You may decide that with additional work you could do better taking the test again.

Contacting the College Board

If you have comments or questions about the tests, please write to us at the College Board SAT Program, P.O. Box 025505, Miami, FL 33102, or e-mail us at sat@info.collegeboard.org.

The Mathematics Subject Tests

Purpose

There are two, one-hour SAT Subject Tests in Mathematics: Mathematics Level 1 and Mathematics Level 2. The purpose of these tests is to measure your knowledge of mathematics through the first three years of college-preparatory mathematics for Level 1 and through precalculus for Level 2.

Mathematics Level 1 Subject Test

Format

Mathematics Level 1 is a one-hour broad survey test that consists of 50 multiple-choice questions. The test has questions in the following areas:

- Number and Operations
- Algebra and Functions
- Geometry and Measurement (plane Euclidean/measurement, coordinate, three-dimensional, and trigonometry)
- Data Analysis, Statistics, and Probability

How to Prepare

The Mathematics Level 1 Subject Test is intended for students who have taken three years of college-preparatory mathematics, including two years of algebra and one year of geometry. You are not expected to have studied every topic on the test. Familiarize yourself with the test directions in advance. The directions in this book are identical to those that appear on the test.

Calculator Use

It is NOT necessary to use a calculator to solve every question on the Level 1 test, but it is important to know when and how to use one. **Students who take the test without a calculator will be at a disadvantage.** For about 50 to 60 percent of the questions, there is no advantage, perhaps even a disadvantage, to using a calculator. For about 40 to 50 percent of the questions, a calculator may be useful or necessary.

A graphing calculator may provide an advantage over a scientific calculator on some questions. However, you should bring the calculator with which you are most familiar. If you are comfortable with both a scientific calculator and a graphing calculator, you should bring the graphing calculator.

Mathematics Level 2 Subject Test

Format

Mathematics Level 2 is also a one-hour test that contains 50 multiple-choice questions that cover the following areas:

- Number and Operations
- Algebra and Functions
- Geometry and Measurement (coordinate geometry, three-dimensional geometry, and trigonometry)
- Data Analysis, Statistics, and Probability

How to Prepare

The Mathematics Level 2 Subject Test is intended for students who have taken college-preparatory mathematics for more than three years, including two years of algebra, one year of geometry, and elementary functions (precalculus) and/or trigonometry. You are not expected to have studied every topic on the test.

Choosing Between Mathematics Levels 1 and 2

If you have taken trigonometry and/or elementary functions (pre-calculus), received grades of B or better in these courses, and are comfortable knowing when and how to use a scientific or a graphing calculator, you should select the Level 2 test. If you are sufficiently prepared to take Level 2, but elect to take Level 1 in hopes of receiving a higher score, you may not do as well as you expect. You may want to consider taking the test that covers the topics you learned most recently, since the material will be fresh in your mind. You should also consider the requirements of the colleges and/or programs you are interested in.

Pages 19 and 20 explain in greater detail the similarities and differences between the two Mathematics tests. Take the time to review this information prior to deciding which Mathematics test to take. Seek advice from your high school math teacher if you are still unsure of which test to take. Keep in mind you can choose to take either test on test day, regardless of what test you registered for.

Calculator Use

It is NOT necessary to use a calculator to solve every question on the Level 2 test, but it is important to know when and how to use one. For about 35 to 45 percent of the questions, there is no advantage, and perhaps even a disadvantage, to using a calculator. For about 55 to 65 percent of the questions, a calculator may be useful or necessary.

As with the Level 1 test, a graphing calculator may provide an advantage over a scientific calculator on some questions. However, you should bring the calculator with which you are most familiar. If you are comfortable with both a scientific calculator and a graphing calculator, you should bring the graphing calculator.

Calculator Policy: You may NOT use a calculator on any Subject Test other than the Mathematics Level 1 and Level 2 Tests.

What Calculator to Bring

- Bring a calculator that you are used to using. If you're comfortable with both a scientific calculator and a graphing calculator, bring the graphing calculator.

- Before you take the test, make sure that your calculator is in good working order. You may bring batteries and a backup calculator to the test center.

- The test center will not have substitute calculators or batteries on hand. Students may not share calculators.

- If your calculator malfunctions during one of the Mathematics Level 1 or Level 2 Tests and you do not have a backup calculator, you must tell your test supervisor when the malfunction occurs. The supervisor will then cancel the scores on that test only, if you desire to do so.

What Is NOT Permitted

- Laptops or other computers, tablets, cell phones, or smartphones, smartwatches, or wearable technology

- Models that can access the internet, have wireless, Bluetooth, cellular, audio/video recording and playing, camera, or any smartphone-type feature

- Models that have typewriter-like keypad, pen-input, or stylus

- Models that use electrical outlets, make noise, or have a paper tape (unless approved by the College Board as an accommodation)

- In addition, the use of hardware peripherals such as a stylus with an approved calculator is not permitted. Some models with touch-screen capability are not permitted (e.g., Casio ClassPad)

Additional information about calculator usage can be found on collegeboard.org.

Using Your Calculator

- Only some questions on these tests require the use of a calculator. First decide how you will solve a problem, then determine if you need a calculator. For many of the questions, there's more than one way to solve the problem. **Don't pick up a calculator if you don't need to**—you might waste time.

- **The answer choices are often rounded**, so the answer you get might not match the answer in the test book. Since the choices are rounded, plugging the choices into the problem might not produce an exact answer.

- **Don't round any intermediate calculations**. For example, if you get a result from your calculator for the first step of a solution, keep the result in the calculator and use it for the second step. If you round the result from the first step and the answer choices are close to each other, you might choose the wrong answer.

- **Read the question carefully** so that you know what you are being asked to do. Sometimes a result that you may get from your calculator is NOT the final answer. If an answer you get is not one of the choices in the question, it may be that you didn't answer the question being asked. You should read the question again. It may also be that you rounded at an intermediate step in solving the problem, and that's why your answer doesn't match any of the choices in the question.

- **Think about how you are going to solve the question** before picking up your calculator. It may be that you only need the calculator for the final step or two and can do the rest in your test book or in your head. Don't waste time by using the calculator more than necessary.

- If you are taking the **Level 1 test, make sure your calculator is in degree mode** ahead of time so you won't have to worry about it during the test. If you're taking the Level 2 test, make sure your calculator is in the correct mode (degree or radian) for the question being asked.

- For some questions on these tests, a **graphing calculator** may provide an advantage. If you use a graphing calculator, you should know how to perform calculations (e.g., exponents, roots, trigonometric values, logarithms), graph functions and analyze the graphs, find zeros of functions, find points of intersection of graphs of functions, find minima/maxima of functions, find numerical solutions to equations, generate a table of values for a function, and perform data analysis features, including finding a regression equation.

- **You will not be allowed to share calculators.** You will be dismissed and your scores canceled if you use your calculator to share information during the test, or to remove test questions or answers from the test room.

Comparing the Two Tests

Although there is some overlap between Mathematics Levels 1 and 2, the emphasis for Level 2 is on more advanced content. Here are the differences in the two tests.

Topics Covered*	Approximate Percentage of Test	
	Level 1	Level 2
Number and Operations	10–14	10–14
Operations, ratio and proportion, complex numbers, counting, elementary number theory, matrices, sequences, *series*, *vectors*		
Algebra and Functions	38–42	48–52
Expressions, equations, inequalities, representation and modeling, properties of functions (linear, polynomial, rational, exponential, *logarithmic*, *trigonometric*, *inverse trigonometric*, *periodic*, *piecewise*, *recursive*, *parametric*)		
Geometry and Measurement	38–42	28–32
Plane Euclidean/Measurement	18–22	—
Coordinate	8–12	10–14
Lines, parabolas, circles, *ellipses*, *hyperbolas*, symmetry, transformations, *polar coordinates*		
Three-dimensional	4–6	4–6
Solids, surface area and volume (cylinders, cones, pyramids, spheres, prisms), *coordinates in three dimensions*		
Trigonometry	6–8	12–16
Right triangles, identities, *radian measure*, *law of cosines*, *law of sines*, *equations*, *double angle formulas*		
Data Analysis, Statistics, and Probability	8–12	8–12
Mean, median, mode, range, interquartile range, *standard deviation*, graphs and plots, least-squares regression (linear, *quadratic*, *exponential*), probability		

* Topics in italics are tested on Level 2 only. The content of Level 1 overlaps somewhat with that on Level 2, but the emphasis on 2 is on more advanced content. Plane Euclidean Geometry is not tested directly on Level 2.

Areas of Overlap

The content of Level 1 has some overlap with Level 2, especially in the following areas:

- elementary algebra
- three-dimensional geometry
- coordinate geometry
- statistics
- basic trigonometry

How Test Content Differs

Although some questions may be appropriate for both tests, the emphasis for Level 2 is on more advanced content. The tests differ significantly in the following areas:

Number and Operations. Level 1 measures a more basic understanding of the topics than Level 2. For example, Level 1 covers the *arithmetic of complex numbers*, but Level 2 also covers *graphical and other properties of complex numbers*. Level 2 also includes *series* and *vectors*.

Algebra and Functions. Level 1 contains mainly *algebraic* equations and functions, whereas Level 2 also contains more advanced equations and functions, such as *exponential*, *logarithmic*, and *trigonometric*.

Geometry and Measurement. A significant percentage of the questions on Level 1 is devoted to *plane Euclidean geometry and measurement*, which is not tested directly on Level 2. On Level 2, the concepts learned in plane geometry are applied in the questions on *coordinate geometry* and *three-dimensional geometry*.

The trigonometry questions on Level 1 are primarily limited to *right triangle trigonometry* (*sine*, *cosine*, *tangent*) and *the fundamental relationships among the trigonometric ratios*. Level 2 includes questions about *ellipses*, *hyperbolas*, *polar coordinates*, and *coordinates in three dimensions*. The trigonometry questions on Level 2 place more emphasis on *the properties and graphs of trigonometric functions*, *the inverse trigonometric functions*, *trigonometric equations and identities*, and *the laws of sines and cosines*.

Data Analysis, Statistics, and Probability. Both Level 1 and Level 2 include *mean*, *median*, *mode*, *range*, *interquartile range*, *data interpretation*, and *probability*. Level 2 also includes *standard deviation*. Both include *least-squares linear regression*, but Level 2 also includes *quadratic and exponential regression*.

Scores

The total score for each test is reported on the 200 to 800 point scale. Because the content measured by Level 1 and Level 2 differs considerably, you should not use your score on one test to predict your score on the other.

Note: Geometric Figures

Figures that accompany problems are intended to provide information useful in solving the problems. They are drawn as accurately as possible EXCEPT when it is stated in a particular problem that the figure is not drawn to scale. Even when figures are not drawn to scale, the relative positions of points and angles may be assumed to be in the order shown. Also, line segments that extend through points and appear to lie on the same line *may be assumed to be* on the same line.

When "Note: Figure not drawn to scale," appears below a figure in a question, it means that degree measures may not be accurately shown and specific lengths may not be drawn proportionately.

Mathematics Level 2

Sample Questions

All questions in the Mathematics Level 2 Test are multiple-choice questions in which you are asked to choose the BEST response from the five choices offered. The directions that follow are the same as those in the Mathematics Level 2 test.

Directions: For each of the following problems, decide which is the BEST of the choices given. If the exact numerical value is not one of the choices, select the choice that best approximates this value. Then fill in the corresponding circle on the answer sheet.

Notes: (1) A scientific or graphing calculator will be necessary for answering some (but not all) of the questions in this test. For each question you will have to decide whether or not you should use a calculator.

(2) For some questions on this test you may have to decide whether your calculator should be in the radian mode or in the degree mode.

(3) Figures that accompany problems in this test are intended to provide information useful in solving the problems. They are drawn as accurately as possible EXCEPT when it is stated in a specific problem that its figure is not drawn to scale. All figures lie in a plane unless otherwise indicated.

(4) Unless otherwise specified, the domain of any function f is assumed to be the set of all real numbers x for which $f(x)$ is a real number. The range of f is assumed to be the set of all real numbers $f(x)$, where x is in the domain of f.

(5) Reference information that may be useful in answering the questions in this test can be found on the following page.

Reference Information: The following information is for your reference in answering some of the questions in this test.

Volume of a right circular cone with radius r and height h: $V = \frac{1}{3}\pi r^2 h$

Volume of a sphere with radius r: $V = \frac{4}{3}\pi r^3$

Volume of a pyramid with base area B and height h: $V = \frac{1}{3}Bh$

Surface Area of a sphere with radius r: $S = 4\pi r^2$

Number and Operations

1

From a group of 6 juniors and 8 seniors on the student council, 2 juniors and 4 seniors will be chosen to make up a 6-person committee. How many different 6-person committees are possible?

A) 84

B) 85

C) 1,050

D) 1,710

E) 1,890

Choice (C) is the correct answer. The 2 juniors on the committee can be chosen from the 6 juniors in $\binom{6}{2} = 15$ ways. The 4 seniors on the committee can be chosen from the 8 seniors in $\binom{8}{4} = 70$ ways. Therefore, there are $(15)(70) = 1{,}050$ possibilities for the 6-person committee.

Algebra and Functions

If $x^4 < |x^3|$, then $0 < x < 1$.

2

Which of the following values for x is a counterexample to the statement above?

A) $-\frac{4}{3}$

B) $-\frac{1}{2}$

C) 0

D) $\frac{1}{2}$

E) 1

Choice (B) is the correct answer. A counterexample to the given statement would be a number x such that the hypothesis $x^4 < |x^3|$ is true, but the conclusion $0 < x < 1$ does not hold. Choice (B), $-\frac{1}{2}$, is a counterexample.

It is true that $\left(-\frac{1}{2}\right)^4 < \left|\left(-\frac{1}{2}\right)^3\right|$, since $\frac{1}{16} < \frac{1}{8}$; but it is not true that $-\frac{1}{2}$ lies

between 0 and 1. Choice (D) is incorrect. It is true that $\left(\frac{1}{2}\right)^4 < \left|\left(\frac{1}{2}\right)^3\right|$, but

the conclusion $0 < \frac{1}{2} < 1$ is also true, so $x = \frac{1}{2}$ is not a counterexample.

Choices (A), (C), and (E) are incorrect. None of these values of x satisfies the hypothesis $x^4 < |x^3|$.

3

If $\ln(x) = 1.25$, then $\ln(3x) =$

A) 1.10

B) 1.37

C) 1.73

D) 2.35

E) 3.75

Choice (D) is the correct answer. By the properties of logarithms, $\ln(3x) =$ $\ln(3) + \ln(x) \approx 1.10 + 1.25 = 2.35$.

4

During a thunderstorm, the distance between a person and the storm varies directly as the time interval between the person seeing a flash of lightning and hearing the sound of thunder. When a storm is 4,000 feet away, the time interval between the person seeing the lightning flash and hearing the sound of the thunder is 3.7 seconds. How far away from the person is the storm when this time interval is 5 seconds?

A) 2,960 ft

B) 4,650 ft

C) 5,405 ft

D) 6,284 ft

E) 7,304 ft

Choice (C) is the correct answer. Since the person's distance from the storm varies directly with the time interval between the flash of lightning and the sound of thunder, the distance can be written as $d = kt$, where d is the distance in feet, t is the time in seconds, and k is a constant. This distance is 4,000 feet when the time interval is 3.7 seconds; therefore,

$4,000 = k(3.7)$, and $k = \frac{4,000}{3.7}$. Thus, when the interval between the

lightning flash and the sound of the thunder is 5 seconds, the storm is

$\frac{4,000}{3.7}(5) \approx 5,405$ feet away.

5

If $x = \dfrac{3}{2}$ is a solution to the equation $5(4x - k)(x - 1) = 0$, what is the value of k?

A) $\dfrac{2}{3}$

B) 1

C) 4

D) 5

E) 6

Choice (E) is the correct answer. The expression $5(4x - k)(x - 1)$ is equal to 0 if and only if $x = 1$ or $4x = k$. If $x = \dfrac{3}{2}$, it cannot be true that $x = 1$.

Thus, if $x = \dfrac{3}{2}$ is a solution to the equation, it must be true that $4x = k$.

It follows that $(4)\left(\dfrac{3}{2}\right) = 6 = k$.

6

$$p(t) = 110 + 20 \sin(160\pi t)$$

A certain person's blood pressure $p(t)$, in millimeters of mercury, is modeled above as a function of time, t, in minutes. According to the model, how many times in the interval $0 \le t \le 1$ does the person's blood pressure reach its maximum of 130?

A) 60

B) 80

C) 100

D) 110

E) 130

Choice (B) is the correct answer. The maximum of 130 millimeters is achieved exactly when $\sin(160\pi t) = 1$. The sine function has a value of 1 exactly for arguments $\dfrac{\pi}{2} + 2n\pi$, where n is any integer. Over the interval $0 \le t \le 1$, the argument of $\sin(160\pi t)$ ranges from 0 to 160π. Thus, over the interval in question, $\sin(160\pi t) = 1$, and $p(t) = 110 + 20 \sin(160\pi) = 130$, for $160\pi t = \dfrac{\pi}{2}, \dfrac{5\pi}{2}, \dfrac{9\pi}{2}, \ldots, \dfrac{317\pi}{2}$. Thus, the maximum blood pressure is reached exactly 80 times in the interval. You can also use the period of p to answer the question. The period of p is $\dfrac{2\pi}{|160\pi|} = \dfrac{1}{80}$. This means that the graph of p has one complete cycle every $\dfrac{1}{80}$. On the interval $0 \le t \le 1$, p has 80 complete cycles.

7

x	*f(x)*
−3	87
0	−15
1	15
3	171
5	455

The table above gives selected values for the function *f*. Which of the following could be the definition of *f*?

A) $f(x) = 30x - 15$

B) $f(x) = 30x + 15$

C) $f(x) = 30x^2 + 15$

D) $f(x) = 16x^2 - 14x + 15$

E) $f(x) = 16x^2 + 14x - 15$

Choice (E) is the correct answer. The function in choice (A) takes on the correct values at $x = 0$ and $x = 1$, but the value at $x = 3$ is 75, not 171, so choice (A) cannot be correct. The function in choice (B) does not take on the correct value at $x = 1$, so choice (B) cannot be correct. (Another way to eliminate choices (A) and (B) is to note that $f(x)$ decreases and then increases, so that *f* cannot be linear.) The function in choice (C) takes on only positive values, so choice (C) cannot be correct. The function in choice (D) does not take on the correct value at $x = 0$, so choice (D) cannot be correct. The values of the function in choice (E) do agree with all the values in the table, so this could be the definition of the function. You can also find a quadratic regression for the values using the graphing calculator, which is $y = 16x^2 + 14x - 15$.

8

If $f(x) = \dfrac{1}{x-5}$ and $g(x) = \sqrt{x + 4}$, what is the domain of $f - g$?

A) All *x* such that $x \neq 5$ and $x \leq 4$

B) All *x* such that $x \neq -5$ and $x \leq 4$

C) All *x* such that $x \neq 5$ and $x \geq -4$

D) All *x* such that $x \neq -4$ and $x \geq -5$

E) All real numbers *x*

Choice (C) is the correct answer. The function $f - g$ will be defined at exactly those points where *f* and *g* are both defined. In other words, the domain of $f - g$ is the intersection of the domain of *f* and the domain of *g*. Since $f(x) = \dfrac{1}{x-5}$ is defined for all $x \neq 5$ and $g(x) = \sqrt{x + 4}$ is defined for all $x \geq -4$, the domain of $f - g$ is all *x* such that $x \neq 5$ and $x \geq -4$. You can also examine the graph of $f - g$. The graph is defined for all real numbers $x \geq -4$ except for $x = 5$, where the graph has a vertical asymptote.

9

A sum of $10,000 is invested at a rate of 10 percent, with interest compounded semiannually. The value, in dollars, of this investment after t years is given by $V(t) = 10,000(1.05)^{2t}$. Approximately how much greater is the value of this investment at the end of 2 years than the same amount invested at the rate of 10 percent compounded annually?

A) $55

B) $200

C) $500

D) $1,075

E) $1,155

Choice (A) is the correct answer. Applying the given function with $t = 2$ shows that the value of the investment compounded semiannually after 2 years would be approximately $12,155. If $10,000 were invested at 10 percent interest compounded annually, then at the end of 2 years the value of this investment would be $10,000(1.10)^2 = $12,100. Thus, difference in the amounts of the investments is approximately $12,155 − $12,100 = $55.

10

For which of the following functions does $f(x, y) = -f(-x, -y)$ for all values of x and y ?

A) $f(x, y) = x + y^2$

B) $f(x, y) = x - y^2$

C) $f(x, y) = x^2 - y$

D) $f(x, y) = x + y^3$

E) $f(x, y) = x - y^4$

Choice (D) is the correct answer. If $f(x, y)$ is a polynomial in x and y, then $f(x, y) = -f(-x, -y)$ if and only if every nonzero term of f is of odd degree. Of the given choices, this is true only for $f(x, y) = x + y^3$. In this case, $f(-x, -y) = (-x) + (-y)^3 = -x - y^3 = -(x + y^3) = -f(x, y)$. So, $f(x, y) = -f(-x, -y)$.

Geometry and Measurement: Coordinate Geometry

11

Which of the following describes the set of points (a, b) for which $|a| + |b| = 5$ in the xy–plane?

A) A circle with radius 5

B) A circle with radius $5\sqrt{2}$

C) A square with sides of length $5\sqrt{2}$

D) A square with sides of length 10

E) A regular hexagon with sides of length 5

If $|a| + |b| = 5$, consider the four cases:

$a > 0, b > 0$: $a + b = 5$ so $b = 5 - a$ is a line with slope –1 and y-intercept 5

$a > 0, b < 0$: $a - b = 5$ so $b = -5 + a$ is a line with slope 1 and y-intercept –5

$a < 0, b > 0$: $-a + b = 5$ so $b = 5 + a$ is a line with slope 1 and y-intercept 5

$a < 0, b < 0$: $-a - b = 5$ so $b = -5 - a$ is a line with slope –1 and y-intercept –5

Sketch the graphs of the 4 lines. The 4 lines intersect to form a square with vertices on the coordinate axes located 5 units from the origin.

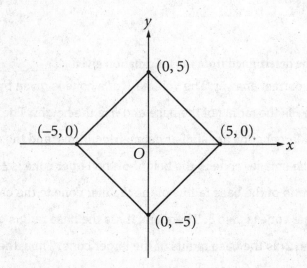

Choice (C) is the correct answer. As shown in the figure above, the set of points (a, b) for which $|a| + |b| = 5$ is the square with vertices (0, 5), (5, 0), (0, –5), and (–5, 0). By the Pythagorean theorem, the sides of this square are of length $5\sqrt{2}$.

Geometry and Measurement: Three-Dimensional Geometry

12

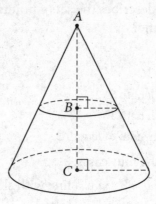

In the figure above, points B and C are the centers of the bases of two right circular cones, each with vertex A. If $AB = 1$ and $AC = 2$, what is the ratio of the volume of the smaller cone to the volume of the larger cone?

A) $\frac{1}{8}$

B) $\frac{1}{4}$

C) $\frac{3}{8}$

D) $\frac{1}{2}$

E) It cannot be determined from the information given.

Choice (A) is the correct answer. The volume V of a cone is given by $V = \frac{1}{3}\pi r^2 h$, where r is the radius of the base and h is the height. The smaller cone and larger cone are similar geometric figures, and the ratio of the height of the smaller cone to the height of the larger cone is $\frac{1}{2}$. It follows that the ratio of the base radius of the smaller cone to the base radius of the larger cone is also $\frac{1}{2}$. Therefore, if r is the base radius of the smaller cone, then $2r$ is the base radius of the larger cone. Thus, the volume of the smaller cone is $V = \frac{1}{3}\pi r^2(1)$, the volume of the larger cone is $V = \frac{1}{3}\pi (2r)^2 (2) = \frac{8}{3}\pi r^2$. Thus, the ratio of the volume of the smaller cone to the volume of the larger cone is $\dfrac{\frac{1}{3}}{\frac{8}{3}} = \frac{1}{8}$.

Geometry and Measurement: Trigonometry

13

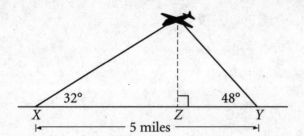

The airplane in the figure above is flying directly over point Z on a straight, level road. The angles of elevation for points X and Y are 32° and 48°, respectively. If points X and Y are 5 miles apart, what is the distance, in miles, from the airplane to point X?

A) 1.60

B) 2.40

C) 2.69

D) 3.77

E) 7.01

Choice (D) is the correct answer. Label the location of the airplane as point W. Then in $\triangle XYW$, the measure of $\angle X$ is 32°, the measure of $\angle Y$ is 48°, and the measure of $\angle W$ is 100°. Let x, y, and w denote the lengths, in miles, of the sides of $\triangle XYW$ opposite $\angle X$, $\angle Y$, and $\angle W$, respectively. Then by the law of sines, $\dfrac{x}{\sin X} = \dfrac{y}{\sin Y} = \dfrac{w}{\sin W}$. Since $w = 5$ and the distance from the plane to point X is y, it follows that $\dfrac{5}{\sin 100°} = \dfrac{y}{\sin 48°}$. This gives $y \approx 3.77$ for the distance, in miles, from the plane to point X.

14

If $\cos \theta = \dfrac{x}{3}$, where $0 < \theta < \dfrac{\pi}{2}$ and $0 < x < 3$, then $\sin \theta =$

A) $\dfrac{\sqrt{9-x^2}}{3}$

B) $\dfrac{\sqrt{x^2-9}}{x}$

C) $\dfrac{\sqrt{9-x^2}}{x}$

D) $\dfrac{\sqrt{3-x^2}}{3}$

E) $\dfrac{\sqrt{3-x^2}}{x}$

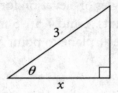

Choice (A) is the correct answer. Since $\cos \theta = \dfrac{x}{3}$, $0 < \theta < \dfrac{\pi}{2}$, and $0 < x < 3$, the figure above can be drawn. By the Pythagorean theorem, the other leg of the right triangle is $\sqrt{9-x^2}$. Thus, $\sin \theta = \dfrac{\sqrt{9-x^2}}{3}$. Alternatively, since $\sin^2 \theta + \cos^2 \theta = 1$,

$$\sin^2 \theta = 1 - \cos^2 \theta$$
$$= 1 - \left(\frac{x}{3}\right)^2$$
$$= \frac{9-x^2}{9}$$
$$\sin \theta = \frac{\sqrt{9-x^2}}{3}$$

since $0 < \theta < \dfrac{\pi}{2}$ and $0 < x < 3$.

Data Analysis, Statistics, and Probability

15

Revenue for Company X	
Years after merger	**Revenue (in billions of dollars)**
0	$3
2	$4
4	$11
7	$25

Two companies merged to form Company X, whose revenues are shown in the table above for selected years after the merger. If a least-squares exponential regression is used to model the data above, what revenue, in billions of dollars, would be predicted for the company 13 years after the merger?

A) $31

B) $43

C) $109

D) $172

E) $208

Choice (D) is the correct answer. A graphing calculator can be used to find the least-squares exponential regression for the data (0, 3), (2, 4), (4, 11), and (7, 25). This gives a function of the form $y = ab^x$, where $a \approx 2.678$ and $b \approx 1.377$. The exponential regression is $y = (2.678)(1.377)^x$. Evaluating this function at $t = 13$, without rounding the values of a and b, gives approximately 172. Thus, the revenue predicted is $172 billion.

Mathematics Level 2 – Practice Test 1

Practice Helps

The test that follows is an actual, previously administered SAT Subject Test in Mathematics Level 2. To get an idea of what it's like to take this test, practice under conditions that are much like those of an actual test administration.

- Set aside an hour when you can take the test uninterrupted.

- Sit at a desk or table with no other books or papers. Dictionaries, other books, or notes are not allowed in the test room.

- Remember to have a scientific or graphing calculator with you.

- Tear out an answer sheet from the back of this book and fill it in just as you would on the day of the test. One answer sheet can be used for up to three Subject Tests.

- Read the instructions that precede the practice test. During the actual administration you will be asked to read them before answering test questions.

- Use a clock or kitchen timer to time yourself.

- After you finish the practice test, read the sections "How to Score the SAT Subject Test in Mathematics Level 2" and "How Did You Do on the Subject Test in Mathematics Level 2?"

- The appearance of the answer sheet in this book may differ from the answer sheet you see on test day.

- The Reference Information at the start of the practice test is slightly different from what appeared on the original test. It has been modified to reflect the language included on tests administered at the time of this book's printing. These changes are minor and will not affect how you answer the questions.

MATHEMATICS LEVEL 2 TEST

The top portion of the page of the answer sheet that you will use to take the Mathematics Level 2 Test must be filled in exactly as illustrated below. When your supervisor tells you to fill in the circle next to the name of the test you are about to take, mark your answer sheet as shown.

○ Literature	○ Mathematics Level 1	○ German	○ Chinese Listening	○ Japanese Listening
○ Biology E	● Mathematics Level 2	○ Italian	○ French Listening	○ Korean Listening
○ Biology M	○ U.S. History	○ Latin	○ German Listening	○ Spanish Listening
○ Chemistry	○ World History	○ Modern Hebrew		
○ Physics	○ French	○ Spanish	Background Questions: ① ② ③ ④ ⑤ ⑥ ⑦ ⑧ ⑨

After filling in the circle next to the name of the test you are taking, locate the Background Questions section, which also appears at the top of your answer sheet (as shown above). This is where you will answer the following Background Questions on your answer sheet.

BACKGROUND QUESTIONS

Please answer Part I and Part II below by filling in the appropriate circle in the Background Questions box on your answer sheet. The information you provide is for statistical purposes only and will not affect your test score.

Part I. Which of the following describes a mathematics course you have taken or are currently taking? (FILL IN **ALL** CIRCLES THAT APPLY.)

- Algebra I or Elementary Algebra **OR** Course I of a college preparatory mathematics sequence — Fill in circle 1.

- Geometry **OR** Course II of a college preparatory mathematics sequence — Fill in circle 2.

- Algebra II or Intermediate Algebra **OR** Course III of a college preparatory mathematics sequence — Fill in circle 3.

- Elementary Functions (Precalculus) and/or Trigonometry **OR** beyond Course III of a college preparatory mathematics sequence — Fill in circle 4.

- Advanced Placement Mathematics (Calculus AB or Calculus BC) — Fill in circle 5.

Part II. What type of calculator did you bring to use for this test? (FILL IN THE **ONE** CIRCLE THAT APPLIES. If you did not bring a scientific or graphing calculator, do not fill in any of circles 6-9.)

- Scientific — Fill in circle 6.

- Graphing (Fill in the circle corresponding to the model you used.)

    Casio 9700, Casio 9750, Casio 9800, Casio 9850, Casio 9860, Casio FX 1.0, Casio CG-10, Sharp 9200, Sharp 9300, Sharp 9600, Sharp 9900, TI-82, TI-83, TI-83 Plus, TI-83 Plus Silver, TI-84 Plus, TI-84 Plus Silver, TI-85, TI-86, TI-Nspire, or TI-Nspire CX — Fill in circle 7.

    Casio 9970, Casio Algebra FX 2.0, HP 38G, HP 39 series, HP 40 series, HP 48 series, HP 49 series, HP 50 series, TI-89, TI-89 Titanium, TI-Nspire CAS, or TI-Nspire CX CAS — Fill in circle 8.

    Some other graphing calculator — Fill in circle 9.

When the supervisor gives the signal, turn the page and begin the Mathematics Level 2 Test. There are 100 numbered circles on the answer sheet and 50 questions in the Mathematics Level 2 Test. Therefore, use only circles 1 to 50 for recording your answers.

MATHEMATICS LEVEL 2 TEST

REFERENCE INFORMATION

THE FOLLOWING INFORMATION IS FOR YOUR REFERENCE IN ANSWERING SOME OF THE QUESTIONS IN THIS TEST.

Volume of a right circular cone with radius r and height h: $V = \frac{1}{3}\pi r^2 h$

Volume of a sphere with radius r: $V = \frac{4}{3}\pi r^3$

Volume of a pyramid with base area B and height h: $V = \frac{1}{3}Bh$

Surface Area of a sphere with radius r: $S = 4\pi r^2$

DO NOT DETACH FROM BOOK.

GO ON TO THE NEXT PAGE

MATHEMATICS LEVEL 2 TEST

For each of the following problems, decide which is the BEST of the choices given. If the exact numerical value is not one of the choices, select the choice that best approximates this value. Then fill in the corresponding circle on the answer sheet.

Notes: (1) A scientific or graphing calculator will be necessary for answering some (but not all) of the questions in this test. For each question you will have to decide whether or not you should use a calculator.

(2) For some questions in this test you may have to decide whether your calculator should be in the radian mode or the degree mode.

(3) Figures that accompany problems in this test are intended to provide information useful in solving the problems. They are drawn as accurately as possible EXCEPT when it is stated in a specific problem that its figure is not drawn to scale. All figures lie in a plane unless otherwise indicated.

(4) Unless otherwise specified, the domain of any function f is assumed to be the set of all real numbers x for which $f(x)$ is a real number. The range of f is assumed to be the set of all real numbers $f(x)$, where x is in the domain of f.

(5) Reference information that may be useful in answering the questions in this test can be found on the page preceding Question 1.

USE THIS SPACE FOR SCRATCH WORK.

1. $x^m x^{-2m} =$

(A) x^m

(B) $\dfrac{1}{x^m}$

(C) $\dfrac{1}{x^{-m}}$

(D) x^{-3m}

(E) x^{-2m^2}

GO ON TO THE NEXT PAGE

MATHEMATICS LEVEL 2 TEST—*Continued*

2. All of the following numbers satisfy the inequality $(2x + 1)(x - 5) < 0$ EXCEPT

   (A) -1 (B) 0   (C) 1   (D) 2   (E) 3

USE THIS SPACE FOR SCRATCH WORK.

3. For all real numbers m, the equation $y = mx + 3$ represents which of the following in the xy-plane?

   (A) Lines whose x-intercept is 3
   (B) Lines whose y-intercept is 3
   (C) Lines whose slope is 3
   (D) Vertical lines through $(3, 0)$
   (E) Horizontal lines through $(0, 3)$

4. If $2^a = 4^b = 64$, what is the value of $a + b$?

   (A) 3   (B) 8   (C) 9   (D) 18   (E) 48

GO ON TO THE NEXT PAGE

MATHEMATICS LEVEL 2 TEST—*Continued*

5. What is the domain of the function f defined by

$$f(x) = \frac{x^2}{x^2 + 1}?$$

(A) $-1 < x \le 1$
(B) $0 \le x < 1$
(C) $x \ge 0$
(D) All real numbers except -1
(E) All real numbers

USE THIS SPACE FOR SCRATCH WORK.

6. If $y = 2x^3 + x^2$, what is the value of $|y|$ when $x = -2$?

(A) -20
(B) $\quad 8$
(C) $\quad 12$
(D) $\quad 20$
(E) $\quad 60$

7. If $f(x) = (x - 3)^2$, what is the greatest value of x for which $f(x) = 5$?

(A) -0.76
(B) $\quad 0.76$
(C) $\quad 3.74$
(D) $\quad 4.00$
(E) $\quad 5.24$

GO ON TO THE NEXT PAGE

MATHEMATICS LEVEL 2 TEST—*Continued*

USE THIS SPACE FOR SCRATCH WORK.

```
2 | 6
3 | 2  7
4 | 5  5
5 | 6  8  8
6 | 1  3  6
```

2 | 6 represents 26.

8. The stem-and-leaf plot above shows the mathematics scores on a national test for a group of juniors at Pacific High School. What is the median score for this group?

(A) 45
(B) 49.7
(C) 50.5
(D) 56
(E) 58

9. If $f(x) = 2x + 1$ and $g(x) = \dfrac{1}{x} - 2$, for what value of x is $g(f(x))$ equal to 0 ?

(A) -1

(B) $-\dfrac{1}{4}$

(C) $\dfrac{1}{4}$

(D) $\dfrac{1}{2}$

(E) $\dfrac{2}{3}$

GO ON TO THE NEXT PAGE

MATHEMATICS LEVEL 2 TEST—*Continued*

10. Let a be a nonzero constant. If $2x^2 - 4 = a$, then $x^2 - 2 =$

(A) $\dfrac{1}{2}$ (B) $\dfrac{a}{2}$ (C) $\dfrac{2}{a}$ (D) 2 (E) $2a$

USE THIS SPACE FOR SCRATCH WORK.

x	Number of months in business	0	1	2	3	4	5
$P(x)$	Profit (in thousands of dollars)	0	1	4.2	9.1	15.8	25.3

11. The table above shows the profit made by a new company. Of the following functions, which best models the relationship between the company's profit and the number of months in business?

(A) $P(x) = 2x - 1$

(B) $P(x) = 5x - 3$

(C) $P(x) = x^2$

(D) $P(x) = 2x^2 - 1$

(E) $P(x) = x^3$

12. If $y_n = 1 - (-1)^n$, where $n = 1, 2, 3, \ldots$, which of the following statements is true?

(A) For all $n, y_n = 0$ only.

(B) For all $n, y_n = 0$ or $y_n = 2$.

(C) For all $n, y_n = 0$ or $y_n = 1$.

(D) For $n \geq 1,000, y_n > 0$.

(E) For $n \geq 1,000, y_n < 0$.

GO ON TO THE NEXT PAGE

13. Which of the following is NOT a graph of y as a function of x ?

USE THIS SPACE FOR SCRATCH WORK.

(A)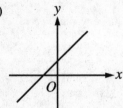

(B)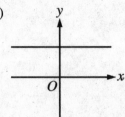

(C)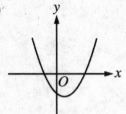

(D)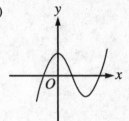

(E)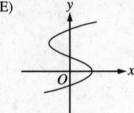

GO ON TO THE NEXT PAGE

MATHEMATICS LEVEL 2 TEST—*Continued*

USE THIS SPACE FOR SCRATCH WORK.

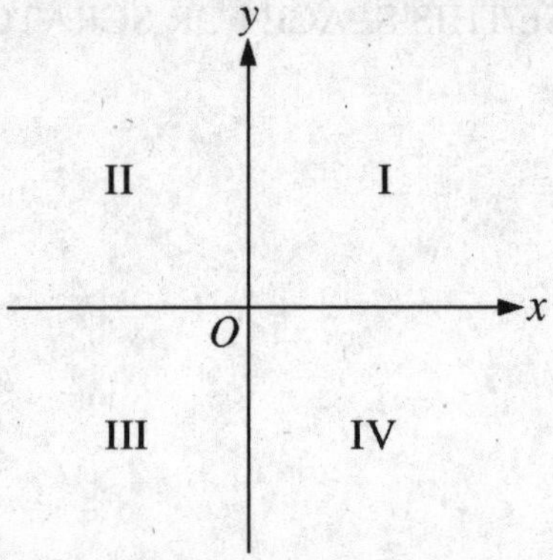

14. The figure above shows the xy-plane. If $f(x) = cx + 3$ and $g(x) = dx + 1$ for $0 < c < d$, which of the following is true about the graphs of f and g ?

(A) The graphs intersect in quadrant I.
(B) The graphs intersect in quadrant II.
(C) The graphs intersect in quadrant III.
(D) The graphs intersect in quadrant IV.
(E) The graphs do not intersect.

15. Eight cars, each of a different color (red, blue, black, gray, white, green, tan, gold), travel one behind the other to a campground. The red car must lead and the green car must be last. How many different orderings of the cars are there?

(A) 6!
(B) 8!
(C) $2 \cdot 6!$
(D) $2 \cdot 8!$
(E) $\dfrac{8!}{2}$

GO ON TO THE NEXT PAGE

MATHEMATICS LEVEL 2 TEST—Continued

16. If $\ln(x) = 1.58$, then $\ln(2x) =$

    (A) 1.15
    (B) 2.27
    (C) 2.49
    (D) 3.16
    (E) 3.58

USE THIS SPACE FOR SCRATCH WORK.

17. An insect population is growing in such a way that the number in each generation is approximately 1.5 times that of the previous generation. If there are 100 insects in the first generation, approximately how many insects will there be in the fourth generation?

    (A)   338
    (B)   475
    (C)   506
    (D)   813
    (E) 1,319

18. Which of the following are true ?

    I. If $x \neq 2$, then $x^2 + 4 \neq 8$.

    II. If $x^2 + 4 \neq 8$, then $x \neq 2$.

    III. If $x^2 + 4 = 8$, then $x = 2$.

    (A) I only
    (B) II only
    (C) I and II only
    (D) I and III only
    (E) I, II, and III

GO ON TO THE NEXT PAGE

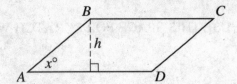

USE THIS SPACE FOR SCRATCH WORK.

Note: Figure not drawn to scale.

19. In parallelogram $ABCD$ above, $AB = 8$ and $AD = 13$. If $x = 42$, what is the value of h?

 (A) 5.35
 (B) 5.95
 (C) 7.20
 (D) 8.70
 (E) 9.66

20. If $f(1) = -3$, $f(3) = 2$, and for all real numbers x, $f(x) = ax + b$, then $(a, b) =$

 (A) $\left(\dfrac{5}{2}, \dfrac{11}{2}\right)$

 (B) $\left(\dfrac{5}{2}, -\dfrac{11}{2}\right)$

 (C) $\left(\dfrac{5}{2}, -\dfrac{13}{2}\right)$

 (D) $\left(-\dfrac{5}{2}, \dfrac{11}{2}\right)$

 (E) $\left(-\dfrac{5}{2}, -\dfrac{13}{2}\right)$

GO ON TO THE NEXT PAGE

21. Which value of x in the interval $-\dfrac{\pi}{2} < x < \dfrac{\pi}{2}$

    satisfies the equation $\cos x = \sec x$?

    (A) $-\dfrac{\pi}{3}$

    (B) $-\dfrac{\pi}{4}$

    (C) 0

    (D) $\dfrac{\pi}{4}$

    (E) $\dfrac{\pi}{3}$

22. The function g is defined by
$$g(x) = 3\sin(2x + 1) - 1.$$

    What is the range of g ?

    (A) $-4 \le g(x) \le 2$

    (B) $-2 \le g(x) \le 4$

    (C) $-1 \le g(x) \le 3$

    (D) $-\dfrac{1}{2} \le g(x) \le 0$

    (E) $2 \le g(x) \le 3$

GO ON TO THE NEXT PAGE

MATHEMATICS LEVEL 2 TEST—*Continued*

23. In the first quadrant of the *xy*-plane, the point of

    intersection of the graphs of the line $y = x$ and

    the ellipse $\dfrac{x^2}{16} + \dfrac{y^2}{25} = 1$ is which of the following?

    (A) $(3.12, 3.12)$
    (B) $(4.47, 4.47)$
    (C) $(4.50, 4.50)$
    (D) $(6.67, 6.67)$
    (E) $(9.76, 9.76)$

USE THIS SPACE FOR SCRATCH WORK.

24. The probability of randomly drawing a piece of
    red candy from a bag containing only red and

    purple candies is $\dfrac{2}{3}$. Which of the following

    could be the number of red and the number of
    purple candies in the bag?

    (A) 10 red, 20 purple
    (B) 20 red, 10 purple
    (C) 20 red, 30 purple
    (D) 20 red, 50 purple
    (E) 30 red, 20 purple

GO ON TO THE NEXT PAGE

MATHEMATICS LEVEL 2 TEST—*Continued*

USE THIS SPACE FOR SCRATCH WORK.

x	$f(x)$
0	3
1	0
2	1
3	4
4	2

25. The table above defines the function f, which has domain $\{0,1,2,3,4\}$. What is the value of $f(f(3))$?

(A) 0　(B) 1　(C) 2　(D) 3　(E) 4

26. Functions f and g are defined for all real numbers. The function f has zeros at -2, 3, and 7; and the function g has zeros at -3, -1, 4, and 7. How many distinct zeros does the product function $f \cdot g$ have?

(A) Three
(B) Four
(C) Six
(D) Seven
(E) Twelve

GO ON TO THE NEXT PAGE

MATHEMATICS LEVEL 2 TEST—Continued

USE THIS SPACE FOR SCRATCH WORK.

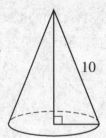

27. In the figure above, the diameter of the base of the right circular cone is 8. What is the volume of the cone?

(A) 153.6
(B) 167.6
(C) 351.9
(D) 402.1
(E) 670.2

28. In the xy-plane, what is the distance between the points whose coordinates are $\left(2\sqrt{3}, 4\sqrt{5}\right)$ and $\left(-\sqrt{3}, 7\sqrt{5}\right)$?

(A) 3.45   (B) 4.24   (C) 6.93   (D) 8.00
    (E) 8.49

GO ON TO THE NEXT PAGE

MATHEMATICS LEVEL 2 TEST—*Continued*

USE THIS SPACE FOR SCRATCH WORK.

29. An isosceles triangle has a base of length 25 centimeters and a vertex angle (the angle opposite the base) of 50°. What is the perimeter of the triangle?

(A) 42.3 cm
(B) 57.9 cm
(C) 67.3 cm
(D) 84.2 cm
(E) 101.0 cm

30. A taxi charges a base fee of \$1.25 plus \$0.75 for each mile (or part thereof). Which of the following would represent the taxi fare for a trip of length x miles? (Let $\lceil x \rceil$ represent the least integer that is greater than or equal to x.)

(A) $\$2.00\lceil x \rceil$
(B) $\$1.25 + \$0.75\lceil x \rceil$
(C) $\$0.75 + \$1.25\lceil x \rceil$
(D) $\$1.25 + \$0.75\lceil x+1 \rceil$
(E) $\$0.75 + \$1.25\lceil x+1 \rceil$

31. If $f(x, y) = \dfrac{x^2 + y^2}{x^2 - y^2}$, then $f(x, -y) =$

(A) -1

(B) 1

(C) $\dfrac{y^2 - x^2}{x^2 + y^2}$

(D) $\dfrac{x^2 + y^2}{y^2 - x^2}$

(E) $\dfrac{x^2 + y^2}{x^2 - y^2}$

GO ON TO THE NEXT PAGE

MATHEMATICS LEVEL 2 TEST—*Continued*

32. Twenty-seven identical cubes are arranged to form a larger cube. The diagonal of each face of each of the 27 identical cubes measures 1.415 centimeters. What is the volume of the larger cube?

    (A) 1.002 cm^3
    (B) 2.833 cm^3
    (C) 9.018 cm^3
    (D) 27.045 cm^3
    (E) 76.495 cm^3

$$t,\ 8,\ 5,\ 4,\ 12,\ 8$$

33. In the list above, t is an integer. For the list, if the mean is equal to the median and the range is less than 10, what is the value of t ?

    (A) 2   (B) 6.5   (C) 8   (D) 11   (E) 14

34. Which of the following are polar coordinates of a point on the graph of $r = \cos\theta$?

    (A) $\left(1, \dfrac{\pi}{2}\right)$

    (B) $\left(0.5, \dfrac{\pi}{3}\right)$

    (C) $(1, \pi)$

    (D) $\left(0.5, \dfrac{2\pi}{3}\right)$

    (E) $\left(1, \dfrac{\pi}{4}\right)$

GO ON TO THE NEXT PAGE

MATHEMATICS LEVEL 2 TEST—*Continued*

35. The prime factorization of a positive integer n is p^3. Which of the following is true?

    I. n cannot be even.
    II. n has only one positive prime factor.
    III. n has exactly three distinct factors.

(A) I only
(B) II only
(C) III only
(D) II and III only
(E) I, II, and III

USE THIS SPACE FOR SCRATCH WORK.

36. In the xy-plane, the asymptotes of a hyperbola are the lines $y = x + 5$ and $y = -x - 5$. What are the coordinates of the center of the hyperbola?

(A) $(0, 0)$
(B) $(-5, 0)$
(C) $(0, -5)$
(D) $(0, 5)$
(E) $(5, 0)$

GO ON TO THE NEXT PAGE

MATHEMATICS LEVEL 2 TEST—*Continued*

USE THIS SPACE FOR SCRATCH WORK.

Test Number	Student's Score	Class Mean	Class Standard Deviation
1	85	76	3
2	87	89	7
3	94	88	4
4	88	80	6
5	82	72	5

37. The table above shows a student's record of performance on five tests. On which test did the student rank the highest in relation to the other students in the class? (Assume that the test scores on each test are normally distributed.)

   (A) Test 1
   (B) Test 2
   (C) Test 3
   (D) Test 4
   (E) Test 5

38. When a positive integer n is divided by 4, the remainder is 3. Which of the following could equal n for some integer t ?

   (A) $4t + 2$
   (B) $4t$
   (C) $4t - 1$
   (D) $4t - 2$
   (E) $4t - 3$

GO ON TO THE NEXT PAGE

MATHEMATICS LEVEL 2 TEST—*Continued*

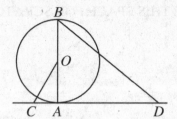

39. In the figure above, O is the center of the circle
with radius 1, and line CD is tangent to the circle
at A. If the measure of $\angle AOC$ is 30° and the
length of $\overline{CD}$ is 3, what is the length of $\overline{BD}$?

(A) 2.53
(B) 2.62
(C) 2.93
(D) 3.14
(E) 3.20

40. Let $f(x) = e^x + x + k$. If $f(x) < 0$ when
$x = 1.27$ and $f(x) > 0$ when $x = 1.28$, which
of the following could be a value of k?

(A) −4.70
(B) −4.75
(C) −4.80
(D) −4.85
(E) −4.90

GO ON TO THE NEXT PAGE

MATHEMATICS LEVEL 2 TEST—*Continued*

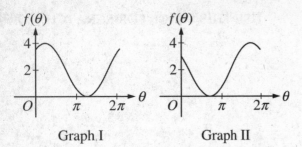

Graph I   Graph II

USE THIS SPACE FOR SCRATCH WORK.

41. In the graphs above, Graph I shows a portion of
the graph of $f(\theta) = A[\sin(B\theta + C)] + D$, where
A, B, C, and D are constants. Graph II could
result from changing which of the constants
in $f(\theta)$?

(A) A only
(B) B only
(C) C only
(D) D only
(E) A and D

42. The number of birds on <u>each</u> of islands X and Y
remains constant from year to year; however, the
birds migrate between islands. After one year,
20 percent of the birds on X have migrated to Y,
and 15 percent of the birds on Y have migrated
to X. If the total number of birds is 14,000, how
many birds are on island X ?

(A) 2,800
(B) 6,000
(C) 6,788
(D) 7,212
(E) 8,000

GO ON TO THE NEXT PAGE

MATHEMATICS LEVEL 2 TEST—*Continued*

USE THIS SPACE FOR SCRATCH WORK.

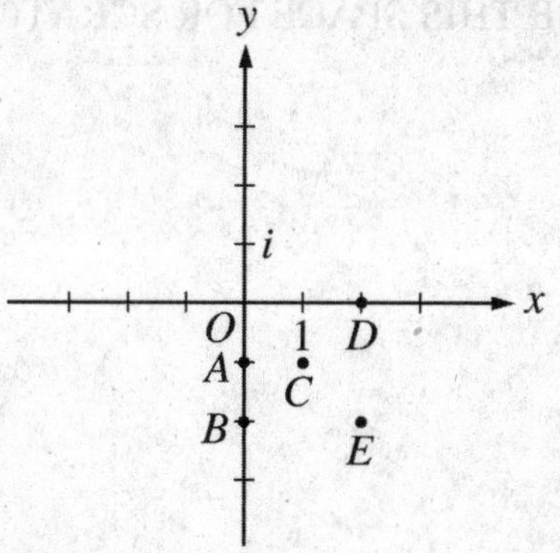

43. If $z = 1 - i$, which of the points in the figure above is the graphical representation of z^2?

(A) A (B) B (C) C (D) D (E) E

44. What is the total surface area of a right circular cylindrical solid if the diameter of its base is $2r$ and its height is $2r$?

(A) $2\pi r + 2r$

(B) $\pi r^2 + 2r$

(C) $8\pi r^2$

(D) $6\pi r^2$

(E) $2\pi r^2$

GO ON TO THE NEXT PAGE

MATHEMATICS LEVEL 2 TEST—*Continued*

USE THIS SPACE FOR SCRATCH WORK.

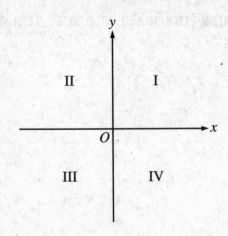

45. If the terminal side of an angle θ, in standard position, lies in quadrant IV of the xy-plane above, which of the following must be true?

(A) $\csc \theta < 0$ and $\sec \theta > 0$
(B) $\csc \theta < 0$ and $\sec \theta < 0$
(C) $\csc \theta < 0$ and $\tan \theta > 0$
(D) $\csc \theta > 0$ and $\sec \theta < 0$
(E) $\csc \theta > 0$ and $\tan \theta < 0$

Time (seconds)	0	0.5	1.5	2
Height (feet)	5	17	20.5	11.9

46. A ball is tossed into the air, and the height of the ball above the ground at different times is recorded in the table above. A quadratic regression equation is obtained for these data, with height expressed as a function of time. According to the regression equation, what is the maximum height of the ball?

(A) 18.8 ft
(B) 20.5 ft
(C) 22.2 ft
(D) 22.4 ft
(E) 30.9 ft

GO ON TO THE NEXT PAGE

MATHEMATICS LEVEL 2 TEST—*Continued*

47. In right triangle ABC, the measure of $\angle A$ is $90°$, $AB = 3$, and $BC = x$. If $\sin C = k$, then, in terms of k, $AC =$

(A) $\sqrt{9k^2 - 9}$

(B) $\sqrt{9 - \left(\dfrac{3}{k}\right)^2}$

(C) $\sqrt{9 - \left(\dfrac{k}{3}\right)^2}$

(D) $\sqrt{\left(\dfrac{k}{3}\right)^2 - 9}$

(E) $\sqrt{\left(\dfrac{3}{k}\right)^2 - 9}$

USE THIS SPACE FOR SCRATCH WORK.

48. If $f(x) = \begin{cases} x & \text{when } 0 \le x < 1 \\ f(x-1) & \text{when } x \ge 1 \end{cases}$,

what is the value of $f(4.7)$?

(A) 4.7
(B) 3.7
(C) 0.7
(D) 0.3
(E) −0.3

GO ON TO THE NEXT PAGE

MATHEMATICS LEVEL 2 TEST—*Continued*

49. How many noncongruent triangles ABC exist such that the measure of $\angle A$ is $42°$, $AB = 6$, and $BC = 4$?

   (A) None
   (B) One
   (C) Two
   (D) Three
   (E) An infinite number

USE THIS SPACE FOR SCRATCH WORK.

50. A magazine article described the growth of a computer network as exponential. The article stated that in 10 years, the number of users of this network had risen from 1 million to 20 million. Assuming that this article was correct, in how many years would the number of users increase from 20 million to 200 million?

   (A) 20   (B) 18   (C) 15   (D) 10   (E) 8

S T O P

**IF YOU FINISH BEFORE TIME IS CALLED, YOU MAY CHECK YOUR WORK ON THIS TEST ONLY.
DO NOT TURN TO ANY OTHER TEST IN THIS BOOK.**

How to Score the SAT Subject Test in Mathematics Level 2

When you take an actual SAT Subject Test in Mathematics Level 2, your answer sheet will be "read" by a scanning machine that will record your response to each question. Then a computer will compare your answers with the correct answers and produce your raw score. You get one point for each correct answer. For each wrong answer, you lose one-fourth of a point. Questions you omit (and any for which you mark more than one answer) are not counted. This raw score is converted to a scaled score that is reported to you and to the colleges you specify.

Worksheet 1. Finding Your Raw Test Score

STEP 1: Table A on the following page lists the correct answers for all the questions on the Subject Test in Mathematics Level 2 that is reproduced in this book. It also serves as a worksheet for you to calculate your raw score.

- Compare your answers with those given in the table.

- Put a check in the column marked "Right" if your answer is correct.

- Put a check in the column marked "Wrong" if your answer is incorrect.

- Leave both columns blank if you omitted the question.

STEP 2: Count the number of right answers.

Enter the total here: _____

STEP 3: Count the number of wrong answers.

Enter the total here: _____

STEP 4: Multiply the number of wrong answers by .250.

Enter the product here: _____

STEP 5: Subtract the result obtained in Step 4 from the total you obtained in Step 2.

Enter the result here: _____

STEP 6: Round the number obtained in Step 5 to the nearest whole number.

Enter the result here: _____

The number you obtained in Step 6 is your raw score.

Answers to Practice Test 1 for Mathematics Level 2

Table A
Answers to the Subject Test in Mathematics Level 2 - Practice Test 1 and Percentage of Students Answering Each Question Correctly

Question Number	Correct Answer	Right	Wrong	Percent Answering Correctly*	Question Number	Correct Answer	Right	Wrong	Percent Answering Correctly*
1	B			90	26	C			51
2	A			95	27	A			63
3	B			92	28	E			76
4	C			94	29	D			78
5	E			87	30	B			84
6	C			93	31	E			75
7	E			86	32	D			61
8	D			71	33	D			51
9	B			88	34	B			45
10	B			94	35	B			37
11	C			89	36	B			62
12	B			87	37	A			44
13	E			82	38	C			53
14	A			86	39	D			56
15	A			80	40	D			73
16	B			76	41	C			61
17	A			76	42	B			30
18	B			68	43	B			51
19	A			85	44	D			56
20	B			83	45	A			64
21	C			84	46	D			29
22	A			74	47	E			43
23	A			70	48	C			43
24	B			84	49	A			26
25	C			77	50	E			45

* These percentages are based on an analysis of the answer sheets for a random sample of 25,344 students who took the original administration of this test and whose mean score was 678. They may be used as an indication of the relative difficulty of a particular question. Each percentage may also be used to predict the likelihood that a typical Subject Test in Mathematics Level 2 candidate will answer correctly that question on this edition of this test.

Finding Your Scaled Score

When you take SAT Subject Tests, the scores sent to the colleges you specify are reported on the College Board scale, which ranges from 200-800. You can convert your practice test score to a scaled score by using Table B. To find your scaled score, locate your raw score in the left-hand column of Table B; the corresponding score in the right-hand column is your scaled score. For example, a raw score of 25 on this particular edition of the Subject Test in Mathematics Level 2 corresponds to a scaled score of 600.

Raw scores are converted to scaled scores to ensure that a score earned on any one edition of a particular Subject Test is comparable to the same scaled score earned on any other edition of the same Subject Test. Because some editions of the tests may be slightly easier or more difficult than others, College Board scaled scores are adjusted so that they indicate the same level of performance regardless of the edition of the test taken and the ability of the group that takes it. Thus, for example, a score of 500 on one edition of a test taken at a particular administration indicates the same level of achievement as a score of 500 on a different edition of the test taken at a different administration.

When you take the SAT Subject Tests during a national administration, your scores are likely to differ somewhat from the scores you obtain on the tests in this book. People perform at different levels at different times for reasons unrelated to the tests themselves. The precision of any test is also limited because it represents only a sample of all the possible questions that could be asked.

Table B
Scaled Score Conversion Table
Subject Test in Mathematics Level 2 - Practice Test 1

Raw Score	Reported Score	Raw Score	Reported Score	Raw Score	Reported Score
50	800	29	640	8	480
49	800	28	630	7	480
48	800	27	620	6	470
47	800	26	610	5	460
46	800	25	600	4	450
45	800	24	600	3	440
44	800	23	590	2	440
43	800	22	580	1	430
42	790	21	570	0	420
41	780	20	570	−1	410
40	770	19	560	−2	400
39	760	18	550	−3	400
38	750	17	550	−4	390
37	730	16	540	−5	380
36	720	15	530	−6	370
35	710	14	530	−7	360
34	690	13	520	−8	350
33	680	12	510	−9	340
32	670	11	500	−10	340
31	660	10	500	−11	320
30	650	9	490	−12	310

How Did You Do on the Subject Test in Mathematics Level 2?

After you score your test and analyze your performance, think about the following questions:

Did you run out of time before reaching the end of the test?

If so, you may need to pace yourself better. For example, maybe you spent too much time on one or two hard questions. A better approach might be to skip the ones you can't answer right away and try answering all the questions that remain on the test. Then if there's time, go back to the questions you skipped.

Did you take a long time reading the directions?

You will save time when you take the test by learning the directions to the Subject Test in Mathematics Level 2 ahead of time. Each minute you spend reading directions during the test is a minute that you could use to answer questions.

How did you handle questions you were unsure of?

If you were able to eliminate one or more of the answer choices as wrong and guess from the remaining ones, your approach probably worked to your advantage. On the other hand, making haphazard guesses or omitting questions without trying to eliminate choices could cost you valuable points.

How difficult were the questions for you compared with other students who took the test?

Table A shows you how difficult the multiple-choice questions were for the group of students who took this test during its national administration. The right-hand column gives the percentage of students that answered each question correctly.

A question answered correctly by almost everyone in the group is obviously an easier question. For example, 84 percent of the students answered question 21 correctly. But only 29 percent answered question 46 correctly.

Keep in mind that these percentages are based on just one group of students. They would probably be different with another group of students taking the test.

If you missed several easier questions, go back and try to find out why: Did the questions cover material you haven't yet reviewed? Did you misunderstand the directions?

Answer Explanations

For Practice Test 1

The solutions presented here provide one method for solving each of the problems on this test. Other mathematically correct approaches are possible.

Question 1

Choice (B) is the correct answer. Since $x^m x^{-2m} = x^{m-2m}$, then
$$x^{m-2m} = x^{-m} = \frac{1}{x^m}.$$

Choice (E) is incorrect. It results from multiplying the exponents m and $-2m$ instead of adding them.

Question 2

Choice (A) is the correct answer. By using a graphing calculator, one can see that the function $y = (2x + 1)(x - 5)$ is a parabola that opens upward and has zeros at $x = -\frac{1}{2}$ and $x = 5$. Thus, the graph below the x-axis corresponds to the negative values of the function; that is, $(2x + 1)(x - 5)$ is negative for $-\frac{1}{2} < x < 5$. So, -1 is the only choice that is NOT a number within that interval. Alternatively, $2x + 1 > 0$ when $x > -\frac{1}{2}$ and $x - 5 < 0$ when $x < 5$. Since the terms in the product $(2x + 1)(x - 5)$ have different signs when $-\frac{1}{2} < x < 5$, this interval includes the numbers for which the product is negative. If $x > 5$ or $x < -\frac{1}{2}$, both terms in the product have the same sign; thus, the product $(2x + 1)(x - 5)$ would be positive in these intervals. Of the numbers in the choices, the only number that is in either of these intervals is -1.

Question 3

Choice (B) is the correct answer. For all real numbers m in the linear equation $y = mx + 3$, if $x = 0$, then $y = 3$ regardless of the value of m. Thus, all equations of this form are lines in the xy-plane that have y-intercept equal to 3.

Choice (C) is incorrect. This results from incorrectly identifying the constant 3 in the equation as the slope of the line.

Question 4

Choice (C) is the correct answer. Since $2^a = 4^b = 2^{2b}$ and $4^b = 64 = 4^3$, equating exponents for expressions that have the same base gives $a = 2b$ and $b = 3$. Thus, $a = 2 \cdot 3 = 6$ and $a + b = 6 + 3 = 9$.

Choice (D) is incorrect. It results from incorrectly multiplying a and b instead of adding them.

Question 5

Choice (E) is the correct answer. The domain of this rational function, f, is all real numbers for which the denominator is not equal to 0. Since the denominator is $x^2 + 1$, it is always positive. Thus, all real numbers are in the domain of f.

Choice (D) is incorrect. It results from substituting -1 into the denominator $x^2 + 1$ to get $(-1)^2 + 1$ and then incorrectly squaring to get $-1 + 1$ or 0.

Question 6

Choice (C) is the correct answer. Since $x = -2$, this value can be substituted for x in the equation $y = 2x^3 + x^2$ to find y. So, $y = 2(-2)^3 + (-2)^2 = 2(-8) + 4 = -12$. Thus, $|y| = |-12| = 12$.

Choice (D) is incorrect. This results from incorrectly thinking $|y|$ is the same as $\left|2x^3\right| + \left|x^2\right|$. Substituting $x = -2$ into this expression then gives $\left|2(-2)^3\right| + \left|(-2)^2\right| = 16 + 4 = 20$, which is incorrect.

Question 7

Choice (E) is the correct answer. One way to solve this problem is to first find the value(s) of x for which $f(x) = 5$. Since $(x - 3)^2 = 5$, you can solve for x by taking the square root of both sides of the equation to get $x - 3 = \pm\sqrt{5}$. Next, add 3 to both sides of the equation to get $x = 3 \pm \sqrt{5}$. Simplifying each outcome gives $3 - \sqrt{5} \approx 0.7639$ and $3 + \sqrt{5} \approx 5.2361$. Thus, there are two values of x such that $f(x) = 5$, and 5.2361 is the greater one of the two.

Choice (D) is incorrect. This results from mistaking $f(x) = 5$ for $x = 5$ and finding $f(5)$, which is 4.

Question 8

Choice (D) is the correct answer. There are 11 scores in the stem-and-leaf plot. The median score is the 6th score when the 11 scores are listed in increasing order. Additionally, there are five scores less than 56 and five scores greater than 56; thus, 56 is the median score.

Choice (A) is incorrect. It could result from incorrectly selecting a mode of the scores instead of selecting the median of the scores.

Question 9

Choice (B) is the correct answer. Since $g(f(x)) = g(2x + 1) =$ $\frac{1}{2x + 1} - 2$, solving $g(f(x)) = 0$ for x is equivalent to solving the equation $\frac{1}{2x + 1} - 2 = 0$ for x. The first step is to add 2 to both sides of the equation to get $\frac{1}{2x + 1} = 2$. The next step could be to multiply both sides of the equation by $2x + 1$ to get $1 = 2(2x + 1)$, which gives $4x + 2 = 1$ or $x = -\frac{1}{4}$.

Choice (E) is incorrect. This results from finding $f(g(x)) = 0$ instead of finding $g(f(x)) = 0$. Since $f(g(x)) = f\left(\frac{1}{x} - 2\right) = 2\left(\frac{1}{x} - 2\right) + 1 = \frac{2}{x} - 3$, then $\frac{2}{x} - 3 = 0$ gives the incorrect value of x to be $\frac{2}{3}$.

Question 10

Choice (B) is the correct answer. Since $2x^2 - 4 = 2(x^2 - 2)$, it follows that $2(x^2 - 2) = a$. Dividing both sides of the equation by 2 gives $x^2 - 2 = \frac{a}{2}$.

Choice (E) is incorrect. This could result from incorrectly multiplying by 2 instead of dividing by 2 on both sides of the equation given.

Question 11

Choice (C) is the correct answer. One way to answer this problem is to evaluate the functions listed in the choices at the values of x given in the table to see which function has outputs that best approximate the corresponding profits for all values of x in the table. For $P(x) = x^2$, each output is less than 1 unit from the corresponding profit for each x-value in the table, while each function in the other choices has outputs, $P(x)$, that are more than 1 unit from the corresponding profits for all $x > 1$. Thus, $P(x) = x^2$ is the best model for the relationship between the company's profit and the number of months in business.

Question 12

Choice (B) is the correct answer. For integer n, $(-1)^n = 1$ when n is an even integer and $(-1)^n = -1$ when n is an odd integer. So, for the y_n defined in the problem, one can see that $y_n = 1 - (-1)^n = 1 - 1 = 0$ if n is an even integer and $y_n = 1 - (-1)^n = 1 - (-1) = 1 + 1 = 2$ if n is an odd integer.

Therefore y_n can only be equal to 0 or 2.

Choice (A) is incorrect. This results from thinking $(-1)^n$ is equal to 1 for any integer n, giving $1 - (-1)^n = 1 - 1 = 0$.

Question 13

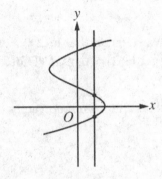

Choice (E) is the correct answer. For each value of x in the graphs in choices (A), (B), (C), and (D), there is only one value of y corresponding to that value. However, in some places in the graph in choice (E), more than one value of y corresponds to a single value of x. It is helpful to use the given figure in the problem and add a vertical line to it to illustrate this, as shown above. The vertical line drawn to the right of the y-axis in the figure above intersects the graph in more than one place (indicated with dots); this line shows an example of multiple values of y on the graph that correspond to one x-value. Thus, this graph cannot display y as a function of x.

Question 14

Choice (A) is the correct answer. In the xy-plane, the graphs of both functions in the problem are lines. If the graphs do not intersect, then they would be parallel. Since the problem states $c < d$, it follows that the slopes of the lines are different; therefore, the lines cannot be parallel and must intersect. Let $x = a$ be the x-coordinate where the lines intersect; thus, the point of intersection can be represented by $(a, f(a))$ and $f(a) = g(a)$. Since $f(a) = ca + 3$ and $g(a) = da + 1$, it follows that $ca + 3 = da + 1$. Solving this equation yields $a = \dfrac{2}{d - c}$.

It is given in the problem that $0 < c < d$; thus, $a > 0$. As a result, $ca + 3 > 0$ or $f(a) > 0$. Since both $a > 0$ and $f(a) > 0$, the point where the lines intersect has both a positive x-coordinate and a positive y-coordinate. Therefore, that point is in Quadrant I.

Question 15

Choice (A) is the correct answer. It is stated that the lead car must be red and the last car must be green. Since this leaves the remaining 6 cars between them to have different positions in the ordering of the cars, it follows that there are 6 choices for the car that could be in the second position, then 5 choices for the third position, and so on. So, the different orderings come from the different possible positions of the 6 remaining cars, which can be in $6 \cdot 5 \cdot 4 \cdot 3 \cdot 2 \cdot 1$ or 6! different orderings.

Choice (C) is incorrect. This could result from incorrectly thinking the red car could also be in the last position and the green car could also be in the lead position.

Question 16

Choice (B) is the correct answer. Recall that $\ln(2x) = \ln(2) + \ln(x)$. Using a calculator, you can get $\ln(2) \approx 0.6931$. Thus, $\ln(2x) \approx 0.6931 + 1.58$ or 2.2731.

Choice (D) is incorrect. This results from incorrectly thinking $\ln(2x)$ is equal to $2\ln(x)$.

Question 17

Choice (A) is the correct answer. According to the information given in the problem, the number of insects in the second generation is approximately $100(1.5)$, the number of insects in the third generation is approximately $100(1.5)^2$, and the number of insects in the fourth generation is approximately $100(1.5)^3$ or approximately 338.

Choice (C) is incorrect. This results from computing $100(1.5)^4$, which is the number of insects in the fifth generation.

Question 18

Choice (B) is the correct answer. Each of the three statements must be analyzed separately. Consider statement I. Since both $x = 2$ and $x = -2$ give $x^2 = 4$ or $x^2 + 4 = 8$, it follows that x could be equal to -2 when $x \neq 2$, and you would get $x^2 + 4 = 8$. Thus, statement I is not true. Consider statement II. When $x^2 + 4 \neq 8$ or $x^2 \neq 4$, x can neither be equal to 2 nor equal to -2. Thus, statement II is true. Consider statement III. When $x^2 + 4 = 8$ or $x^2 = 4$, taking the square root of both sides of this equation gives x is either equal to 2 or equal to -2. Thus, statement III is not true. So, only choice II is correct.

Choice (E) is incorrect. It is likely the result of forgetting that when $x^2 = 4$, x could be -2.

Question 19

Choice (A) is the correct answer. In the figure shown, the dashed vertical line of length h is perpendicular to side AD and the right triangle in the parallelogram contains an acute $\angle A$ of measure 42°. In the right triangle, the dashed line is a leg opposite $\angle A$, and side AB is the hypotenuse of length 8. Thus, $\sin 42° = \dfrac{h}{8}$ or $h = 8\sin 42°$. By using your calculator in degree mode or the degree symbol if your calculator is in radian mode, you get $h = 8\sin 42° \approx 5.3530$.

Choice (B) is incorrect. This comes from using the cosine function instead of the sine function and getting $\cos 42° = \dfrac{h}{8}$, so $h = 8\cos 42° \approx 5.9452$.

Question 20

Choice (B) is the correct answer. Since $-3 = f(1) = a \cdot 1 + b$ and $2 = f(3) = a \cdot 3 + b$, the system of equations that results can be solved for a and b. So with $\begin{cases} a + b = -3 \\ 3a + b = 2 \end{cases}$, subtract the first equation from the second equation to eliminate the variable b. This results in the equation $5 = 2a$ or $a = \dfrac{5}{2}$. Substituting this into the first equation gives $\dfrac{5}{2} + b = -3$ or $b = -\dfrac{11}{2}$. Thus, $(a, b) = \left(\dfrac{5}{2}, -\dfrac{11}{2}\right)$.

Choice (A) is incorrect. This may result from solving the equation $\dfrac{5}{2} + b = -3$ for b and missing a negative sign to get $\dfrac{11}{2}$.

Question 21

Choice (C) is the correct answer. Recall when $-\dfrac{\pi}{2} < x < \dfrac{\pi}{2}$, $\sec x = \dfrac{1}{\cos x}$; substituting this into the equation $\cos x = \sec x$ gives $\cos x = \dfrac{1}{\cos x}$ or $\cos^2 x = 1$. Taking the square root of both sides of this equation gives $\cos x = \pm 1$. So, x can be any integer multiple of π. Alternatively, use your calculator in radian mode to get x by finding the $\cos^{-1}(-1) = \pi$ and $\cos^{-1}(1) = 0$. Since $-\dfrac{\pi}{2} < x < \dfrac{\pi}{2}$, the only one of these values within that interval is 0.

Choice (D) is incorrect. This likely results from mistaking the function $\sin x$ for $\sec x$. If $\cos x = \sin x$ and $-\dfrac{\pi}{2} < x < \dfrac{\pi}{2}$, then you get the incorrect solution, $x = \dfrac{\pi}{4}$.

Question 22

Choice (A) is the correct answer. In order to find the range of the function g, it is helpful to begin with the range of the function $y = \sin(2x + 1)$. Since the range of the sine function is $[-1, 1]$, it follows that $-1 \leq \sin(2x + 1) \leq 1$ for all values of x. Therefore, $3(-1) - 1 \leq 3\sin(2x + 1) - 1 \leq 3(1) - 1$ or $-4 \leq 3\sin(2x + 1) - 1 \leq 2$. Thus, $-4 \leq g(x) \leq 2$. Alternatively, one could graph $y = g(x)$ on a graphing calculator in radian mode; a suitable viewing window is $[0, 2\pi]$ for x-values and $[-5, 5]$ for y-values. Under a menu on the graphing calculator there are features that can be used to find the minimum y-value of the graph, -4, and the maximum y-value of the graph, 2. Thus, $-4 \leq g(x) \leq 2$.

Choice (C) is incorrect. This may result from incorrectly thinking the minimum value of g occurs when $\sin(2x + 1) = 0$ and the maximum value of g is the coefficient of the sine function.

Question 23

Choice (A) is the correct answer. One way to answer this problem is to solve the system of the two equations, $y = x$ and $\dfrac{x^2}{16} + \dfrac{y^2}{25} = 1$.

Plugging $y = x$ into the second equation yields $\dfrac{y^2}{16} + \dfrac{y^2}{25} = 1$.

Multiplying both sides of the equation by 400 gives $25y^2 + 16y^2 = 400$ or $y^2 = \dfrac{400}{41}$. Since the point of intersection is in the first quadrant, only the positive y value is considered. Thus, $y \approx 3.1235$. And it follows from $y = x$ that $x \approx 3.1235$.

Choice (C) is incorrect. This might result from considering the graphs of the line $y = x$ and the ellipse $\dfrac{x^2}{16} + \dfrac{y^2}{25} = 1$ in the xy-plane. Since the ellipse intersects the positive axes at $x = 4$ and $y = 5$, the line $y = x$ may appear to intersect the ellipse in Quadrant I at a point whose coordinates are halfway between 4 and 5.

Question 24

Choice (B) is the correct answer. From the information given, you can determine an equation that relates the number of red candies, r, to the number of purple candies, p. Since these are the only candies in the bag, the total number of candies in the bag is $r + p$. The probability of randomly selecting a red candy from the bag can then be expressed as $\dfrac{r}{r + p}$. Thus, $\dfrac{r}{r + p} = \dfrac{2}{3}$ or $r = 2p$. The only choice in which the number of red candies is twice the number of purple candies is choice B.

Choice (C) is incorrect. It could result from mistaking the probability $\dfrac{2}{3}$ for the ratio of the number of red candies to the number of purple candies.

Question 25

Choice (C) is the correct answer. From the table, you can see that $f(3) = 4$. Thus, $f(f(3)) = f(4)$. You can also see from the table that $f(4) = 2$. So, $f(f(3)) = 2$.

Choice (B) is incorrect. This could result from incorrectly interchanging the x values and the $f(x)$ values in the table; that is, $f(3) = 0$, which results in $f(0) = 1$.

Question 26

Choice (C) is the correct answer. Since $f(x) = 0$ only when x is equal to -2, 3, or 7, and $g(x) = 0$ only when x is equal to -3, -1, 4, or 7, it follows that $f(x) \cdot g(x) = 0$ only when x is equal to $-3, -2, -1, 3, 4$, or 7. On the other hand, if $f(x) \cdot g(x) = 0$, then either one of the two functions is equal to 0 or both functions are equal to 0. Since there are no other values of x aside from the six listed above such that $f(x) = 0$ or $g(x) = 0$, these six values are the zeros of $f \cdot g$.

Choice (D) is incorrect. This results from missing the fact that the number 7 is repeated as a zero of both functions and the question is to identify the number of zeros that are distinct or different.

Question 27

Choice (A) is the correct answer. From the reference information given at the beginning of the Level 2 Subject Test, you can find the formula for the volume of a right circular cone to be $V = \frac{1}{3}\pi r^2 h$, where r is the radius of the base of the cone and h is the height of the cone. In the given figure, the slant height of the cone, the height of the cone, and a radius of the base of the cone form a right triangle. Thus, the height of the cone can be calculated using the Pythagorean Theorem. Note that the radius of the base of the cone is $\frac{8}{2}$ or 4. So $h^2 + 4^2 = 10^2$ or $h = \sqrt{100 - 16} = \sqrt{84}$. Thus, the volume of the cone is $\frac{1}{3}\pi\left(4^2\right)\sqrt{84} \approx 153.5636$ or 153.6 rounded to the nearest tenth.

Choice (B) is incorrect. This results from mistakenly taking the slant height of the cone to be the height of the cone and using 10 in place of h in the formula for the volume. Thus, getting the volume to be $\frac{1}{3}\pi\left(4^2\right) \cdot 10 \approx 167.5516$ or 167.6 rounded to the nearest tenth.

Question 28

Choice (E) is the correct answer. One way to find the distance between the two points is to start by finding the absolute difference between each pair of coordinates. The absolute difference between the x-coordinates is $\left|2\sqrt{3} - \left(-\sqrt{3}\right)\right| = 3\sqrt{3}$. The absolute difference between the y-coordinates is $\left|4\sqrt{5} - 7\sqrt{5}\right| = 3\sqrt{5}$. These amounts are the lengths of the legs of a right triangle in which the hypotenuse is the segment that has the two points given in the question as its endpoints. Thus, the length of the hypotenuse is the distance between the two points. So, by the Pythagorean Theorem, the distance between the two points is $\sqrt{\left(3\sqrt{3}\right)^2 + \left(3\sqrt{5}\right)^2}$ or $\sqrt{72}$. Alternatively, using the distance formula gives $\sqrt{\left(2\sqrt{3} - \left(-\sqrt{3}\right)\right)^2 + \left(4\sqrt{5} - 7\sqrt{5}\right)^2} = \sqrt{\left(3\sqrt{3}\right)^2 + \left(-3\sqrt{5}\right)^2} \approx 8.4853$ or 8.49 rounded to the nearest hundredth.

Choice (C) is incorrect. It results from incorrectly subtracting the x-coordinates to get $\sqrt{3}$ by missing the negative sign, which leads to $\sqrt{\left(\sqrt{3}\right)^2 + \left(3\sqrt{5}\right)^2} \approx 6.9282$ or 6.93 rounded to the nearest hundredth.

Question 29

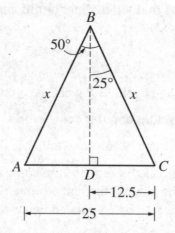

Choice (D) is the correct answer. It is helpful to draw an isosceles triangle ABC with the information given. In the figure shown above, sides AB and BC have equal length of x, and the dashed vertical segment BD is perpendicular to base AC. It can be proved that segment BD bisects the vertex angle B and that D is the midpoint of base AC. To find the perimeter of the triangle, you need to find the value of x. Since $\triangle ABC$ is an isosceles triangle, the base angles $\angle A$ and $\angle C$ are congruent. The two right triangles formed have congruent hypotenuses ($\overline{AB}$ and $\overline{BC}$) and congruent acute angles (A and C); thus, the right triangles ADB and CDB are congruent. Since corresponding parts of congruent triangles are congruent, the altitude bisects both $\angle B$ and $\overline{AC}$, giving an acute angle of measure $25°$ with opposite side of length 12.5 in each right triangle. Using a calculator in degree mode or the degree symbol if your calculator is in radian mode with these measures, you can see that $\sin 25° = \dfrac{12.5}{x}$ or $x = \dfrac{12.5}{\sin 25°} \approx 29.5775$ or 29.6. So, the perimeter of $\triangle ABC$ is approximately $29.6 + 29.6 + 25 = 84.2$.

Alternatively, the law of sines can be used. The base angles of isosceles triangle ABC each have measure 65° This gives you $\dfrac{\sin 50°}{25} = \dfrac{\sin 65°}{x}$, where $x \approx 29.5775$. The perimeter is $2x + 25 \approx 84.1550$, which rounds to 84.2.

Choice (B) is incorrect. This results from incorrectly thinking that cosine has a similar relationship as sine does with the law of sines. Using the incorrect relationship $\dfrac{\cos 50°}{25} = \dfrac{\cos 65°}{x}$ results in $x \approx 16.4369$. Using this value for x gives an approximate perimeter of 57.8739, which rounds to 57.9.

Question 30

Choice (B) is the correct answer. In the problem, the taxi charges include both a base fee of $1.25 and a variable fee that is $0.75 for each mile or part of a mile. Thus, for each full mile in a trip $0.75 goes toward the variable fee and, if there is any additional fraction of a mile in the trip, an additional $0.75 is added to the variable fee. So, using the function $\lceil x \rceil$, defined in the parenthetical as the least integer greater than or equal to x, the variable fee for a trip of length x miles is $\$0.75\lceil x \rceil$. Thus, the taxi fare for a trip of length x miles is $\$1.25 + \$0.75\lceil x \rceil$.

Choice (D) is incorrect. This results from incorrectly thinking the function $\lceil x \rceil$ is the greatest integer less than or equal to x, which is generally denoted by $\lfloor x \rfloor$. Note the differences in these functions from these examples: $\lfloor 8.7 \rfloor = 8$, whereas $\lceil 8.7 \rceil = 9$.

Question 31

Choice (E) is the correct answer. Since the function f is defined as $f(x, y) = \dfrac{x^2 + y^2}{x^2 - y^2}$, you can substitute $-y$ for y into the function to get

$$f(x, -y) = \dfrac{x^2 + (-y)^2}{x^2 - (-y)^2} = \dfrac{x^2 + y^2}{x^2 - y^2}.$$

Choice (C) is incorrect. This may result from incorrectly thinking $f(x, -y) \cdot f(x, y) = -1$, so that $f(x, -y)$ is determined to be equivalent

to $\dfrac{-1}{\dfrac{x^2 + y^2}{x^2 - y^2}} = \dfrac{(-1) \cdot \left(x^2 - y^2\right)}{x^2 + y^2} = \dfrac{y^2 - x^2}{x^2 + y^2}.$

Question 32

Choice (D) is the correct answer. Since each face of the smaller cubes is a square and the diagonal of the face is 1.415 centimeters, if the length of a side of the face is x centimeters, then by the Pythagorean Theorem, x can be calculated from $x^2 + x^2 = 1.415^2$ or $x \approx 1.00056$. Thus, the volume of each smaller cube is 1.00056^3 or 1.00167. Since the larger cube consists of 27 of these smaller cubes, the larger cube has volume $27 \cdot 1.00167 \approx 27.045$.

Choice (E) is incorrect. This results from incorrectly thinking the diagonal of a face of a smaller cube is the length of a side of that face; thus, the edge of a smaller cube is 1.415, giving a volume for the smaller cubes of 1.415^3 or 2.8331. So, the volume of the larger cube would be approximately $27 \cdot 2.8331$ or 76.495.

Question 33

Choice (D) is the correct answer. One way to answer this problem is to consider cases for potential integer values for t. In the first case, consider $t \geq 8$. When $t \geq 8$, the ordered list would have 8 in the middle; thus, the median of the list would be 8. The problem indicates that the mean is equal to the median; so, for $t \geq 8$, then $\dfrac{37 + t}{6} = 8$ or $t = 11$. In the second case, consider $5 \leq t < 8$. After ordering the list with the assumption that $5 \leq t < 8$, you see that the median is $\dfrac{t + 8}{2}$. Given that the mean is equal to the median for $5 \leq t < 8$, then $\dfrac{t + 8}{2} = \dfrac{37 + t}{6}$ or $t = 6.5$. However, the problem states that t is an integer; thus, the assumption that $5 \leq t < 8$ cannot be true. In the third and final case, consider $t < 5$. After ordering the list with the assumption that $t < 5$, you see the median is $\dfrac{5 + 8}{2} = 6.5$. So, given the mean is equal to the median for $t < 5$, then $\dfrac{37 + t}{6} = 6.5$ or $t = 2$. However, the problem states that the range of the list is less than 10 and when $t = 2$, the range would be $12 - 2 = 10$; thus, the assumption that $t < 5$ cannot be true. Since the assumptions in the latter two cases cannot be true, $t \geq 8$ and $t = 11$.

Question 34

Choice (B) is the correct answer. Since polar notation for polar coordinates would be (r, θ), every point on the graph of the polar equation $r = \cos \theta$ must have polar coordinates $(\cos \theta, \theta)$. Of the choices given, only $\left(0.5, \dfrac{\pi}{3}\right)$ are the coordinates that satisfy this condition.

Choice (C) is incorrect. Note that $\cos \pi = -1 \neq 1$.

Question 35

Choice (B) is the correct answer. Consider each statement individually. Statement I indicates that n cannot be an even number. Since 2 is a prime number, 2^3 or 8 could be the value of n. Because 8 is an even number that is the cube of a prime number, it is a counterexample of the statement. Thus, statement I is false. Statement II indicates that n has only 1 positive prime factor; suppose this is not true. The problem gives the prime factorization of n is p^3; thus, p is a prime number. Let s be a different prime number that is also a factor of n. Since $n = p^3$, it follows that s must also be a factor of p^3. The only positive factors of p^3 are 1, p, p^2, and p^3. Therefore, s must be equivalent to one of those factors. Since s is a prime number, it cannot be equal to 1, p^2, or p^3. Therefore, $s = p$, which contradicts the fact that such a prime number s different from p exists. So, the statement must be true. Statement III indicates that n has exactly three distinct factors. As previously stated, the factors of n are 1, p, p^2, and p^3. So, there are four distinct factors of n. Thus, the statement is false. So, only statement II is true.

Question 36

Choice (B) is the correct answer. The center of the hyperbola is by definition the point of intersection of the hyperbola's asymptotes. Thus, solving the system of equations for the asymptotes will give you the coordinates of the center of the hyperbola. From the system $\begin{cases} y = x + 5 \\ y = -x - 5 \end{cases}$ you get $x + 5 = -x - 5$ or $x = -5$. By substituting -5 for x into an equation in the system and solving for y you get $y = 0$. So, the coordinates of the center are $(-5, 0)$.

Choice (A) is incorrect. This results from the assumption that all hyperbolas are centered at the origin.

Question 37

Choice (A) is the correct answer. One way to see how high the student's score is relative to the other students' scores in the class is to see how far the student's score is above the class mean in terms of the standard deviation of the scores on the test. For example, on Test Number 1 the student's score of 85 is 9 points more than the class mean score of 76, which is 3 standard deviations above the class mean. Since the test scores are normally distributed, this score is greater than approximately 99.87% of the other scores. Similarly, one can check to find that the student's test score on any of the other tests is below 3 standard deviations of the class mean. Thus, the student ranked highest on Test Number 1 relative to the other students in the class.

Choice (E) is incorrect. This results from incorrectly considering just the difference between the student's test score and the class mean. For Test Number 5, the student received a score that was 10 points higher than the class mean, which is the greatest difference among the five differences.

Question 38

Choice (C) is the correct answer. Since n has a remainder of 3 when it is divided by 4, it can be written as $n = 4k + 3$ for some integer k. One way to answer this question is to examine each choice and identify if an integer value of t exists such that the expression in the choice can be written as $4k + 3$ for some integer k. If so, then that expression could be equal to n.

For choice (A): If $4t + 2 = 4k + 3$, then $t = k + \frac{1}{4}$. Since k is an integer, $k + \frac{1}{4}$ is not an integer. So, no integer value of t exists for which $4t + 2$ could be written as $4k + 3$. Thus, $4t + 2$ could not be n, and choice (A) is incorrect.

For choice (B): If $4t = 4k + 3$, then $t = k + \frac{3}{4}$. Since k is an integer, $k + \frac{3}{4}$ is not an integer. So, no integer value of t exists for which $4t$ could be written as $4k + 3$. Thus, $4t$ could not be n, and choice (B) is incorrect.

For choice (C): If $4t - 1 = 4k + 3$, then $t = k + 1$. Since k is an integer, $k + 1$ is an integer. So, there exists an integer value of t for which $4t - 1$ can be written as $4k + 3$. Thus, $4t - 1$ could be n, and choice (C) is correct.

For choice (D): If $4t - 2 = 4k + 3$, then $t = k + \frac{5}{4}$. Since k is an integer, $k + \frac{5}{4}$ is not an integer. So, no integer value of t exists for which $4t - 2$ could be written as $4k + 3$. Thus, $4t - 2$ could not be n, and choice (D) is incorrect.

For choice (E): If $4t - 3 = 4k + 3$, then $t = k + \frac{3}{2}$. Since k is an integer, $k + \frac{3}{2}$ is not an integer. So, no integer value of t exists for which $4t - 3$ could be written as $4k + 3$. Thus, $4t - 3$ could not be n, and choice (E) is incorrect.

Question 39

Choice (D) is the correct answer. Since line CD is tangent to the circle at A, $\overline{AB}$ is perpendicular to $\overline{CD}$. Thus, $\triangle ABD$ and $\triangle COA$ are right triangles. You can see that $\overline{AO}$ is a radius of the circle; so, $AO = 1$. Given that the measure of $\angle AOC$ is 30°, the measure of the side $\overline{CA}$, opposite $\angle AOC$, can be found by dividing the length of the longer leg, $\overline{AO}$, by $\sqrt{3}$ to get a length of $\frac{1}{\sqrt{3}}$. Since $CD = 3$, it follows that $AD = 3 - \frac{1}{\sqrt{3}} \approx 2.4227$. Since $\overline{AB}$ is a diameter of the circle, $AB = 2$. So, from the right triangle ABD, you can use the Pythagorean Theorem to show that $BD^2 \approx 2.423^2 + 2^2 \approx 9.8792$. So, $BD \approx 3.1415$.

Choice (E) is incorrect. This may result from incorrectly thinking that the side opposite the 30° angle in the right triangle COA is half the length of the longer leg. This would give AD is $3 - 0.5 = 2.5$ and then give BD is $\sqrt{2.5^2 + 2^2} \approx 3.2016$.

Question 40

Choice (D) is the correct answer. By substituting 1.27 for x in the function you get $e^{1.27} + 1.27 + k < 0$, and by substituting 1.28 for x in the function you get $e^{1.28} + 1.28 + k > 0$. Thus, solving each inequality for k and combining the statements gives $-e^{1.28} - 1.28 < k < -e^{1.27} - 1.27$ or $-4.8766 < k < -4.8308$. Among the choices, the only value that is within this interval is -4.85.

Choice (E) is incorrect. This could come as a result of incorrectly thinking that the function is negative for both given values of x. Then among the choices, the only value that would solve $k < -e^{-1.28} - 1.28 < -e^{-1.27} - 1.27$ is -4.90.

Question 41

Choice (C) is the correct answer. Comparing Graph II with Graph I, one can see that Graph II is a horizontal shift of Graph I. The function f is given by $f(\theta) = A[\sin(B\theta + C)] + D$. Constant A determines the amplitude of the function. Constant B determines the period of the function. Both constants B and C have an affect on the horizontal shift of the graph of the function. Constant D determines the vertical shift of the graph of the function. Since the range, amplitude, and period in Graph II remain the same as in Graph I, there is no change to A, B, or D. Therefore, a change in C would result in shifting Graph I to Graph II.

Question 42

Choice (B) is the correct answer. One way to answer this problem is to set up a system of equations that represent the constraints described in the problem. Let x represent the number of birds on island X before the migration begins. Let y represent the number of birds on island Y before the migration begins. Since the total number of birds is 14,000, it follows that $x + y = 14,000$. After one year, island X has lost 20% of the original birds on the island and gained 15% of the birds that were originally on island Y. Thus, after one year, island X has $0.80x + 0.15y$ birds. Also, the problem states that the number of birds on an island remains constant from year to year. Thus, $0.80x + 0.15y = x$. So, solving the system $\begin{cases} x + y = 14,000 \\ 0.80x + 0.15y = x \end{cases}$ gives $0.80x + 0.15(14,000 - x) = x$ or $x = 6,000$.

Choice (E) is incorrect. This results from incorrectly finding the value of y from the prior system, which would give the number of birds on island Y after one year.

Choice (C) is incorrect. This results from incorrectly representing the number of birds on island X after one year as $0.85y + 0.2x$ instead of the number of birds on island Y after one year. This incorrectly gives the number of birds on island X to be about 6,788.

Qeustion 43

Choice (B) is the correct answer. Since $z = 1 - i$, it follows that $z^2 = (1 - i)^2 = 1 - 2i + i^2 = 1 - 2i + (-1) = -2i$.

Choice (D) is incorrect. This results from incorrectly squaring z to get $1^2 - i^2 = 1 - (-1) = 2$.

Question 44.

Choice (D) is the correct answer. The total surface area of a right circular cylindrical solid is the area of the 2 circular bases plus the lateral surface area. Each circular base has a diameter of $2r$, so they each have a radius of r or area πr^2. The lateral surface area is the height of the cylindrical solid times the circumference of a base. The circumference of the base is $2\pi r$, and the height of the solid is given to be $2r$. So, the lateral surface area is $(2\pi r)(2r) = 4\pi r^2$. Thus, the total surface area is $2\pi r^2 + 4\pi r^2 = 6\pi r^2$.

Choice (C) is incorrect. This may result from incorrectly using the diameter instead of the radius in calculating the area of the circular bases.

Question 45

Choice (A) is the correct answer. If the terminal side of angle θ in standard position terminates in Quadrant IV, then a point (x, y) on its terminal side has a positive x-coordinate and a negative y-coordinate. Considering a point 1 unit from the origin on the terminal side of angle θ, then x and y can be expressed as $x = \cos\theta$ and $y = \sin\theta$. Thus, $\cos\theta > 0$ and $\sin\theta < 0$. Since $\sec\theta = \dfrac{1}{\cos\theta}$ and $\csc\theta = \dfrac{1}{\sin\theta}$, it follows that $\sec\theta > 0$ and $\csc\theta < 0$.

Choice (B) is incorrect. This could come as a result of incorrectly thinking that the reciprocal of the sine function is the secant function and that the reciprocal of the cosine function is the cosecant function.

Question 46

Choice (D) is the correct answer. Using your graphing calculator, enter the data from the table in lists in order to obtain a regression equation that best models the data. Enter the values from the table for time in the first list that will correspond to your x-values, and enter their corresponding heights in a second list as your y-values. The quadratic regression function that is determined for the values is $f(x) \approx -13.73x^2 + 30.93x + 4.99$. You can graph this function on your calculator and then select a feature that will allow you to analyze the graph and find the maximum of the function. The maximum value of the function is approximately 22.4.

Choice (B) is incorrect. This is the result of incorrectly choosing the greatest height given in the table.

Question 47

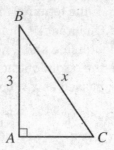

Choice (E) is the correct answer. It is helpful to draw a right triangle ABC as described in the problem. In the figure, the leg opposite angle C has length 3, and the hypotenuse of the triangle $\overline{BC}$ has length x. From this information, you get $\sin C = \dfrac{3}{x}$. Since it is given that $\sin C = k$, you have $\dfrac{3}{x} = k$ or $x = \dfrac{3}{k}$. Using the Pythagorean Theorem, $AC = \sqrt{x^2 - 3^2}$. Substituting $\dfrac{3}{k}$ for x in the expression gives

$$AC = \sqrt{\left(\frac{3}{k}\right)^2 - 3^2} = \sqrt{\left(\frac{3}{k}\right)^2 - 9}.$$

Choice (D) is incorrect. This may result from solving the equation $\dfrac{3}{x} = k$ for x and incorrectly getting $x = \dfrac{k}{3}$.

Question 48

Choice (C) is the correct answer. Since $4.7 > 1$, by definition $f(4.7) = f(4.7 - 1) = f(3.7)$. But $3.7 > 1$, so by definition again $f(3.7) = f(3.7 - 1) = f(2.7)$. Continue this process until the value of x is less than 1 and yields $f(2.7) = f(2.7 - 1) = f(1.7) = f(1.7 - 1) = f(0.7) = 0.7$. Thus, $f(4.7) = 0.7$.

Choice (B) is incorrect. This may result from incorrectly interpreting the definition for $f(x)$ to be equal to $x - 1$ for $x \geq 1$.

Question 49

Choice (A) is the correct answer. If at least one triangle that fits the characteristics described in the problem exists, one can observe that side BC would be opposite angle A in this triangle. Let the angle opposite side AB have measure $x°$. Given that $AB = 6$ and the measure of $\angle A$ is $42°$, then by the law of sines, $\dfrac{\sin x°}{6} = \dfrac{\sin 42°}{4}$. By using a calculator in degree mode or by using the degree symbol if the calculator is in radian mode, you will find that this equation gives

$$\sin x° = \frac{6\sin 42°}{4} = \frac{6(0.6691)}{4} \approx 1.0037.$$ However, $\sin x°$ must be less than or equal to 1. Therefore, no such triangle exists. Additionally, the fact that no such triangle exists can be observed by first considering the right triangle in the diagram below with altitude of length h. The closest point on ray $\overrightarrow{AC}$ to point B is the point on ray $\overrightarrow{AC}$ that is h units directly below B.

Since this is a right triangle, $h = 6\sin 42° = 4.0148$. So, there are no points on ray $\overrightarrow{AC}$ that would be 4 units from point B. The dashed circle drawn on top of the triangle has radius 4 and is centered at B, thus also showing that no point 4 units from point B or on the circle intersects ray $\overrightarrow{AC}$.

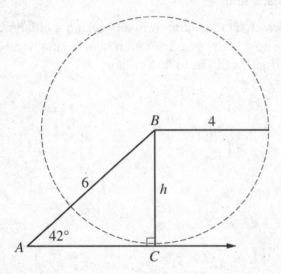

Choice (C) is incorrect. This may result from incorrectly sketching the triangle described without considering constraints. It may appear that the segment BC drawn from vertex B to side AB could result in an obtuse angle C or an acute angle C; however, since BC would be 4, it will not intersect side AC.

Question 50

Choice (E) is the correct answer. The problem indicates that the growth of the computer network is exponential. Thus, the number of users of the computer network x years after counting the number of users began can be modeled by a function of the form $f(x) = ab^x$, where a and b are constants. The problem states that in 10 years the number of users went from 1 million to 10 million. So, there were 1 million users at the start of counting or $f(0) = 1,000,000$, and there were 20 million users after 10 years or $f(10) = 20,000,000$. Based on the definition of the function, $f(0) = ab^0 = a$ and $f(10) = ab^{10}$. So, $\begin{cases} a = 1,000,000 \\ ab^{10} = 20,000,000 \end{cases}$, which gives $1,000,000b^{10} = 20,000,000$ or $b^{10} = 20$. Thus, $b \approx 1.3493$ and $f(x) = 1,000,000(1.3493^x)$. So for 200 million users, solving $200,000,000 = 1,000,000(1.3493^x)$ for x gives $200 = 1.3493^x$ or $\ln(200) = x\ln(1.3493)$ or $x = \dfrac{\ln(200)}{\ln(1.3493)} \approx 17.6862$. Thus, after 17.6862 or 18 years, the number of users was 200 million users. The problem states that it took 10 years for the number of users to rise to 20 million. Therefore, it took $18 - 10$ or 8 years for the number of users to increase from 20 million to 200 million.

Choice (B) is incorrect. This results from answering a different question, which is how many years would it take for the number of users to increase from 1 million to 200 million.

Mathematics Level 2 – Practice Test 2

Practice Helps

The test that follows is an actual, previously administered SAT Subject Test in Mathematics Level 2. To get an idea of what it's like to take this test, practice under conditions that are much like those of an actual test administration.

- Set aside an hour when you can take the test uninterrupted.

- Sit at a desk or table with no other books or papers. Dictionaries, other books, or notes are not allowed in the test room.

- Remember to have a scientific or graphing calculator with you.

- Tear out an answer sheet from the back of this book and fill it in just as you would on the day of the test. One answer sheet can be used for up to three Subject Tests.

- Read the instructions that precede the practice test. During the actual administration you will be asked to read them before answering test questions.

- Use a clock or kitchen timer to time yourself.

- After you finish the practice test, read the sections "How to Score the SAT Subject Test in Mathematics Level 2" and "How Did You Do on the Subject Test in Mathematics Level 2?"

- The appearance of the answer sheet in this book may differ from the answer sheet you see on test day.

- The Reference Information at the start of the practice test is slightly different from what appeared on the original test. It has been modified to reflect the language included on tests administered at the time of this book's printing. These changes are minor and will not affect how you answer the questions.

MATHEMATICS LEVEL 2 TEST

The top portion of the page of the answer sheet that you will use to take the Mathematics Level 2 Test must be filled in exactly as illustrated below. When your supervisor tells you to fill in the circle next to the name of the test you are about to take, mark your answer sheet as shown.

After filling in the circle next to the name of the test you are taking, locate the Background Questions section, which also appears at the top of your answer sheet (as shown above). This is where you will answer the following Background Questions on your answer sheet.

BACKGROUND QUESTIONS

Please answer Part I and Part II below by filling in the appropriate circle in the Background Questions box on your answer sheet. <u>The information you provide is for statistical purposes only and will not affect your test score.</u>

<u>Part I.</u> Which of the following describes a mathematics course you have taken or are currently taking? (FILL IN **ALL** CIRCLES THAT APPLY.)

- Algebra I or Elementary Algebra **OR** Course I of a college preparatory mathematics sequence　　—Fill in circle 1.

- Geometry **OR** Course II of a college preparatory mathematics sequence　　—Fill in circle 2.

- Algebra II or Intermediate Algebra **OR** Course III of a college preparatory mathematics sequence　　—Fill in circle 3.

- Elementary Functions (Precalculus) and/or Trigonometry **OR** beyond Course III of a college preparatory mathematics sequence　　—Fill in circle 4.

- Advanced Placement Mathematics (Calculus AB or Calculus BC)　　—Fill in circle 5.

<u>Part II.</u> What type of calculator did you bring to use for this test? (FILL IN THE **ONE** CIRCLE THAT APPLIES. If you did not bring a scientific or graphing calculator, do not fill in any of circles 6-9.)

- Scientific　　—Fill in circle 6.

- Graphing (Fill in the circle corresponding to the model you used.)

   Casio 9700, Casio 9750, Casio 9800, Casio 9850, Casio 9860, Casio FX 1.0, Casio CG-10, Sharp 9200, Sharp 9300, Sharp 9600, Sharp 9900, TI-82, TI-83, TI-83 Plus, TI-83 Plus Silver, TI-84 Plus, TI-84 Plus Silver, TI-85, TI-86, TI-Nspire, or TI-Nspire CX　　—Fill in circle 7.

   Casio 9970, Casio Algebra FX 2.0, HP 38G, HP 39 series, HP 40 series, HP 48 series, HP 49 series, HP 50 series, TI-89, TI-89 Titanium, TI-Nspire CAS, or TI-Nspire CX CAS　　—Fill in circle 8.

   Some other graphing calculator　　—Fill in circle 9.

When the supervisor gives the signal, turn the page and begin the Mathematics Level 2 Test. There are 100 numbered circles on the answer sheet and 50 questions in the Mathematics Level 2 Test. Therefore, use only circles 1 to 50 for recording your answers.

MATHEMATICS LEVEL 2 TEST

REFERENCE INFORMATION

THE FOLLOWING INFORMATION IS FOR YOUR REFERENCE IN ANSWERING SOME OF THE QUESTIONS IN THIS TEST.

Volume of a right circular cone with radius r and height h: $V = \frac{1}{3}\pi r^2 h$

Volume of a sphere with radius r: $V = \frac{4}{3}\pi r^3$

Volume of a pyramid with base area B and height h: $V = \frac{1}{3}Bh$

Surface area of a sphere with radius r: $S = 4\pi r^2$

DO NOT DETACH FROM BOOK.

GO ON TO THE NEXT PAGE

MATHEMATICS LEVEL 2 TEST

For each of the following problems, decide which is the BEST of the choices given. If the exact numerical value is not one of the choices, select the choice that best approximates this value. Then fill in the corresponding circle on the answer sheet.

<u>Notes:</u> (1) A scientific or graphing calculator will be necessary for answering some (but not all) of the questions in this test. For each question you will have to decide whether or not you should use a calculator.

(2) For some questions in this test you may have to decide whether your calculator should be in the radian mode or the degree mode.

(3) Figures that accompany problems in this test are intended to provide information useful in solving the problems. They are drawn as accurately as possible EXCEPT when it is stated in a specific problem that its figure is not drawn to scale. All figures lie in a plane unless otherwise indicated.

(4) Unless otherwise specified, the domain of any function f is assumed to be the set of all real numbers x for which $f(x)$ is a real number. The range of f is assumed to be the set of all real numbers $f(x)$, where x is in the domain of f.

(5) Reference information that may be useful in answering the questions in this test can be found on the page preceding Question 1.

USE THIS SPACE FOR SCRATCH WORK.

1. If $a = 2^{\frac{1}{5}}$, then $a^3 =$

(A) 0.064
(B) 1.047
(C) 1.516
(D) 2.828
(E) 3.175

GO ON TO THE NEXT PAGE

MATHEMATICS LEVEL 2 TEST—*Continued*

2. In the *xy*-plane, the graph of which of the
   following has a positive *y*-intercept?

   (A) $y = 2x - 6$
   (B) $y = -2x + 1$
   (C) $y = -3$
   (D) $x = -4$
   (E) $x = 5$

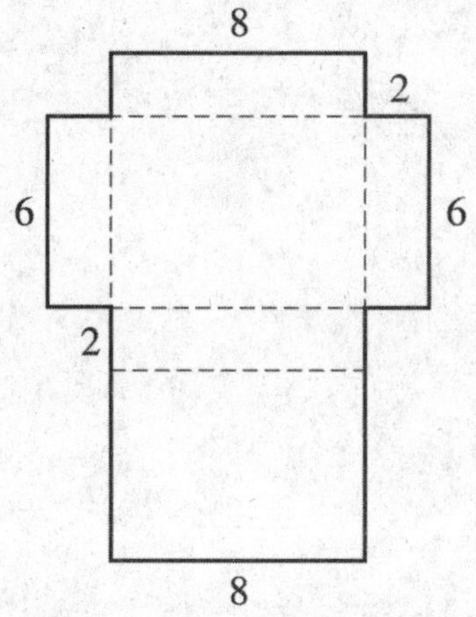

USE THIS SPACE FOR SCRATCH WORK.

3. The net for a rectangular solid is shown in the
   figure above. When the solid is formed, what
   is its volume?

   (A) 32　(B) 96　(C) 144　(D) 152　(E) 192

> If *p* is a prime number, then
> $2p + 1$ is a prime number.

4. Which of the following prime numbers could be a
   value of *p* that yields a COUNTEREXAMPLE to
   the statement above?

   (A) 19　(B) 11　(C) 5　(D) 3　(E) 2

GO ON TO THE NEXT PAGE

USE THIS SPACE FOR SCRATCH WORK.

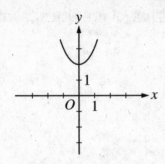

5. If the parabola in the figure above is translated
3 units to the right, which of the following could
represent the equation of this translated parabola?

(A) $y = (x - 3)^2 + 2$

(B) $y = (x + 3)^2 + 2$

(C) $y = (x - 3)^2 - 2$

(D) $y = (x + 3)^2 - 2$

(E) $y = (x - 3)^2 + 5$

6. In the xy-plane, the graph of the linear function f
has slope -3. If the graph of f passes through the
point $(2, 6)$, which of the following could be an
expression for $f(x)$?

(A) $-3x$
(B) $-3x + 12$
(C) $-3x + 20$
(D) $3x$
(E) $3x - 16$

GO ON TO THE NEXT PAGE

MATHEMATICS LEVEL 2 TEST—*Continued*

USE THIS SPACE FOR SCRATCH WORK.

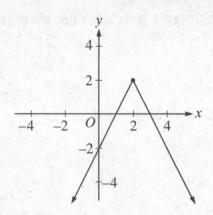

7. What is the range of the function whose graph is shown above?

(A) The set of all real numbers less than or equal to 2
(B) The set of all real numbers greater than or equal to −2
(C) The set of all real numbers greater than or equal to 2
(D) The set of all real numbers between 1 and 3
(E) The set of all real numbers

GO ON TO THE NEXT PAGE

MATHEMATICS LEVEL 2 TEST—*Continued*

Year	Subscribers (in millions)
1995	34
1996	44
1997	55
1998	69
1999	86
2000	109
2001	128
2002	141
2003	159
2004	182
2005	208

USE THIS SPACE FOR SCRATCH WORK.

8. The table above gives the number of cellular phone subscribers in the United States for 1995–2005. Which of the following scatterplots best represents the data above?

(A)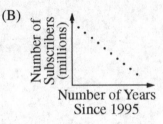

(B)

(C)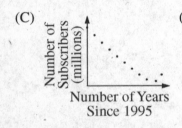

(D)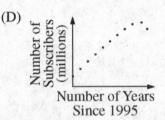

(E)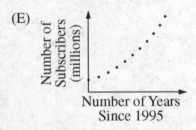

GO ON TO THE NEXT PAGE

MATHEMATICS LEVEL 2 TEST—*Continued*

9. If $f(x) = x^2 - 1$, what are the zeros of f?

(A) f has no zeros.
(B) -1 only
(C) $\ \ 0$ only
(D) $\ \ 1$ only
(E) -1 and 1

USE THIS SPACE FOR SCRATCH WORK.

10. A bag contains 5 black balls and 20 white balls. If a person draws 4 white balls out of the bag without replacing them, what is the probability that the next ball drawn at random will be black?

(A) $\ 0$

(B) $\dfrac{5}{21}$

(C) $\dfrac{4}{5}$

(D) $\ 1$

(E) It cannot be determined from the information given.

11. If $\sin x = 0.90$ and $0 < x < \dfrac{\pi}{2}$, then $\cos\dfrac{x}{2} =$

(A) 0.22
(B) 0.45
(C) 0.56
(D) 0.85
(E) 0.97

GO ON TO THE NEXT PAGE

MATHEMATICS LEVEL 2 TEST—*Continued*

12. What are all values of y that satisfy the inequality
$-y|y| < -y|-y|$?

(A) 0 only
(B) All negative real numbers
(C) All positive real numbers
(D) All real numbers
(E) No real numbers

USE THIS SPACE FOR SCRATCH WORK.

13. In the xy-plane, a parabola is symmetric about the line $x = 2$ and passes through the point $(4, 2)$. Which of the following points must also be on the parabola?

(A) $(0, 2)$

(B) $(2, 4)$

(C) $(4, -2)$

(D) $(-4, 2)$

(E) $(-2, 4)$

14. The function p, given by $p(t) = 3123e^{0.143t}$, can be used to model the population of a town at time t years after the last census, where $t \geq 0$. How many years from the last census will it take for the town's population to double?

(A) 2.11
(B) 4.85
(C) 13.99
(D) 56.27
(E) 61.12

GO ON TO THE NEXT PAGE

MATHEMATICS LEVEL 2 TEST—*Continued*

15. The deviation of an observation x_i is calculated by the formula $x_i - \overline{x}$, where $\overline{x}$ is the arithmetic mean of all of the observations. What is the deviation of 15 in the set of observations 10, 12, 14, 15, and 18 ?

    (A) −54
    (B) −1.2
    (C)   1
    (D)   1.2
    (E)   54

USE THIS SPACE FOR SCRATCH WORK.

16. If $y = 4x - 12$, what is the value of y when it is twice the value of x ?

    (A) 4   (B) 6   (C) 12   (D) 24   (E) 30

17. If $g(x) = x - 1$ and $f(g(x)) = \dfrac{2}{\sqrt{x - 1}}$,

    what is $f(x)$?

    (A) $x - 1$

    (B) $\dfrac{2}{\sqrt{x - 1}} - 1$

    (C) $\dfrac{2}{\sqrt{x - 1}} + 1$

    (D) $\dfrac{2}{\sqrt{x}}$

    (E) $\dfrac{2}{\sqrt{x - 2}}$

GO ON TO THE NEXT PAGE

MATHEMATICS LEVEL 2 TEST—*Continued*

Score	Frequency
10	3
15	4
20	7
25	2
30	8
Total	24

USE THIS SPACE FOR SCRATCH WORK.

18. What is the mean of the scores in the frequency distribution shown above?

(A) 20
(B) 20.42
(C) 21.67
(D) 22.92
(E) 30

19. Point P has coordinates (x, y), where $x = \cos 22.5°$ and $y = \sin 22.5°$. The point P is on the graphs of which of the following?

I. $x^2 y^2 = 1$

II. $x^2 + y^2 = 1$

III. $x^2 - y^2 = 0$

(A) I only
(B) II only
(C) III only
(D) I and II only
(E) I, II, and III

GO ON TO THE NEXT PAGE

MATHEMATICS LEVEL 2 TEST—*Continued*

$$t_1 = 4$$
$$t_n = 2t_{n-1} + 1 \text{ for } n \geq 2$$

USE THIS SPACE FOR SCRATCH WORK.

20. In the recursively defined sequence above, t_1 is the first term of the sequence. What is the sum of the first four terms of the sequence?

(A) 16
(B) 56
(C) 71
(D) 82
(E) 146

21. Which of the following expressions approaches 2 for large values of n ?

(A) $\dfrac{n}{n+2}$

(B) $\dfrac{n-1}{n}$

(C) $\dfrac{2n}{2n-1}$

(D) $\dfrac{2n+1}{n}$

(E) $\dfrac{n^2+1}{n}$

GO ON TO THE NEXT PAGE

MATHEMATICS LEVEL 2 TEST—*Continued*

USE THIS SPACE FOR SCRATCH WORK.

22. What is the value of $f\left(g\left(\dfrac{\pi}{4}\right)\right)$

    if $f(x) = \dfrac{x}{\sqrt{1-x^2}}$ for $-1 < x < 1$,

    and $g(x) = \sin x$ for all x ?

    (A) 0.89
    (B) 0.95
    (C) 1.00
    (D) 1.27
    (E) 2.05

23. A pair of sneakers at a store originally sold for n dollars. After one month, the original price was reduced by 20 percent. After another month, the discounted price was reduced by 25 percent. What was the price of the sneakers, including a 5 percent tax, after the second discount?

    (A) $0.05n$
    (B) $0.0525n$
    (C) $0.5n$
    (D) $0.6n$
    (E) $0.63n$

24. In the xy-plane, the line through $(1, 3)$ and $(3, -1)$ is perpendicular to the line through $(5, 2)$ and $(-1, y)$. What is the value of y ?

    (A) -5 (B) -1 (C) 1   (D) 3   (E) 5

GO ON TO THE NEXT PAGE

MATHEMATICS LEVEL 2 TEST—*Continued*

x	$f(x)$
−2	9
−1	3
0	1
2	9
2.5	−13.5

25. Five values for function f are given in the table above. If f is a polynomial function, which of the following conclusions can be inferred from the given values?

    (A) The graph of f has at least one x-intercept.
    (B) The graph of f is not symmetric with respect to the y-axis.
    (C) f has an inverse function.
    (D) f is increasing for $0 < x < 2$.
    (E) The degree of f is at least 4.

26. If $\dfrac{2}{1-x} = k$, which of the following equals $\dfrac{k}{4}$?

    (A) $\dfrac{8}{1-x}$

    (B) $\dfrac{1}{2-2x}$

    (C) $\dfrac{2}{4-x}$

    (D) $\dfrac{2}{1-4x}$

    (E) $\dfrac{1}{4-4x}$

GO ON TO THE NEXT PAGE

MATHEMATICS LEVEL 2 TEST—*Continued*

27. If one zero of a function with period 8 occurs at
    $x = -1$, another zero must occur at $x =$

    (A) 9   (B) 15   (C) 18   (D) 21   (E) 24

USE THIS SPACE FOR SCRATCH WORK.

28. If f is defined for all numbers x by

    $f(x) = 1 - x^2$, for which of the following

    values of x does $f(x) = \dfrac{f(x)}{3}$?

    (A) 0
    (B) 1
    (C) 2
    (D) 3
    (E) 6

29. Let a, b, x, and y represent real numbers greater
    than 1. If $y = b^{ax}$, which of the following must
    be true?

    (A) $x \log_a y = b$
    (B) $x \log_b y = a$
    (C) $\log_{ax} y = b$
    (D) $\log_y b = ax$
    (E) $\log_b y = ax$

GO ON TO THE NEXT PAGE

MATHEMATICS LEVEL 2 TEST—*Continued*

USE THIS SPACE FOR SCRATCH WORK.

30. For all x and y such that $xy \neq 0$, let

$f(x,y) = \dfrac{xy}{x^2 + y^2}$. Then $f(x,-x) =$

(A) $-x^2$

(B) $-\dfrac{1}{x^2}$

(C) $-\dfrac{1}{2}$

(D) 0

(E) $\dfrac{1}{2}$

31. The lengths of the sides of an isosceles triangle are 5, 10, and 10. What is the measure of the angle formed by the two congruent sides of the triangle?

(A) 29.0°
(B) 60.0°
(C) 75.5°
(D) 104.5°
(E) 151.0°

GO ON TO THE NEXT PAGE

MATHEMATICS LEVEL 2 TEST—*Continued*

32. The 355 students in a school are to be seated on chairs in the gymnasium. The chairs are set up in rows so that each row contains the same number of chairs. If each row is fully occupied except for the last row, which has five empty chairs, which of the following could NOT be the number of chairs in each row?

    (A) 10   (B) 15   (C) 20   (D) 24   (E) 25

33. The rate R of decomposition, in moles per liter per second, of a certain chemical is given by the formula $R = kC^m$, where C is the chemical's concentration, in moles per liter, and k and m are constants. If $R = 1.0$ when $C = 0.2$ and $R = 16.0$ when $C = 0.8$, what is the value of m?

    (A) 2   (B) 4   (C) 8   (D) 16   (E) 32

USE THIS SPACE FOR SCRATCH WORK.

GO ON TO THE NEXT PAGE

MATHEMATICS LEVEL 2 TEST—*Continued*

USE THIS SPACE FOR SCRATCH WORK.

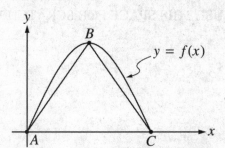

34. The figure above shows a portion of the graph of a function f, where $f(x) = 2\sin(2x)$. One of the vertices of $\triangle ABC$ is a maximum point of the graph of f, and the other two vertices are consecutive x-intercepts of this graph. What is the area of $\triangle ABC$?

(A) $\dfrac{\pi}{2}$

(B) π

(C) 2π

(D) 3π

(E) 4π

35. A piece of paper is 0.03 inch thick. Each time the paper is folded in half, the thickness is doubled. Someone claims that the paper can be folded in half 12 times. If this were true, how thick, to the nearest <u>foot</u>, would the folded paper be?
(1 foot = 12 inches)

(A) 1,475 ft
(B) 1,229 ft
(C)   123 ft
(D)   10 ft
(E)   5 ft

GO ON TO THE NEXT PAGE

MATHEMATICS LEVEL 2 TEST—*Continued*

36. In 3-space, point A has coordinates $(1,5,-1)$ and point B has coordinates $(-2,3,5)$. What is the distance between A and B?

    (A) 6.4   (B) 7   (C) 7.8   (D) 9   (E) 11

USE THIS SPACE FOR SCRATCH WORK.

37. Which of the following is equivalent to

    $\cos\theta - \dfrac{1}{\cos\theta}$, where $0 \le \theta < \dfrac{\pi}{2}$?

    (A) $\dfrac{\cos\theta - 1}{\cos\theta}$

    (B) $\cos^2\theta - 1$

    (C) $\tan\theta$

    (D) $-\tan\theta$

    (E) $-\tan\theta\sin\theta$

GO ON TO THE NEXT PAGE

MATHEMATICS LEVEL 2 TEST—*Continued*

USE THIS SPACE FOR SCRATCH WORK.

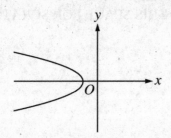

38. The graph in the figure above could be a portion of the graph of which of the following pairs of parametric equations?

(A) $x = t$
     $y = t^2 + 1$

(B) $x = t$
     $y = t^2 - 1$

(C) $x = t^2 - 1$
     $y = t$

(D) $x = -t^2 + 1$
     $y = t$

(E) $x = -t^2 - 1$
     $y = t$

GO ON TO THE NEXT PAGE

USE THIS SPACE FOR SCRATCH WORK.

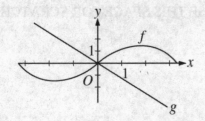

39. The graphs of f and g are shown in the figure above. Which of the following is the graph of $f - g$?

(A)

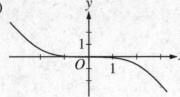

(B)

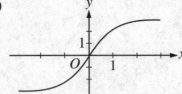

(C)

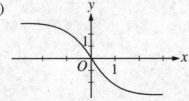

(D)

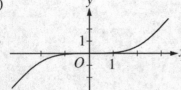

(E)

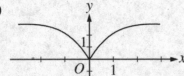

GO ON TO THE NEXT PAGE

MATHEMATICS LEVEL 2 TEST—*Continued*

USE THIS SPACE FOR SCRATCH WORK.

40. If $\sin\theta = \frac{x}{4}$, where $0° < \theta < 90°$ and $0 < x < 4$, then $\cos\theta =$

(A) $\frac{\sqrt{16 - x^2}}{4}$

(B) $\frac{\sqrt{x^2 - 16}}{x}$

(C) $\frac{\sqrt{16 - x^2}}{x}$

(D) $\frac{\sqrt{4 - x^2}}{4}$

(E) $\frac{\sqrt{4 - x^2}}{x}$

41. In the *xy*-plane, what is the center of the circle with equation $x^2 - 10x + y^2 + 6y = 2$?

(A) $(5, 3)$
(B) $(5, -3)$
(C) $(3, -5)$
(D) $(-3, -5)$
(E) $(-5, 3)$

42. Which of the following equations has exactly two distinct real roots?

(A) $(x^2 + 8)(x^2 + 4) = 0$

(B) $(x^3 - 8)(x^2 + 5) = 0$

(C) $(x^2 - 1)(x^2 + 1) = 0$

(D) $(x^4 - 1)(x + 2) = 0$

(E) $(x^2 - 4)(x^2 - 9) = 0$

GO ON TO THE NEXT PAGE

MATHEMATICS LEVEL 2 TEST—*Continued*

USE THIS SPACE FOR SCRATCH WORK.

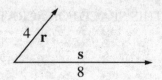

43. In the figure above, **r** and **s** are vectors of
    magnitude 4 and 8, respectively. If the angle
    between the two vectors is 50°, what is the
    magnitude of vector **r** + **s** ?

    (A) 5.5
    (B) 6.2
    (C) 8.9
    (D) 11.0
    (E) 12.0

44. If the points $(2b,3)$, $(b+3,-2)$, and $(b,7)$ lie on
    the same line, what is the value of b ?

    (A) -2

    (B) $-\dfrac{4}{3}$

    (C) $-\dfrac{1}{3}$

    (D) $\dfrac{3}{4}$

    (E) $\dfrac{4}{3}$

GO ON TO THE NEXT PAGE

MATHEMATICS LEVEL 2 TEST—*Continued*

45. Which of the following functions is the same as its inverse function?

   I. $f(x) = \dfrac{1}{x}$

   II. $g(x) = \dfrac{1}{x} + 1$

   III. $h(x) = \dfrac{1}{x-1} + 1$

(A) I only
(B) I and II only
(C) I and III only
(D) II and III only
(E) I, II, and III

USE THIS SPACE FOR SCRATCH WORK.

$$f(t) = 24.62\sin(0.53t - 2.57) + 27.27$$

46. The function f above can be used to approximate the average monthly temperature, in degrees Fahrenheit, for Nome, Alaska. Integer values of t represent the first day of each month (e.g., $t = 1$ represents January 1, $t = 2$ represents February 1, etc.) Using the calendar year, during what month does the average temperature first reach 32°F ?

(A) March
(B) April
(C) May
(D) June
(E) July

GO ON TO THE NEXT PAGE

MATHEMATICS LEVEL 2 TEST—*Continued*

USE THIS SPACE FOR SCRATCH WORK.

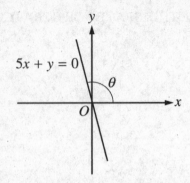

47. The terminal side of an angle θ in standard position coincides with the line with equation $5x + y = 0$ as shown in the figure above. Which of the following equals $\sec \theta$?

(A) $-\sqrt{26}$

(B) $-\sqrt{24}$

(C) $-\dfrac{1}{\sqrt{26}}$

(D) $\sqrt{24}$

(E) $\sqrt{26}$

48. A deposit of $1,000 is used to open an account that pays 8 percent annual interest compounded monthly. Assuming that no withdrawals or other deposits are made, how many months after the original deposit will the amount of money in the account first reach $2,000 ?

(A) 109
(B) 108
(C) 105
(D) 11
(E) 10

GO ON TO THE NEXT PAGE

MATHEMATICS LEVEL 2 TEST—*Continued*

49. Let a, b, w, x, y, and z represent real numbers greater than 1. If $a^x = b^y$ and $a^w = b^z$, which of the following statements must be true?

    (A) $x + w = y + z$
    (B) $x + y = w + z$
    (C) $x + z = w + y$
    (D) $xy = wz$
    (E) $xz = wy$

USE THIS SPACE FOR SCRATCH WORK.

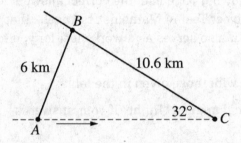

Note: Figure not drawn to scale.

50. In the figure above, points B and C represent two different radar stations. A ship starts at point A, which is 6 kilometers from point B, and sails in a straight line toward point C. When the ship is once again 6 kilometers from point B, how far is it from point C?

    (A)   5.62 km
    (B)   6.88 km
    (C)   8.99 km
    (D)   11.10 km
    (E)   12.18 km

S T O P

**IF YOU FINISH BEFORE TIME IS CALLED, YOU MAY CHECK YOUR WORK ON THIS TEST ONLY.
DO NOT TURN TO ANY OTHER TEST IN THIS BOOK.**

How to Score the SAT Subject Test in Mathematics Level 2

When you take an actual SAT Subject Test in Mathematics Level 2, your answer sheet will be "read" by a scanning machine that will record your response to each question. Then a computer will compare your answers with the correct answers and produce your raw score. You get one point for each correct answer. For each wrong answer, you lose one-fourth of a point. Questions you omit (and any for which you mark more than one answer) are not counted. This raw score is converted to a scaled score that is reported to you and to the colleges you specify.

Worksheet 1. Finding Your Raw Test Score

STEP 1: Table A on the following page lists the correct answers for all the questions on the Subject Test in Mathematics Level 2 that is reproduced in this book. It also serves as a worksheet for you to calculate your raw score.

- Compare your answers with those given in the table.

- Put a check in the column marked "Right" if your answer is correct.

- Put a check in the column marked "Wrong" if your answer is incorrect.

- Leave both columns blank if you omitted the question.

STEP 2: Count the number of right answers.

Enter the total here: _____

STEP 3: Count the number of wrong answers.

Enter the total here: _____

STEP 4: Multiply the number of wrong answers by .250.

Enter the product here: _____

STEP 5: Subtract the result obtained in Step 4 from the total you obtained in Step 2.

Enter the result here: _____

STEP 6: Round the number obtained in Step 5 to the nearest whole number.

Enter the result here: _____

The number you obtained in Step 6 is your raw score.

Answers to Practice Test 2 for Mathematics Level 2

Table A
Answers to the Subject Test in Mathematics Level 2 - Practice Test 2 and Percentage of Students Answering
Each Question Correctly

Question Number	Correct Answer	Right	Wrong	Percent Answering Correctly*	Question Number	Correct Answer	Right	Wrong	Percent Answering Correctly*
1	C			93	26	B			77
2	B			94	27	B			60
3	B			93	28	B			81
4	A			86	29	E			74
5	A			88	30	C			70
6	B			86	31	A			59
7	A			88	32	E			56
8	E			98	33	A			52
9	E			94	34	A			51
10	B			93	35	D			62
11	D			81	36	B			67
12	E			78	37	E			52
13	A			78	38	E			47
14	B			71	39	B			36
15	D			79	40	A			54
16	C			65	41	B			55
17	D			82	42	C			54
18	C			76	43	D			31
19	B			80	44	E			37
20	C			70	45	C			47
21	D			75	46	C			37
22	C			80	47	A			22
23	E			69	48	C			16
24	B			74	49	E			34
25	A			48	50	B			32

* These percentages are based on an analysis of the answer sheets for a random sample of 29,386 students who took the original administration of this test and whose mean score was 684. They may be used as an indication of the relative difficulty of a particular question. Each percentage may also be used to predict the likelihood that a typical Subject Test in Mathematics Level 2 candidate will answer correctly that question on this edition of this test.

Finding Your Scaled Score

When you take SAT Subject Tests, the scores sent to the colleges you specify are reported on the College Board scale, which ranges from 200-800. You can convert your practice test score to a scaled score by using Table B. To find your scaled score, locate your raw score in the left-hand column of Table B; the corresponding score in the right-hand column is your scaled score. For example, a raw score of 25 on this particular edition of the Subject Test in Mathematics Level 2 corresponds to a scaled score of 630.

Raw scores are converted to scaled scores to ensure that a score earned on any one edition of a particular Subject Test is comparable to the same scaled score earned on any other edition of the same Subject Test. Because some editions of the tests may be slightly easier or more difficult than others, College Board scaled scores are adjusted so that they indicate the same level of performance regardless of the edition of the test taken and the ability of the group that takes it. Thus, for example, a score of 500 on one edition of a test taken at a particular administration indicates the same level of achievement as a score of 500 on a different edition of the test taken at a different administration.

When you take the SAT Subject Tests during a national administration, your scores are likely to differ somewhat from the scores you obtain on the tests in this book. People perform at different levels at different times for reasons unrelated to the tests themselves. The precision of any test is also limited because it represents only a sample of all the possible questions that could be asked.

Table B
Scaled Score Conversion Table
Subject Test in Mathematics Level 2 - Practice Test 2

Raw Score	Reported Score	Raw Score	Reported Score	Raw Score	Reported Score
50	800	29	670	8	490
49	800	28	660	7	480
48	800	27	650	6	470
47	800	26	640	5	460
46	800	25	630	4	450
45	800	24	620	3	440
44	800	23	610	2	430
43	800	22	600	1	410
42	800	21	590	0	390
41	800	20	580	−1	370
40	800	19	580	−2	340
39	790	18	570	−3	330
38	780	17	560	−4	320
37	770	16	550	−5	320
36	760	15	540	−6	320
35	740	14	540	−7	320
34	730	13	530	−8	320
33	710	12	520	−9	320
32	700	11	510	−10	320
31	690	10	500	−11	320
30	680	9	500	−12	320

How Did You Do on the Subject Test in Mathematics Level 2?

After you score your test and analyze your performance, think about the following questions:

Did you run out of time before reaching the end of the test?

If so, you may need to pace yourself better. For example, maybe you spent too much time on one or two hard questions. A better approach might be to skip the ones you can't answer right away and try answering all the questions that remain on the test. Then if there's time, go back to the questions you skipped.

Did you take a long time reading the directions?

You will save time when you take the test by learning the directions to the Subject Test in Mathematics Level 2 ahead of time. Each minute you spend reading directions during the test is a minute that you could use to answer questions.

How did you handle questions you were unsure of?

If you were able to eliminate one or more of the answer choices as wrong and guess from the remaining ones, your approach probably worked to your advantage. On the other hand, making haphazard guesses or omitting questions without trying to eliminate choices could cost you valuable points.

How difficult were the questions for you compared with other students who took the test?

Table A shows you how difficult the multiple-choice questions were for the group of students who took this test during its national administration. The right-hand column gives the percentage of students that answered each question correctly.

A question answered correctly by almost everyone in the group is obviously an easier question. For example, 80 percent of the students answered question 22 correctly. But only 31 percent answered question 43 correctly.

Keep in mind that these percentages are based on just one group of students. They would probably be different with another group of students taking the test.

If you missed several easier questions, go back and try to find out why: Did the questions cover material you haven't yet reviewed? Did you misunderstand the directions?

Answer Explanations

For Practice Test 2

The solutions presented here provide one method for solving each of the problems on this test. Other mathematically correct approaches are possible.

Question 1

Choice (C) is the correct answer. Since $a = 2^{\frac{1}{5}}$, then

$$a^3 = \left(2^{\frac{1}{5}}\right)^3 \approx 1.5157,$$ which rounds to 1.516.

The other choices result from an incorrect application of exponents.

Choice (B) is incorrect. This results from $\left(2^{\frac{1}{5}}\right)^{\frac{1}{3}} \approx 1.047$.

Choice (E) is incorrect. This results from $\left(2^5\right)^{\frac{1}{3}} \approx 3.175$.

Question 2

Choice (B) is the correct answer. Each of the five choices is an equation for a line and must be examined.

Choice (B) is written in slope-intercept form, $y = mx + b$, where m is the slope and b is the y-intercept. The y-intercept in this case is 1.

Choice (A) is incorrect, since the y-intercept is −6. Choice (C) is incorrect, since this is an equation of a horizontal line with y-intercept −3.

Choices (D) and (E) are incorrect, since these are both equations of vertical lines that do not intersect the y-axis.

Question 3

Choice (B) is the correct answer. The volume V for a rectangular solid is found by the product of the length, width, and height of the solid. In this case, $V = 8 \cdot 2 \cdot 6 = 96$.

Choice (D) is incorrect. This represents the total surface area of the rectangular solid, the sum of the areas of the six faces of the solid:
$2 \cdot (6 \cdot 8) + 2 \cdot (6 \cdot 2) + 2 \cdot (2 \cdot 8) = 152$.

Question 4

Choice (A) is the correct answer. Each of the five choices is a prime number and must be examined. This problem asks for a COUNTEREXAMPLE to the given statement. This requires identification of a prime number p for which the result $2p + 1$ is NOT a prime number. $2(19) + 1 = 39$, which is not a prime number. The factors of 39 are 1, 3, 13, and 39.

Choice (B) is incorrect because $2(11) + 1 = 23$ is a prime number.

Choice (C) is incorrect because $2(5) + 1 = 11$ is a prime number.

Choice (D) is incorrect because $2(3) + 1 = 7$ is a prime number.

Choice (E) is incorrect because $2(2) + 1 = 5$ is a prime number.

Question 5

Choice (A) is the correct answer. An equation for the given parabola in the figure is $y = x^2 + 2$, since the vertex of the parabola is $(0, 2)$. A graphing calculator may be helpful to you to confirm the answer. If the parabola is translated 3 units to the right, the vertex of the translated parabola is $(3, 2)$. If (h, k) is the vertex, the vertex form of the parabola's equation is given by $y = a(x - h)^2 + k$. Thus, $y = (x - 3)^2 + 2$.

Choice (B) is incorrect. This results from using $(-3, 2)$ as the vertex, a translation of 3 units to the left. It also results from thinking that a parabola with vertex (h, k) has an equation given by $y = a(x + h)^2 + k$.

Question 6

Choice (B) is the correct answer. Since f is a linear function, the slope and a point on the graph can be used to find an expression for $f(x)$. The point-slope form of a line $y - y_1 = m(x - x_1)$ can be used with $m = -3$ and $(x_1, y_1) = (2, 6)$. Thus, $y - 6 = -3(x - 2)$, which simplifies to $y = -3x + 12$. The linear function is given by $f(x) = -3x + 12$.

Choice (A) is incorrect. This results from an arithmetic error with signs in simplifying $y - 6 = -3(x - 2)$.

Choice (C) is incorrect. This results from reversing the order of the coordinates and using $y - 2 = -3(x - 6)$.

Question 7

Choice (A) is the correct answer. The range of a function f is the set of all real numbers $f(x)$, where x is in the domain of f. The maximum value of the function whose graph is shown is 2. The graph indicates that the function continues in the third and fourth quadrants. The y-values of the function (or $f(x)$ values) are all real numbers less than or equal to 2.

Choice (E) is incorrect. The <u>domain</u> of the function is the set of all real numbers.

Question 8

Choice (E) is the correct answer. The data in the table show growth in the number of cellular phone subscribers, and the growth rate is increasing. The scatterplot that best represents the data is the one that shows exponential growth.

Choice (D) is incorrect. The scatterplot shows a maximum after which there is a decrease in the number of subscribers. This is not consistent with the data in the table.

Question 9

Choice (E) is the correct answer. Setting $f(x) = 0$ and solving for x gives you the zeros of the function.

$$x^2 - 1 = 0$$
$$(x - 1)(x + 1) = 0$$
$$x = -1, \ x = 1$$

Another approach is for you to look at the graph of f using your graphing calculator. The graph of f has two x-intercepts, -1 and 1. The x-intercepts of the graph are the zeros of the function.

Choices (B) and (D) are incorrect. The graph of f has two x-intercepts, and thus the function f has two zeros.

Question 10

Choice (B) is the correct answer. If 4 white balls are removed from the bag without replacement, the total number of balls in the bag is 21. The probability that the next ball drawn at random will be black can be determined as follows:

$$\text{Probability} = \frac{\text{the number of black balls in the bag}}{\text{the total number of balls in the bag}} = \frac{5}{21}.$$

Choice (C) is incorrect. If no balls have been drawn from the bag, the probability of drawing a white ball at random can be determined as follows: $\text{Probability} = \frac{\text{the number of white balls in the bag}}{\text{the total number of balls in the bag}} = \frac{20}{25} = \frac{4}{5}.$

Question 11

Choice (D) is the correct answer. For this problem it is important that your calculator is in radian mode. Since $\sin x = 0.90$, $\sin^{-1}(0.90) \approx 1.1198$. Store this intermediate result in calculator memory in order to avoid intermediate rounding errors. Let

$1.1198.... = X$. Evaluate $\cos\left(\dfrac{X}{2}\right)$ to get 0.8473, which rounds to 0.85.

Choice (A) is incorrect. This results from $\dfrac{\cos(X)}{2} \approx 0.2179$, which rounds to 0.22.

Question 12

Choice (E) is the correct answer. For this type of problem, it is helpful for you to examine the inequality for three cases: (1) $y = 0$, (2) $y < 0$, and (3) $y > 0$. For case (1), if $y = 0$, then the inequality becomes $0 < 0$, which is false. For case (2), if $y < 0$, then the inequality becomes $-y \cdot -y < -y \cdot -y$. This simplifies to $0 < 0$, which is false. For case (3), if $y > 0$, then the inequality becomes $-y \cdot y < -y \cdot y$. This simplifies to $0 < 0$, which is false. Thus, no real numbers satisfy the inequality given. The other choices are incorrect because of this reasoning.

Question 13

Choice (A) is the correct answer. The vertical line $x = 2$ is the axis of symmetry of the parabola. This vertical line passes through the vertex of the parabola and divides the parabola into two congruent halves that are reflections of each other. If the point $(4, 2)$ is on the graph of the parabola, then its reflection about the line $x = 2$ is the point $(0, 2)$. The point $(0, 2)$ must also be on the graph of the parabola.

Choice (D) is incorrect. The point $(-4, 2)$ would be on the graph of the parabola if the axis of symmetry was the y-axis.

Question 14

Choice (B) is the correct answer. The population of the town after the last census is given by $p(0) = 3123$. To find the number of years it will take for the population to double, you can solve the following equation:

$$2 \cdot 3123 = 3123e^{0.143t}$$
$$2 = e^{0.143t}$$
$$t \approx 4.8472,$$

which rounds to $t \approx 4.85$. You can also use your graphing calculator to solve the equation graphically or numerically.

Choice (C) is incorrect. This results from omitting the base e and solving the equation $2 = 0.143t$. This produces a value of 13.9860 for t.

Question 15

Choice (D) is the correct answer. The arithmetic mean of the observations given is $\dfrac{10 + 12 + 14 + 15 + 18}{5} = 13.8$. Using the given formula to find the deviation of the observation 15 results in $x_i - \bar{x} = 15 - 13.8 = 1.2$.

Choice (B) is incorrect. This results from an error in the order of terms in the formula, $13.8 - 15 = -1.2$.

Question 16

Choice (C) is the correct answer. To find the value of y when it is twice the value of x, you substitute $y = 2x$ into the given equation. This results in

$$2x = 4x - 12$$
$$-2x = -12$$
$$x = 6.$$

Since $x = 6$, it follows that $y = 4x - 12 = 4(6) - 12 = 12$.

Choice (B) is incorrect. 6 is the value for x.

Question 17

Choice (D) is the correct answer. Since $f(g(x))$ and $g(x)$ are given, the problem asks you to find an expression for $f(x)$. This requires you to find an expression for the function f where $x - 1$ is the input and $\dfrac{2}{\sqrt{x-1}}$ is the output. This is true for $f(x) = \dfrac{2}{\sqrt{x}}$, since $f(x-1) = \dfrac{2}{\sqrt{x-1}}$.

Choice (E) is incorrect. If $f(x) = \dfrac{2}{\sqrt{x-2}}$, then

$$f(x-1) = \dfrac{2}{\sqrt{(x-1)-2}} = \dfrac{2}{\sqrt{x-3}} \neq f(g(x)).$$

Question 18

Choice (C) is the correct answer. The mean of the scores is $\dfrac{10 \cdot 3 + 15 \cdot 4 + 20 \cdot 7 + 25 \cdot 2 + 30 \cdot 8}{24} = 21.\overline{6}$, which rounds to 21.67.

Choice (A) is incorrect. This is the median of the scores and also results from ignoring the frequency of the scores: $\dfrac{10 + 15 + 20 + 25 + 30}{5} = 20$.

Question 19

Choice (B) is the correct answer. Each of the three statements must be analyzed separately. For statement I, if $x = \cos 22.5°$ and $y = \sin 22.5°$, then $x^2 y^2 \neq 1$. This can be verified with your calculator. The calculator should be in degree mode, or the degree symbol can be used if the calculator is in radian mode. Statement I is false because point P is <u>not</u> on the graph. For statement II, $x^2 + y^2 = (\cos 22.5°)^2 + (\sin 22.5°)^2 = 1$. This is the identity $\sin^2 \theta + \cos^2 \theta = 1$. Thus, statement II is true because point P is on the graph. For statement III, $x^2 - y^2 = (\cos 22.5°)^2 - (\sin 22.5°)^2 \neq 0$. This can be verified with the calculator. Statement III is false because point P is <u>not</u> on the graph. Thus, point P is only on the graph of $x^2 + y^2 = 1$.

Question 20

Choice (C) is the correct answer. Using the definition of t_n, the second, third, and fourth terms of the sequence are as follows.

$$t_2 = 2t_1 + 1 = 2(4) + 1 = 9$$
$$t_3 = 2t_2 + 1 = 2(9) + 1 = 19$$
$$t_4 = 2t_3 + 1 = 2(19) + 1 = 39$$

The sum of the first four terms is $4 + 9 + 19 + 39 = 71$.

Choice (B) is incorrect. This results from calculating t_2, t_3, and t_4 without including the +1 and forgetting to include t_1. This method produces $8 + 16 + 32 = 56$.

Question 21

Choice (D) is the correct answer. Each of the expressions must be examined separately. As n increases without bound, $\dfrac{2n+1}{n} \to \dfrac{2n}{n} \to 2$.

Choice (A) is incorrect. As n increases without bound, $\dfrac{n}{n+2} \to \dfrac{n}{n} \to 1$.

Choice (B) is incorrect. As n increases without bound, $\dfrac{n-1}{n} \to \dfrac{n}{n} \to 1$.

Choice (C) is incorrect. As n increases without bound, $\dfrac{2n}{2n-1} \to \dfrac{2n}{2n} \to 1$.

Choice (E) is incorrect. As n increases without bound, $\dfrac{n^2+1}{n} \to \dfrac{n^2}{n} \to n$.

Question 22

Choice (C) is the correct answer. For this problem it is important that your

calculator is in radian mode. The value of $f\!\left(g\!\left(\dfrac{\pi}{4}\right)\right) = \dfrac{\sin\!\left(\dfrac{\pi}{4}\right)}{\sqrt{1 - \left(\sin\!\left(\dfrac{\pi}{4}\right)\right)^2}} =$

$\dfrac{\dfrac{\sqrt{2}}{2}}{\sqrt{1 - \left(\dfrac{\sqrt{2}}{2}\right)^2}} = \dfrac{\sqrt{2}}{2} \cdot \dfrac{\sqrt{2}}{1} = 1.$ A calculator can also be used to

approximate $\sin\!\left(\dfrac{\pi}{4}\right) \approx 0.7071$ in the expression above.

Choice (B) is incorrect. This results from calculating the value

of $g\!\left(f\!\left(\dfrac{\pi}{4}\right)\right) \approx 0.9548.$

Choice (D) is incorrect. This is the value of $f\!\left(\dfrac{\pi}{4}\right) \approx 1.2688.$

Question 23

Choice (E) is the correct answer. After one month, the price of the sneakers was $0.8n$, which is a 20 percent reduction from the original price. After another month, the price of the sneakers was $0.75(0.8n)$, which is a 25 percent reduction. After the second discount and including a 5 percent tax, the price of the sneakers was $0.75(0.8n) + 0.05(0.75(0.8n)) = 0.75(0.8n)(1.05) = 0.63n.$

Choice (D) is incorrect. This results from not including the 5 percent tax on $0.75(0.8n)$. It also results from assuming a discounted price of $0.55n$ after the two months, which is a 45 percent reduction from the original price. An incorrect application of the 5 percent tax on the original price results in $0.55n + 0.05n = 0.60n.$

Question 24

Choice (B) is the correct answer. The slope of the line through $(1, 3)$ and $(3, -1)$ is given by $m = \dfrac{3 - (-1)}{1 - 3} = \dfrac{4}{-2} = -2$. Since the product of the slopes of a pair of perpendicular lines is -1, a line that is perpendicular to the given line has slope $\dfrac{1}{2}$. Thus,

$$\frac{1}{2} = \frac{2 - y}{5 - (-1)}$$
$$4 - 2y = 6$$
$$-2y = 2$$
$$y = -1.$$

Choice (E) is incorrect. This results from incorrectly concluding that the line that is perpendicular to the given line has slope $-\dfrac{1}{2}$.

Question 25

Choice (A) is the correct answer. The graph of f must intersect the x-axis in the interval $2 < x < 2.5$ because f is a polynomial function with $f(2) > 0$ and $f(2.5) < 0$. Thus, the graph of f has at least one x-intercept. The other choices are incorrect. Not enough information has been provided to determine if choices (B), (D), or (E) are correct. For example, the graph of f could intersect the x-axis on the interval $0 < x < 2$, and as a result f would not be increasing on the interval.

Choice (C) is incorrect. The function f is not a one-to-one function, and its graph does not pass the horizontal line test. Thus, f does not have an inverse function.

Question 26

Choice (B) is the correct answer. Using the given information,

$$\frac{k}{4} = \frac{\dfrac{2}{1 - x}}{4} = \frac{2}{1 - x} \cdot \frac{1}{4} = \frac{2}{4 - 4x} = \frac{2}{2(2 - 2x)} = \frac{1}{2 - 2x}.$$

Choice (A) is incorrect. This results from incorrectly interpreting $\dfrac{k}{4}$ as $\dfrac{2}{1 - x} \cdot 4 = \dfrac{8}{1 - x}.$

Question 27

Choice (B) is the correct answer. For ease of reference, you can identify the function as f. Since f is a periodic function with period 8, then $f(x) = f(x + 8)$. If $x = -1$ is a zero of f, then $f(-1) = f(-1 + 8) = f(7) = 0$. Since $f(7) = 0$, then $f(7) = f(7 + 8) = f(15) = 0$.

Choice (A) is incorrect. This results from an incorrect definition of a periodic function, $f(x) = f(8 - x)$. Thus, $f(-1) = f(8 - (-1))$, which leads to incorrectly concluding that $f(9)$ is equal to 0.

Question 28

Choice (B) is the correct answer. Consider $1 - x^2 = \dfrac{1 - x^2}{3}$. By inspection, these two expressions can only be equal if they are both equal to 0. If $1 - x^2 = 0$, then $x = 1$ or $x = -1$.

Choice (A) is incorrect. This results from using the "output" value, which is 0, rather than the "input" values of $x = 1$ or $x = -1$ that produce a result of 0.

Question 29

Choice (E) is the correct answer. This is a direct application of the definition of logarithm. The logarithm of a number is the exponent to which the base must be raised to produce that number. By taking the base b logarithm of both sides of the given equation, you will find that the result is $\log_b y = ax$.

The other choices are incorrect. These result from an incorrect understanding of the definition of logarithm.

Question 30

Choice (C) is the correct answer. Using the function definition given, you can determine $f(x, -x) = \dfrac{x \cdot -x}{x^2 + x^2} = \dfrac{-x^2}{2x^2} = -\dfrac{1}{2}$.

Choice (B) is incorrect. This results from algebraic errors and incorrectly thinking that $f(x, -x) = \dfrac{x \cdot -x}{x^2 + x^2} = \dfrac{-x^2}{x^2 + x^2} = \dfrac{-1}{x^2}$. This is not a true statement.

Question 31

Choice (A) is the correct answer. It may be helpful to draw a figure.

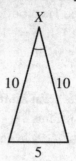

The law of cosines can be used to find the measure of the angle, as shown below. The calculator should be in degree mode.

$$5^2 = 10^2 + 10^2 - 2 \cdot 10 \cdot 10 \cos X$$

$$\cos X = \frac{175}{200}$$

$$X = \cos^{-1}\left(\frac{175}{200}\right)$$

$$X \approx 28.9550°$$

Choice (C) is incorrect. This results from working with an incorrect pair of sides and angle.

$$10^2 = 5^2 + 10^2 - 2 \cdot 5 \cdot 10 \cos X$$

$$\cos X = \frac{25}{100}$$

$$X = \cos^{-1}\left(\frac{25}{100}\right)$$

$$X \approx 75.5225°$$

Question 32

Choice (E) is the correct answer. Each of the five choices must be examined to determine if that is a possible value for the number of chairs in each row. The problem asks for which is NOT possible. Based on the information given, 360 chairs are needed.

Consider choice (A). If there are 10 chairs in each row, $360 = 10 \cdot 35 + 10$. This is a possibility, since there would be 36 rows, and the last row would have 5 students and 5 empty chairs.

Consider choice (B). If there are 15 chairs in each row, $360 = 15 \cdot 23 + 15$. This is a possibility, since there would be 24 rows, and the last row would have 10 students and 5 empty chairs.

Consider choice (C). If there are 20 chairs in each row, $360 = 20 \cdot 17 + 20$. This is a possibility, since there would be 18 rows, and the last row would have 15 students and 5 empty chairs.

Consider choice (D). If there are 24 chairs in each row, $360 = 24 \cdot 14 + 24$. This is a possibility, since there would be 15 rows, and the last row would have 19 students and 5 empty chairs.

Consider choice (E). If there are 25 chairs in each row, $375 = 25 \cdot 14 + 25$. This is NOT a possibility, since there would be 15 rows, and the last row would have 5 students and 20 empty chairs, which does not meet the requirement.

Question 33

Choice (A) is the correct answer. Using the formula $R = kC^m$ and the given information produces two equations: $1 = k(0.2)^m$ and $16 = k(0.8)^m$. Thus, you can solve for k in both equations and set those equal to one another: $k = \dfrac{1}{(0.2)^m}$ and $k = \dfrac{16}{(0.8)^m}$.

$$\frac{1}{(0.2)^m} = \frac{16}{(0.8)^m}$$

$$\frac{(0.8)^m}{(0.2)^m} = 16$$

$$4^m = 16$$

$$m = 2$$

Choice (B) is incorrect. This results from an algebraic error in incorrectly simplifying $\dfrac{(0.8)^m}{(0.2)^m} = 16$ as $4m = 16$ and $m = 4$. This is not a true statement.

Question 34

Choice (A) is the correct answer. Your graphing calculator can be used to examine the graph of $y = 2\sin(2x)$ in the first quadrant. Point A is at the origin, and Point C is at $x = \dfrac{\pi}{2}$. The base of the triangle has a length of $\dfrac{\pi}{2}$. The coordinates of point B are $\left(\dfrac{\pi}{4}, 2\right)$, so the height of the triangle is 2. The area of the triangle is found by

$$A = \frac{1}{2}bh = \frac{1}{2}\left(\frac{\pi}{2}\right)(2) = \frac{\pi}{2}.$$

Choice (B) is incorrect. This results from either forgetting the $\dfrac{1}{2}$ in the area formula or by working with $y = 2\sin(x)$. The area found from using this incorrect function is $A = \dfrac{1}{2}bh = \dfrac{1}{2}(\pi)(2) = \pi$.

Question 35

Choice (D) is the correct answer. Since the problem asks for the answer to the nearest foot, it is helpful for you to convert 0.03 inch to feet:

$$0.03 \text{ in} \cdot \frac{1 \text{ ft}}{12 \text{ in}} = 0.0025 \text{ ft.}$$ Using the claim that the paper can be folded in half 12 times results in a thickness of $(0.0025)2^{12} = 10.24$ ft. This rounds to 10 ft.

Choice (E) is incorrect. This results from taking the result of 10.24 ft and thinking that half of that is the thickness of the paper: 5.12 rounds to 5 ft.

Choice (C) is incorrect. This results from not converting 0.03 inch to feet and computing $(0.03)2^{12} = 122.88$ ft, which rounds to 123 ft.

Question 36

Choice (B) is the correct answer. The distance in 3-space between point A and point B is given by

$$\text{Distance} = \sqrt{(1-(-2))^2 + (5-3)^2 + (-1-5)^2} = \sqrt{49} = 7.$$

Choice (C) is incorrect. This results from incorrectly thinking that the distance is found by taking the square of the sum of the coordinates in an individual point:

$$\text{Distance} = \sqrt{(1+5+(-1))^2 + ((-2)+3+5)^2} = \sqrt{61} \approx 7.8102.$$

Choice (D) is incorrect. This results from incorrectly thinking that the distance is found by taking the sum of the squares of the coordinates rather than the difference:

$$\text{Distance} = \sqrt{(1+(-2))^2 + (5+3)^2 + (-1+5)^2} = \sqrt{81} = 9.$$

Question 37

Choice (E) is the correct answer. $\cos\theta - \dfrac{1}{\cos\theta} = \cos\theta \cdot \dfrac{\cos\theta}{\cos\theta} - \dfrac{1}{\cos\theta} =$
$\dfrac{\cos^2\theta - 1}{\cos\theta} = \dfrac{-\sin^2\theta}{\cos\theta} = \dfrac{-\sin\theta}{\cos\theta} \cdot \sin\theta = -\tan\theta\sin\theta.$ This makes use of

the identity $\sin^2\theta + \cos^2\theta = 1$ and the definition $\tan\theta = \dfrac{\sin\theta}{\cos\theta}.$

Choice (B) is incorrect. This results from an algebraic error, as follows:

$\cos\theta - \dfrac{1}{\cos\theta} = \cos\theta \cdot \dfrac{\cos\theta}{\cos\theta} - \dfrac{1}{\cos\theta} = \dfrac{\cos^2\theta - \cancel{\cos\theta}}{\cancel{\cos\theta}} = \cos^2\theta - 1.$

This is not a true statement.

Question 38

Choice (E) is the correct answer. This is a parabolic curve that opens to the left with an x-intercept of -1 that occurs when $t = 0$. A graphing calculator is helpful for this problem in order to graph the parametric equations in parametric mode. In order to produce a complete graph, you must consider negative and positive values for t.

Since this is a parabolic curve that opens to the left, choices (A) and (B) are incorrect. These are parabolic curves that open up.

Choice (C) is incorrect, since it is a parabolic curve that opens to the right.

Choice (D) is incorrect, since it is a parabolic curve that opens to the left with an x-intercept of 1, and the graph is also in Quadrants I and IV.

Question 39

Choice (B) is the correct answer. This choice is the graph of $f - g$. The values of $f(x)$ are positive in Quadrant I and negative in Quadrant III; f is increasing from its minimum value in Quadrant III to its maximum value in Quadrant I. The values of $g(x)$ are positive in Quadrant II and negative in Quadrant IV; g is decreasing. You can use this information to consider the values of $(f - g)(x)$. For $x < 0$, $(f - g)(x) < 0$ and the values are increasing. For $x > 0$, $(f - g)(x) > 0$ and the values are increasing. Based on this information, choices (A), (C), and (E) are incorrect.

Choice (D) is incorrect. This graph does not reflect the correct behavior of the graph of $f - g$. This is particularly noticeable on the interval $[-1, 1]$.

Question 40

Choice (A) is the correct answer. It may be helpful to draw a figure.

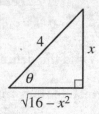

In the right triangle, since $\sin \theta = \dfrac{x}{4}$, x is the length of the leg opposite θ and 4 is the hypotenuse. Using the Pythagorean Theorem, you can determine that the other leg has length $\sqrt{16 - x^2}$. Using the definition, you find that $\cos \theta = \dfrac{\sqrt{16 - x^2}}{4}$.

Choice (C) is incorrect. This results from using the leg of length x instead of the hypotenuse 4 and incorrectly thinking that $\cos \theta = \dfrac{\sqrt{16 - x^2}}{x}$. This is not a true statement.

Question 41

Choice (B) is the correct answer. The center of the circle can be found by completing the square of x and completing the square of y. This will produce an equation for the circle in center-radius form $(x - h)^2 + (y - k)^2 = r^2$, where (h, k) is the center and r is the radius, as shown below:

$$\left(x^2 - 10x + (-5)^2\right) + \left(y^2 + 6y + 3^2\right) = 2 + (-5)^2 + 3^2$$
$$(x - 5)^2 + (y + 3)^2 = 36$$

Thus, the center of the circle is $(5, -3)$.

Choice (A) is incorrect. This results from an error in use of the center-radius form, which concludes from the equation that $(5, 3)$ is the center.

Question 42

Choice (C) is the correct answer. This problem requires examining each of the answer choices. The equation $\left(x^2 - 1\right)\left(x^2 + 1\right) = 0$ has two distinct real roots: $x = -1$ and $x = 1$. The graph of $y = \left(x^2 - 1\right)\left(x^2 + 1\right)$ has two x-intercepts.

Choice (A) is incorrect. This equation has no real roots. The graph of $y = \left(x^2 + 8\right)\left(x^2 + 4\right)$ has no x-intercepts.

Choice (B) is incorrect. This equation has one real root: $x = 2$. The graph of $y = \left(x^3 - 8\right)\left(x^2 + 5\right)$ has one x-intercept.

Choice (D) is incorrect. This equation has three real roots: $x = -1$, $x = 1$, and $x = -2$. The graph of $y = \left(x^4 - 1\right)(x + 2)$ has three x-intercepts.

Choice (E) is incorrect. This equation has four real roots: $x = -3$, $x = -2$, $x = 2$, and $x = 3$. The graph of $y = \left(x^2 - 4\right)\left(x^2 - 9\right)$ has four x-intercepts.

Question 43

Choice (D) is the correct answer. It is helpful to use the given figure to draw a parallelogram where vector $\mathbf{r} + \mathbf{s}$ is the diagonal of the parallelogram.

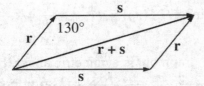

The law of cosines can be used where the magnitude of $\mathbf{r} + \mathbf{s}$ is the unknown side of the triangle with sides 4 and 8. The angle between $\mathbf{r}$ and $\mathbf{s}$ in the parallelogram is 130°, since adjacent angles in a parallelogram are supplementary. If x is the magnitude of $\mathbf{r} + \mathbf{s}$,

$$x^2 = 4^2 + 8^2 - 2(4)(8)\cos 130°$$
$$x^2 \approx 121.1384$$
$$x \approx 11.0063,$$

which rounds to $x \approx 11.0$.

Choice (E) is incorrect. This results from incorrectly reasoning that the magnitude of the sum of the vectors is the sum of the magnitudes of the individual vectors, $4 + 8 = 12$.

Question 44

Choice (E) is the correct answer. If the three given points lie on the same line, then the slopes found by using any two of the points are equal. The slope of the line containing $(2b, 3)$ and $(b + 3, -2)$ is equal to the slope of the line containing $(b + 3, -2)$ and $(b, 7)$. Thus, $\dfrac{3 - (-2)}{2b - (b + 3)} = \dfrac{-2 - 7}{b + 3 - b}$. This simplifies to

$$\frac{5}{b - 3} = \frac{-9}{3}$$

$$\frac{5}{b - 3} = -3$$

$$-3b + 9 = 5$$

$$-3b = -4$$

$$b = \frac{4}{3}.$$

Choice (B) is incorrect. The solution $b = -\dfrac{4}{3}$ results from an arithmetic error in the above calculations.

Question 45

Choice (C) is the correct answer. Each of the three statements must be analyzed separately. If a function f is its own inverse, then $f(f(x)) = x$ for all x in the domain of f.

Consider statement I. Since $f(f(x)) = f\left(\dfrac{1}{x}\right) = \dfrac{1}{\frac{1}{x}} = x$,

f is its own inverse. The graph of f is symmetric about the line $y = x$. Statement I is true. Consider statement II. Since

$$g(g(x)) = g\left(\frac{1}{x} + 1\right) = \frac{1}{\frac{1}{x} + 1} + 1 = \frac{x}{1 + x} + 1 = \frac{x + 1 + x}{1 + x} \neq x, \, g \text{ is not}$$

its own inverse. Statement II is false. Consider statement III. Since

$$h(h(x)) = h\left(\frac{1}{x - 1} + 1\right) = \frac{1}{\left(\frac{1}{x - 1} + 1\right) - 1} + 1 = \frac{1}{\frac{1}{x - 1}} + 1 = x - 1 + 1 = x,$$

h is its own inverse. The graph of h is symmetric about the line $y = x$. Statement III is true. Since statements I and III are true, choice (C) is correct.

Question 46

Choice (C) is the correct answer. For this problem it is important that your calculator is in radian mode. Graph $y = 24.62\sin(0.53x - 2.57) + 27.57$ using the graphing calculator. A suitable viewing window is $[0, 12]$ for x-values and $[0, 60]$ for y-values. Integer x-values represent the first day of each month of the calendar year. The y-values represent temperature, in degrees Fahrenheit, for Nome, Alaska. Graph the horizontal line $y = 32$. The two intersection points of the two graphs give information about when the average temperature in Nome is 32°F. Since the problem asks during which month does the average temperature <u>first</u> reach 32°F, the result is found by examining the first intersection point. This point has coordinates $(5.2138, 32)$, which means that 5.2138 is during the fifth month of the calendar year, May.

Choice (D) is incorrect. This results from an incorrect interpretation of 5.2138 as applying to the sixth month of the calendar year, June.

Question 47

Choice (A) is the correct answer. Consider a point (x, y) on the circle centered at the origin $x^2 + y^2 = r^2$. If θ is an angle in standard position and (x, y) is on the terminal side of the angle, then $\cos\theta = \dfrac{x}{r}$ and $\sin\theta = \dfrac{y}{r}$. In this problem, $(-1, 5)$ is a point that lies on the line with equation $5x + y = 0$ and is on the terminal side of θ. If $(-1, 5)$ is on the circle centered at the origin, then the radius of the circle r is $r = \sqrt{x^2 + y^2} = \sqrt{(-1)^2 + 5^2} = \sqrt{26}$. Using the definition,

$\sec\theta = \dfrac{1}{\cos\theta} = \dfrac{r}{x} = \dfrac{\sqrt{26}}{-1} = -\sqrt{26}$.

Choice (C) is incorrect. This is the value of $\dfrac{x}{r} = \dfrac{-1}{\sqrt{26}} = \cos\theta$.

Question 48

Choice (C) is the correct answer. This problem focuses on compound interest, an example of exponential growth. Since the annual interest is 8 percent, the monthly interest is $\dfrac{0.08}{12}$. To find the number of months needed to reach \$2,000 in the account, solve the equation

$$2000 = 1000\left(1 + \frac{0.08}{12}\right)^{x}.$$

Use your graphing calculator to find the point of intersection of the graphs $y = 2000$ and $y = 1000\left(1 + \dfrac{0.08}{12}\right)^{x}$. A suitable viewing window is $[0, 120]$ for x-values and $[0, 2{,}500]$ for y-values. Alternately, an equation solver can be used. The two graphs intersect at $x \approx 104.3183$, which means 105 months are needed.

Choice (E) is incorrect. This results from using 0.08 as the monthly interest rate and solving $2000 = 1000(1 + 0.08)^{x}$. Using this equation leads to an incorrect conclusion that $x \approx 9.0065$, which can be interpreted as 10 months are needed.

Question 49

Choice (E) is the correct answer. Since the given variables all represent real numbers greater than 1, the equations $a^{x} = b^{y}$ and $a^{w} = b^{z}$ can be manipulated by taking the logarithm of both sides. This results in

$$\begin{array}{ll} \log\left(a^{x}\right) = \log\left(b^{y}\right) & \log\left(a^{w}\right) = \log\left(b^{z}\right) \\ x\log a = y\log b & w\log a = z\log b \end{array}$$

and . Thus, $(x + w)\log a = (y + z)\log b$. This means that choices (A), (B), and (C) are not possible, since additive expressions with the exponents will involve logarithms. To find a relationship between the exponents without involving logarithms consider:

$$x\log a \cdot z\log b = w\log a \cdot y\log b$$
$$xz\log a \cdot \log b = wy\log a \cdot \log b$$
$$xz = wy.$$

In this case you know that $\log a$ and $\log b$ are nonzero. Choice (E) is the correct result. A concrete example of this property can be seen with $3^{4} = 9^{2}$ and $3^{6} = 9^{3}$. In this case $4 \cdot 3 = 2 \cdot 6$.

Question 50

Choice (B) is the correct answer. It is helpful to use the given figure.

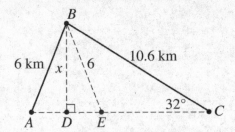

To find the height x of triangle ABC, solve $\sin 32° = \dfrac{x}{10.6}$, which results in $x \approx 5.6171$. Use degree mode or the degree symbol if the calculator is in radian mode. Store this value for x in the calculator as X. Label the point D, where the height of the triangle intersects side $\overline{AC}$. To find DC, solve $\cos 32° = \dfrac{DC}{10.6}$, which results in $DC \approx 8.9893$.

Store this value for DC in the calculator as Y. Label the point E in the smaller right triangle with hypotenuse 6. Then $DE = \sqrt{36 - X^2}$, which results in $DE \approx 2.1090$. Store this value for DE in the calculator as Z. Then EC, the distance when the ship is 6 kilometers from point B, is $Y - Z \approx 6.8804$ kilometers.

Choice (D) is incorrect.

This results from $Y + Z \approx 11.0983$. This is also the value of AC.

Mathematics Level 2 – Practice Test 3

Practice Helps

The test that follows is an actual, previously administered SAT Subject Test in Mathematics Level 2. To get an idea of what it's like to take this test, practice under conditions that are much like those of an actual test administration.

- Set aside an hour when you can take the test uninterrupted.

- Sit at a desk or table with no other books or papers. Dictionaries, other books, or notes are not allowed in the test room.

- Remember to have a scientific or graphing calculator with you.

- Tear out an answer sheet from the back of this book and fill it in just as you would on the day of the test. One answer sheet can be used for up to three Subject Tests.

- Read the instructions that precede the practice test. During the actual administration you will be asked to read them before answering test questions.

- Use a clock or kitchen timer to time yourself.

- After you finish the practice test, read the sections "How to Score the SAT Subject Test in Mathematics Level 2" and "How Did You Do on the Subject Test in Mathematics Level 2?"

- The appearance of the answer sheet in this book may differ from the answer sheet you see on test day.

- The Reference Information at the start of the practice test is slightly different from what appeared on the original test. It has been modified to reflect the language included on tests administered at the time of this book's printing. These changes are minor and will not affect how you answer the questions.

MATHEMATICS LEVEL 2 TEST

The top portion of the page of the answer sheet that you will use to take the Mathematics Level 2 Test must be filled in exactly as illustrated below. When your supervisor tells you to fill in the circle next to the name of the test you are about to take, mark your answer sheet as shown.

After filling in the circle next to the name of the test you are taking, locate the Background Questions section, which also appears at the top of your answer sheet (as shown above). This is where you will answer the following Background Questions on your answer sheet.

BACKGROUND QUESTIONS

Please answer Part I and Part II below by filling in the appropriate circle in the Background Questions box on your answer sheet. <u>The information you provide is for statistical purposes only and will not affect your test score.</u>

<u>Part I.</u> Which of the following describes a mathematics course you have taken or are currently taking? (FILL IN **ALL** CIRCLES THAT APPLY.)

- Algebra I or Elementary Algebra **OR** Course I of a college preparatory mathematics sequence   —Fill in circle 1.

- Geometry **OR** Course II of a college preparatory mathematics sequence   —Fill in circle 2.

- Algebra II or Intermediate Algebra **OR** Course III of a college preparatory mathematics sequence   —Fill in circle 3.

- Elementary Functions (Precalculus) and/or Trigonometry **OR** beyond Course III of a college preparatory mathematics sequence   —Fill in circle 4.

- Advanced Placement Mathematics (Calculus AB or Calculus BC)   —Fill in circle 5.

<u>Part II.</u> What type of calculator did you bring to use for this test? (FILL IN THE **ONE** CIRCLE THAT APPLIES. If you did not bring a scientific or graphing calculator, do not fill in any of circles 6-9.)

- Scientific   —Fill in circle 6.

- Graphing (Fill in the circle corresponding to the model you used.)

  Casio 9700, Casio 9750, Casio 9800, Casio 9850, Casio 9860, Casio FX 1.0, Casio CG-10, Sharp 9200, Sharp 9300, Sharp 9600, Sharp 9900, TI-82, TI-83, TI-83 Plus, TI-83 Plus Silver, TI-84 Plus, TI-84 Plus Silver, TI-85, TI-86, TI-Nspire, or TI-Nspire CX   —Fill in circle 7.

  Casio 9970, Casio Algebra FX 2.0, HP 38G, HP 39 series, HP 40 series, HP 48 series, HP 49 series, HP 50 series, TI-89, TI-89 Titanium, TI-Nspire CAS, or TI-Nspire CX CAS   —Fill in circle 8.

  Some other graphing calculator   —Fill in circle 9.

When the supervisor gives the signal, turn the page and begin the Mathematics Level 2 Test. There are 100 numbered circles on the answer sheet and 50 questions in the Mathematics Level 2 Test. Therefore, use only circles 1 to 50 for recording your answers.

MATHEMATICS LEVEL 2 TEST

REFERENCE INFORMATION

THE FOLLOWING INFORMATION IS FOR YOUR REFERENCE IN ANSWERING SOME OF THE QUESTIONS IN THIS TEST.

Volume of a right circular cone with radius r and height h: $V = \frac{1}{3}\pi r^2 h$

Volume of a sphere with radius r: $V = \frac{4}{3}\pi r^3$

Volume of a pyramid with base area B and height h: $V = \frac{1}{3}Bh$

Surface Area of a sphere with radius r: $S = 4\pi r^2$

DO NOT DETACH FROM BOOK.

GO ON TO THE NEXT PAGE

MATHEMATICS LEVEL 2 TEST

For each of the following problems, decide which is the BEST of the choices given. If the exact numerical value is not one of the choices, select the choice that best approximates this value. Then fill in the corresponding circle on the answer sheet.

<u>Notes:</u> (1) A scientific or graphing calculator will be necessary for answering some (but not all) of the questions in this test. For each question you will have to decide whether or not you should use a calculator.

(2) For some questions in this test you may have to decide whether your calculator should be in the radian mode or the degree mode.

(3) Figures that accompany problems in this test are intended to provide information useful in solving the problems. They are drawn as accurately as possible EXCEPT when it is stated in a specific problem that its figure is not drawn to scale. All figures lie in a plane unless otherwise indicated.

(4) Unless otherwise specified, the domain of any function f is assumed to be the set of all real numbers x for which $f(x)$ is a real number. The range of f is assumed to be the set of all real numbers $f(x)$, where x is in the domain of f.

(5) Reference information that may be useful in answering the questions in this test can be found on the page preceding Question 1.

USE THIS SPACE FOR SCRATCHWORK.

1. If $3x + 6 = \dfrac{k}{4}(x + 2)$ for all x, then $k =$

(A) $\dfrac{1}{4}$ (B) 3   (C) 4   (D) 12   (E) 24

GO ON TO THE NEXT PAGE

MATHEMATICS LEVEL 2 TEST—*Continued*

USE THIS SPACE FOR SCRATCHWORK.

2. The relationship between a reading C on the Celsius temperature scale and a reading F on the Fahrenheit temperature scale is $C = \frac{5}{9}(F - 32)$, and the relationship between a reading on the Celsius temperature scale and a reading K on the Kelvin temperature scale is $K = C + 273$. Which of the following expresses the relationship between readings on the Kelvin and Fahrenheit temperature scales?

(A) $K = \frac{5}{9}(F - 241)$

(B) $K = \frac{5}{9}(F + 305)$

(C) $K = \frac{5}{9}(F - 32) + 273$

(D) $K = \frac{5}{9}(F - 32) - 273$

(E) $K = \frac{5}{9}(F + 32) + 273$

3. What is the slope of the line containing the points $(3, 11)$ and $(-2, 5)$?

(A) 0.17
(B) 0.83
(C) 1.14
(D) 1.20
(E) 6

4. If $x + y = 2$, $y + z = 5$, and $x + y + z = 10$, then $y =$

(A) -3

(B) $\frac{3}{17}$

(C) 1

(D) 3

(E) $\frac{17}{3}$

GO ON TO THE NEXT PAGE

MATHEMATICS LEVEL 2 TEST—*Continued*

USE THIS SPACE FOR SCRATCHWORK.

5. If $f(x) = 3\ln(x) - 1$ and $g(x) = e^x$,
   then $f(g(5)) =$

   (A)   6.83
   (B)   12
   (C)   14
   (D)   45.98
   (E)   568.17

6. The intersection of a cube with a plane could
   be which of the following?

   I. A square
   II. A parallelogram
   III. A triangle

   (A) I only
   (B) II only
   (C) III only
   (D) I and III only
   (E) I, II, and III

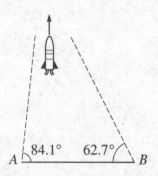

7. The figure above shows a rocket taking off
   vertically. When the rocket reaches a height of
   12 kilometers, the angles of elevation from points
   A and B on level ground are 84.1° and 62.7°,
   respectively. What is the distance between
   points A and B?

   (A)   0.97 km
   (B)   6.36 km
   (C)   7.43 km
   (D)   22.60 km
   (E)   139.37 km

GO ON TO THE NEXT PAGE

MATHEMATICS LEVEL 2 TEST—*Continued*

USE THIS SPACE FOR SCRATCHWORK.

8. What is the value of x^2 if $x = \sqrt{15^2 - 12^2}$?

(A) $\sqrt{3}$ (B) 3 (C) 9 (D) 81 (E) 81^2

9. The points in the rectangular coordinate plane are transformed in such a way that each point $P(x, y)$ is moved to the point $P'(2x, 2y)$. If the distance between a point P and the origin is d, then the distance between the point P' and the origin is

(A) $\frac{1}{d}$

(B) $\frac{d}{2}$

(C) d

(D) $2d$

(E) d^2

10. If $f(g(x)) = \dfrac{2\sqrt{x^2 + 1} - 1}{\sqrt{x^2 + 1} + 1}$ and $f(x) = \dfrac{2x - 1}{x + 1}$, then $g(x) =$

(A) $\sqrt{x}$

(B) $\sqrt{x^2 + 1}$

(C) x

(D) x^2

(E) $x^2 + 1$

GO ON TO THE NEXT PAGE

MATHEMATICS LEVEL 2 TEST—*Continued*

USE THIS SPACE FOR SCRATCHWORK.

11. If A is the degree measure of an acute angle and $\sin A = 0.8$, then $\cos(90° - A) =$

(A) 0.2
(B) 0.4
(C) 0.5
(D) 0.6
(E) 0.8

12. The set of points (x, y, z) such that
$x^2 + y^2 + z^2 = 1$ is

(A) empty
(B) a point
(C) a sphere
(D) a circle
(E) a plane

13. The graph of the rational function f, where
$f(x) = \dfrac{5}{x^2 - 8x + 16}$, has a vertical asymptote at $x =$

(A) 0 only
(B) 4 only
(C) 5 only
(D) 0 and 4 only
(E) 0, 4, and 5

GO ON TO THE NEXT PAGE

MATHEMATICS LEVEL 2 TEST—*Continued*

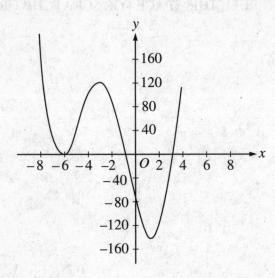

14. The graph of $y = x^4 + 10x^3 + 10x^2 - 96x + c$
    is shown above. Which of the following could be
    the value of c ?

    (A)   3,240
    (B)   1,080
    (C)   72
    (D)   −72
    (E) −3,240

15. If $\cos x = 0.4697$, then $\sec x =$

    (A) 2.1290
    (B) 2.0452
    (C) 1.0818
    (D) 0.9243
    (E) 0.4890

GO ON TO THE NEXT PAGE

16. A club is planning a trip to a museum that has an admission price of $7 per person. The club members going on the trip must share the $200 cost of a bus and the admission price for 2 chaperones who will accompany them on the trip. Which of the following correctly expresses the cost, in dollars, for each club member as a function of n, the number of club members going on the trip?

(A) $c(n) = \dfrac{200 + 7n}{n}$

(B) $c(n) = \dfrac{214 + 7n}{n}$

(C) $c(n) = \dfrac{200 + 7n}{n + 2}$

(D) $c(n) = \dfrac{200 + 7n}{n - 2}$

(E) $c(n) = \dfrac{214 + 7n}{n - 2}$

17. Which of the following is an equation whose graph is the set of points equidistant from the points $(0, 0)$ and $(0, 4)$?

(A) $x = 2$
(B) $y = 2$
(C) $x = 2y$
(D) $y = 2x$
(E) $y = x + 2$

18. What is the sum of the infinite geometric series

$$\frac{1}{4} + \frac{1}{8} + \frac{1}{16} + \frac{1}{32} + \ldots ?$$

(A) $\dfrac{1}{2}$ (B) 1   (C) $\dfrac{3}{2}$ (D) 2   (E) $\dfrac{5}{2}$

GO ON TO THE NEXT PAGE

MATHEMATICS LEVEL 2 TEST—*Continued*

USE THIS SPACE FOR SCRATCHWORK.

19. Which of the following is equivalent to
$p + s > p - s$?

   (A) $p > s$
   (B) $p > 0$
   (C) $s > p$
   (D) $s > 0$
   (E) $s < 0$

20. If a and b are in the domain of a function f and
$f(a) < f(b)$, which of the following must be true?

   (A) $a = 0$ or $b = 0$
   (B) $a < b$
   (C) $a > b$
   (D) $a \neq b$
   (E) $a = b$

21. In a recent survey, it was reported that 75 percent
of the population of a certain state lived within ten
miles of its largest city and that 40 percent of those
who lived within ten miles of the largest city lived
in single-family houses. If a resident of this state
is selected at random, what is the probability that
the person lives in a single-family house within
ten miles of the largest city?

   (A) 0.10
   (B) 0.15
   (C) 0.30
   (D) 0.35
   (E) 0.53

22. To the nearest degree, what is the measure of the
smallest angle in a right triangle with sides of
lengths 3, 4, and 5 ?

   (A) 27°
   (B) 30°
   (C) 37°
   (D) 45°
   (E) 53°

GO ON TO THE NEXT PAGE

MATHEMATICS LEVEL 2 TEST—*Continued*

USE THIS SPACE FOR SCRATCHWORK.

23. Which of the following is an equation of a line perpendicular to $y = -2x + 3$?

(A) $y = 3x - 2$

(B) $y = 2x - 3$

(C) $y = \frac{1}{2}x + 4$

(D) $y = -\frac{1}{2}x + 3$

(E) $y = \frac{1}{-2x + 3}$

24. What is the range of the function f, where $f(x) = -4 + 3\sin(2x + 5\pi)$?

(A) $-7 \le f(x) \le 3$
(B) $-7 \le f(x) \le -1$
(C) $-3 \le f(x) \le 3$
(D) $-3 \le f(x) \le -1$
(E) $-1 \le f(x) \le 1$

25. Of the following lists of numbers, which has the smallest standard deviation?

(A) 1, 5, 9
(B) 3, 5, 8
(C) 4, 5, 8
(D) 7, 8, 9
(E) 8, 8, 8

GO ON TO THE NEXT PAGE

MATHEMATICS LEVEL 2 TEST—*Continued*

USE THIS SPACE FOR SCRATCHWORK.

26. The formula $A = Pe^{0.08t}$ gives the amount A that a savings account will be worth after an initial investment P is compounded continuously at an annual rate of 8 percent for t years. Under these conditions, how many years will it take an initial investment of $1,000 to be worth approximately $5,000 ?

(A) 4.1
(B) 5.0
(C) 8.7
(D) 20.1
(E) 23.0

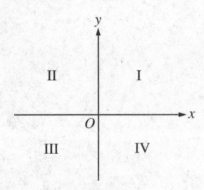

27. If $\sin \theta > 0$ and $\sin \theta \cos \theta < 0$, then θ must be in which quadrant in the figure above?

(A) I
(B) II
(C) III
(D) IV
(E) There is no quadrant in which both conditions are true.

GO ON TO THE NEXT PAGE

MATHEMATICS LEVEL 2 TEST—*Continued*

USE THIS SPACE FOR SCRATCHWORK.

28. If $f(-x) = f(x)$ for all real numbers x and if $(3, 8)$ is a point on the graph of f, which of the following points must also be on the graph of f ?

(A) $(-8, -3)$
(B) $(-3, -8)$
(C) $(-3, 8)$
(D) $(3, -8)$
(E) $(8, 3)$

If $x = y$, then $x^2 = y^2$.

29. If x and y are real numbers, which of the following CANNOT be inferred from the statement above?

(A) In order for x^2 to be equal to y^2, it is sufficient that x be equal to y.
(B) A necessary condition for x to be equal to y is that x^2 be equal to y^2.
(C) x is equal to y implies that x^2 is equal to y^2.
(D) If x^2 is not equal to y^2, then x is not equal to y.
(E) If x^2 is equal to y^2, then x is equal to y.

30. In how many different orders can 9 students arrange themselves in a straight line?

(A) 9
(B) 81
(C) 181,440
(D) 362,880
(E) 387,420,489

GO ON TO THE NEXT PAGE ⇨

MATHEMATICS LEVEL 2 TEST—*Continued*

USE THIS SPACE FOR SCRATCHWORK.

31. What value does $\dfrac{\ln x}{x-1}$ approach as x approaches 1 ?

(A) 0
(B) 0.43
(C) 1
(D) 2
(E) It does not approach a unique value.

32. If $f(x) = |5 - 3x|$, then $f(2) =$

(A) $f(-2)$

(B) $f(-1)$

(C) $f(1)$

(D) $f\left(\dfrac{4}{3}\right)$

(E) $f\left(\dfrac{7}{3}\right)$

33. What is the period of the graph of
$y = 2\tan(3\pi x + 4)$?

(A) $\dfrac{2\pi}{3}$

(B) $\dfrac{2}{3}$

(C) 2

(D) $\dfrac{1}{3}$

(E) $\dfrac{\pi}{3}$

GO ON TO THE NEXT PAGE

USE THIS SPACE FOR SCRATCHWORK.

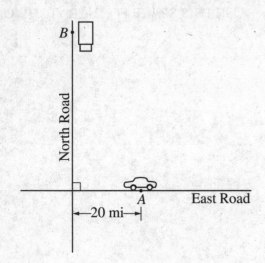

34. The figure above shows a car that has broken
down on East Road. A tow truck leaves a garage
on North Road at point *B*. The straight-line distance
between points *A* and *B* is 50 miles. If the tow
truck travels at an average speed of 45 miles per
hour along North and East Roads, how long will
it take the tow truck to get to the car?

(A) 27 minutes
(B) 1 hour and 7 minutes
(C) 1 hour and 28 minutes
(D) 1 hour and 33 minutes
(E) 1 hour and 46 minutes

GO ON TO THE NEXT PAGE

USE THIS SPACE FOR SCRATCHWORK.

x	$f(x)$
−1	0
0	1
1	−1
2	0

35. If f is a polynomial of degree 3, four of whose values are shown in the table above, then $f(x)$ could equal

(A) $\left(x + \frac{1}{2}\right)(x + 1)(x + 2)$

(B) $(x + 1)(x - 2)\left(x - \frac{1}{2}\right)$

(C) $(x + 1)(x - 2)(x - 1)$

(D) $(x + 2)\left(x - \frac{1}{2}\right)(x - 1)$

(E) $(x + 2)(x + 1)(x - 2)$

36. The only prime factors of a number n are 2, 5, 7, and 17. Which of the following could NOT be a factor of n?

(A) 10   (B) 20   (C) 25   (D) 30   (E) 34

37. If $0 \le x \le \frac{\pi}{2}$ and $\sin x = 3 \cos x$, what is the value of x?

(A) 0.322
(B) 0.333
(C) 0.340
(D) 1.231
(E) 1.249

GO ON TO THE NEXT PAGE

USE THIS SPACE FOR SCRATCHWORK.

38. If $f(x) = 5\sqrt{2x}$, what is the value of $f^{-1}(10)$?

(A)   0.04
(B)   0.89
(C)   2.00
(D)   2.23
(E)   22.36

39. The Fibonacci sequence can be defined recursively as

$$a_1 = 1$$

$$a_2 = 1$$

$$a_n = a_{n-1} + a_{n-2} \text{ for } n \geq 3.$$

What is the 10th term of this sequence?

(A)   21
(B)   34
(C)   55
(D)   89
(E)   144

40. If $f(x) = x^3 - 4x^2 - 3x + 2$, which of the following statements are true?

  I. The function f is increasing for $x \geq 3$.
  II. The equation $f(x) = 0$ has two nonreal solutions.
  III. $f(x) \geq -16$ for all $x \geq 0$.

(A) I only
(B) II only
(C) I and II
(D) I and III
(E) II and III

GO ON TO THE NEXT PAGE

MATHEMATICS LEVEL 2 TEST—*Continued*

USE THIS SPACE FOR SCRATCHWORK.

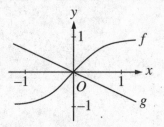

41. Portions of the graphs of *f* and *g* are shown above. Which of the following could be a portion of the graph of *fg* ?

(A)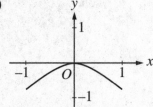

(B)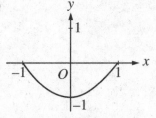

(C)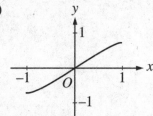

(D)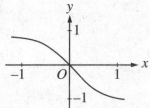

(E)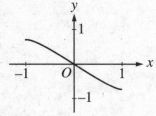

GO ON TO THE NEXT PAGE

MATHEMATICS LEVEL 2 TEST—*Continued*

USE THIS SPACE FOR SCRATCHWORK.

42. The set of all real numbers x such that $\sqrt{x^2} = -x$ consists of

(A) zero only
(B) nonpositive real numbers only
(C) positive real numbers only
(D) all real numbers
(E) no real numbers

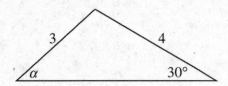

43. In the triangle shown above, $\sin \alpha =$

(A) $\dfrac{3}{8}$

(B) $\dfrac{1}{2}$

(C) $\dfrac{2}{3}$

(D) $\dfrac{3}{4}$

(E) $\dfrac{4}{5}$

44. The length, width, and height of a rectangular solid are 8, 4, and 1, respectively. What is the length of the longest line segment whose end points are two vertices of this solid?

(A) $4\sqrt{5}$
(B) 9
(C) $3\sqrt{10}$
(D) 10
(E) 12

GO ON TO THE NEXT PAGE

MATHEMATICS LEVEL 2 TEST—*Continued*

USE THIS SPACE FOR SCRATCHWORK.

45. If $\log_a 3 = x$ and $\log_a 5 = y$, then $\log_a 45 =$

(A) $2x + y$
(B) $x^2 + y$
(C) $x^2 y$
(D) $x + y$
(E) $9x + y$

46. If $\sin\theta = t$, then, for all θ in the interval $0 < \theta < \frac{\pi}{2}$, $\tan\theta =$

(A) $\frac{1}{\sqrt{1 - t^2}}$
(B) $\frac{t}{\sqrt{1 - t^2}}$
(C) $\frac{1}{1 - t^2}$
(D) $\frac{t}{1 - t^2}$
(E) 1

47. Which of the following shifts of the graph of $y = x^2$ would result in the graph of $y = x^2 - 2x + k$, where k is a constant greater than 2 ?

(A) Left 2 units and up k units
(B) Left 1 unit and up $k + 1$ units
(C) Right 1 unit and up $k + 1$ units
(D) Left 1 unit and up $k - 1$ units
(E) Right 1 unit and up $k - 1$ units

GO ON TO THE NEXT PAGE

MATHEMATICS LEVEL 2 TEST—*Continued*

USE THIS SPACE FOR SCRATCHWORK.

48. If the height of a right circular cone is decreased by 8 percent, by what percent must the radius of the base be decreased so that the volume of the cone is decreased by 15 percent?

(A) 4%
(B) 7%
(C) 8%
(D) 30%
(E) 45%

49. If matrix A has dimensions $m \times n$ and matrix B has dimensions $n \times p$, where m, n, and p are distinct positive integers, which of the following statements must be true?

I. The product BA does not exist.
II. The product AB exists and has dimensions $m \times p$.
III. The product AB exists and has dimensions $n \times n$.

(A) I only
(B) II only
(C) III only
(D) I and II
(E) I and III

GO ON TO THE NEXT PAGE

MATHEMATICS LEVEL 2 TEST—Continued

USE THIS SPACE FOR SCRATCHWORK.

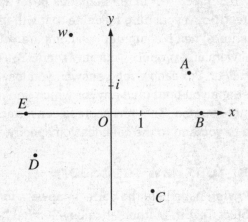

50. If w is the complex number shown in the figure above, which of the following points could be $-iw$?

(A) A (B) B (C) C (D) D (E) E

STOP

IF YOU FINISH BEFORE TIME IS CALLED, YOU MAY CHECK YOUR WORK ON THIS TEST ONLY. DO NOT TURN TO ANY OTHER TEST IN THIS BOOK.

How to Score the SAT Subject Test in Mathematics Level 2

When you take an actual SAT Subject Test in Mathematics Level 2, your answer sheet will be "read" by a scanning machine that will record your responses to each question. Then a computer will compare your answers with the correct answers and produce your raw score. You get one point for each correct answer. For each wrong answer, you lose one-quarter of a point. Questions you omit (and any for which you mark more than one answer) are not counted. This raw score is converted to a scaled score that is reported to you and to the colleges you specify.

Worksheet 1. Finding Your Raw Test Score

STEP 1: Table A on the following page lists the correct answers for all the questions on the Subject Test in Mathematics Level 2 that is reproduced in this book. It also serves as a worksheet for you to calculate your raw score.

- Compare your answers with those given in the table.

- Put a check in the column marked "Right" if your answer is correct.

- Put a check in the column marked "Wrong" if your answer is incorrect.

- Leave both columns blank if you omitted the question.

STEP 2: Count the number of right answers.

Enter the total here: _____

STEP 3: Count the number of wrong answers.

Enter the total here: _____

STEP 4: Multiply the number of wrong answers by .250.

Enter the product here: _____

STEP 5: Subtract the result obtained in Step 4 from the total you obtained in Step 2.

Enter the result here: _____

STEP 6: Round the number obtained in Step 5 to the nearest whole number.

Enter the result here: _____

The number you obtained in Step 6 is your raw score.

Answers to Practice Test 3 for Mathematics Level 2

Table A
Answers to the Subject Test in Mathematics Level 2 - Practice Test 3 and Percentage of Students Answering
Each Question Correctly

Question Number	Correct Answer	Right	Wrong	Percentage of Students Answering the Question Correctly*	Question Number	Correct Answer	Right	Wrong	Percentage of Students Answering the Question Correctly*
1	D			88	26	D			85
2	C			91	27	B			70
3	D			90	28	C			65
4	A			87	29	E			47
5	C			90	30	D			73
6	E			54	31	C			54
7	C			62	32	D			72
8	D			93	33	D			23
9	D			85	34	C			62
10	B			89	35	B			57
11	E			84	36	D			51
12	C			54	37	E			63
13	B			87	38	C			52
14	D			75	39	C			52
15	A			88	40	D			48
16	B			67	41	A			42
17	B			62	42	B			33
18	A			70	43	C			63
19	D			76	44	B			54
20	D			72	45	A			46
21	C			82	46	B			46
22	C			67	47	E			44
23	C			70	48	A			35
24	B			66	49	D			25
25	E			60	50	A			26

* These percentages are based on an analysis of the answer sheets of a representative sample of 15,855 students who took the original administration of this test and whose mean score was 652. They may be used as an indication of the relative difficulty of a particular question.

Finding Your Scaled Score

When you take SAT Subject Tests, the scores sent to the colleges you specify are reported on the College Board scale, which ranges from 200 to 800. You can convert your practice test raw score to a scaled score by using Table B. To find your scaled score, locate your raw score in the left-hand column of Table B; the corresponding score in the right-hand column is your scaled score. For example, a raw score of 26 on this particular edition of the Subject Test in Mathematics Level 2 corresponds to a scaled score of 620.

Raw scores are converted to scaled scores to ensure that a score earned on any one edition of a particular Subject Test is comparable to the same scaled score earned on any other edition of the same Subject Test. Because some editions of the tests may be slightly easier or more difficult than others, College Board scaled scores are adjusted so that they indicate the same level of performance regardless of the edition of the test taken and the ability of the group that takes it. Thus, for example, a score of 400 on one edition of a test taken at a particular administration indicates the same level of achievement as a score of 400 on a different edition of the test taken at a different administration.

When you take the SAT Subject Tests during a national administration, your scores are likely to differ somewhat from the scores you obtain on the tests in this book. People perform at different levels at different times for reasons unrelated to the tests themselves. The precision of any test is also limited because it represents only a sample of all the possible questions that could be asked.

Table B
Scaled Score Conversion Table
Subject Test in Mathematics Level 2 - Practice Test 3

Raw Score	Scaled Score	Raw Score	Scaled Score	Raw Score	Scaled Score
50	800	28	630	6	470
49	800	27	630	5	460
48	800	26	620	4	450
47	800	25	610	3	440
46	800	24	600	2	430
45	800	23	600	1	420
44	800	22	590	0	410
43	790	21	580	−1	400
42	780	20	580	−2	390
41	770	19	570	−3	370
40	760	18	560	−4	360
39	750	17	560	−5	350
38	740	16	550	−6	340
37	730	15	540	−7	340
36	710	14	530	−8	330
35	700	13	530	−9	330
34	690	12	520	−10	320
33	680	11	510	−11	310
32	670	10	500	−12	300
31	660	9	490		
30	650	8	480		
29	640	7	480		

How Did You Do on the Subject Test in Mathematics Level 2?

After you score your test and analyze your performance, think about the following questions:

Did you run out of time before reaching the end of the test?

If so, you may need to pace yourself better. For example, maybe you spent too much time on one or two hard questions. A better approach might be to skip the ones you can't answer right away and try answering all the remaining questions on the test. Then if there's time, go back to the questions you skipped.

Did you take a long time reading the directions?

You will save time when you take the test by learning the directions to the Subject Test in Mathematics Level 2 ahead of time. Each minute you spend reading directions during the test is a minute that you could use to answer questions.

How did you handle questions you were unsure of?

If you were able to eliminate one or more of the answer choices as wrong and guess from the remaining ones, your approach probably worked to your advantage. On the other hand, making haphazard guesses or omitting questions without trying to eliminate choices could cost you valuable points.

How difficult were the questions for you compared with other students who took the test?

Table A shows you how difficult the multiple-choice questions were for the group of students who took this test during its national administration. The right-hand column gives the percentage of students that answered each question correctly.

A question answered correctly by almost everyone in the group is obviously an easier question. For example, 93 percent of the students answered question 8 correctly. However, only 23 percent answered question 33 correctly.

Keep in mind that these percentages are based on just one group of students. They would probably be different with another group of students taking the test.

If you missed several easier questions, go back and try to find out why: Did the questions cover material you haven't yet reviewed? Did you misunderstand the directions?

Answer Explanations

For Practice Test 3

The solutions presented here provide one method for solving each of the problems on this test. Other mathematically correct approaches are possible.

Question 1

Choice (D) is the correct answer. You need to solve the equation $3x + 6 = \frac{k}{4}(x + 2)$ for k.

$$3x + 6 = \frac{k}{4}(x + 2)$$
$$4(3x + 6) = k(x + 2)$$
$$12x + 24 = k(x + 2)$$
$$12(x + 2) = k(x + 2)$$
$$12 = k$$

Question 2

Choice (C) is the correct answer. Since $C = \frac{5}{9}(F - 32)$, you can substitute for C in the equation $K = C + 273$. Thus, $K = \frac{5}{9}(F - 32) + 273$.

Question 3

Choice (D) is the correct answer. The slope of the line is $\frac{11 - 5}{3 - (-2)} = \frac{6}{5} = 1.2$.

Question 4

Choice (A) is the correct answer. One way to find the value of y is to notice that if $x + y = 2$ and $y + z = 5$, then $x + y + y + z = 2 + 5 = 7$. Since $x + y + z = 10$, you can conclude that $y = 7 - 10 = -3$.

Question 5

Choice (C) is the correct answer. $g(5) = e^5$, and $f(e^5) = 3\ell n(e^5) - 1 = 3 \cdot 5 - 1 = 14$. Thus, $f(g(5)) = 14$.

Question 6

Choice (E) is the correct answer. If a plane intersects a cube such that the plane is parallel to a face of the cube, the intersection will be a square, so I is possible. Since a square is a type of parallelogram, II is possible. If a plane intersects a cube so that it slices through three adjacent faces at a corner of the cube, the intersection will be a triangle, so III is possible. Since I, II, and III are all possible.

Question 7

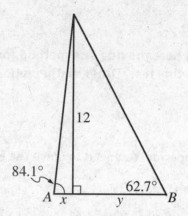

Choice (C) is the correct answer. It is helpful to draw a figure with the information given in the problem. The distance between A and B is $x + y$, so you need to find x and y. Since $\tan 84.1° = \dfrac{12}{x}$, $x = \dfrac{12}{\tan 84.1°}$, which is approximately 1.24. Since $\tan 62.7° = \dfrac{12}{y}$, $y = \dfrac{12}{\tan 62.7°}$, which is approximately 6.19. Thus, $AB = x + y \approx 1.24 + 6.19 = 7.43$ km.

Choice (A) is incorrect. $0.97 \approx \dfrac{\tan 84.1°}{12} + \dfrac{\tan 62.7°}{12}$. Choice (D) is incorrect. This results from using incorrect ratios.

$$\sin 84.1° = \frac{x}{12} \qquad\qquad \sin 62.7° = \frac{y}{12}$$
$$x = 12 \sin 84.1° \qquad\qquad y = 12 \sin 62.7°$$
$$AB = x + y$$
$$= 12 \sin 84.1° + 12 \sin 62.7°$$
$$\approx 22.60$$

Choice (E) is incorrect. This results from using incorrect ratios.

$$\tan 84.1° = \frac{x}{12} \qquad\qquad \tan 62.7° = \frac{y}{12}$$
$$x = 12 \tan 84.1° \qquad\qquad y = 12 \tan 62.7°$$
$$AB = x + y$$
$$= 12 \tan 84.1° + 12 \tan 62.7°$$
$$\approx 139.37$$

Question 8

Choice (D) is the correct answer. If $x = \sqrt{15^2 - 12^2}$, then $x^2 = 15^2 - 12^2$, which is equal to $225 - 144 = 81$.

Question 9

Choice (D) is the correct answer. The distance d from the origin to point $P(x, y)$ is equal to $\sqrt{x^2 + y^2}$. The distance from the origin to point $P'(2x, 2y)$ is equal to $\sqrt{4x^2 + 4y^2} = \sqrt{4(x^2 + y^2)} = 2\sqrt{x^2 + y^2}$, which is $2d$.

Question 10

Choice (B) is the correct answer. You are looking for the input value that gives an output value of $\dfrac{2\sqrt{x^2+1}-1}{\sqrt{x^2+1}+1}$. In this case, $f\left(\sqrt{x^2+1}\right) = \dfrac{2\sqrt{x^2+1}-1}{\sqrt{x^2+1}+1}$. Thus, $g(x) = \sqrt{x^2+1}$.

Question 11

Choice (E) is the correct answer. Since $\sin A = \cos(90° - A)$, it follows that if $\sin A = 0.8$, then $\cos(90° - A)$ is also equal to 0.8.

Question 12

Choice (C) is the correct answer. $x^2 + y^2 + z^2 = r^2$ is the standard form for the equation of a sphere with center (0, 0, 0) and radius r. Thus, $x^2 + y^2 + z^2 = 1$ is a sphere with center (0, 0, 0) and radius 1.

Question 13

Choice (B) is the correct answer. The graph of f has vertical asymptotes at x values for which $f(x)$ is undefined. This occurs when the denominator equals 0. Since $x^2 - 8x + 16 = (x - 4)^2 = 0$ when $x = 4$, the graph has a vertical asymptote at $x = 4$ only. Choice (A) is incorrect. Since $f(0)$ is defined, $x = 0$ is not a vertical asymptote. The graph of f has a horizontal asymptote at $y = 0$. Choice (C) is incorrect. The numerator does not give information about vertical asymptotes. Since $f(5)$ is defined, $x = 5$ is not a vertical asymptote.

Question 14

Choice (D) is the correct answer. To answer this question, it is helpful to realize that finding c in the equation is equivalent to finding the y-intercept of the graph, since $y = c$ when $x = 0$. From the figure shown, the graph appears to intersect the y-axis near –80. Only –72 is near –80. Since (–6, 0) is a point on the graph, you can verify that –72 is correct by substituting –6 for x in the equation $(-6)^4 + 10(-6)^3 + 10(-6)^2 - 96(-6) - 72 = 0$.

Question 15

Choice (A) is the correct answer. Since the secant of an angle is the reciprocal of the cosine, $\sec x = \dfrac{1}{\cos x} = \dfrac{1}{0.4697} \approx 2.1290$.

Question 16

Choice (B) is the correct answer. The question asks for the cost for each club member to go on the trip. Each club member must pay the admission price of $7. The n club members must share the $200 cost of the bus, so each member must pay $\dfrac{200}{n}$ dollars. In addition, the n club members must share the $14 for admission for the 2 chaperones. So each member must pay a total of $7 + \dfrac{200}{n} + \dfrac{14}{n}$ dollars. This is equal to $7 + \dfrac{214}{n}$ or $\dfrac{7n + 214}{n}$ dollars. Choice (A) is incorrect. This answer does not include the $14 for admission for the 2 chaperones. Each member must pay $\dfrac{14}{n}$ dollars of that amount.

Question 17

Choice (B) is the correct answer. For any point (x, y) on the graph, the distance between (x, y) and $(0, 0)$ should equal the distance between (x, y) and $(0, 4)$. That is, $\sqrt{x^2 + y^2} = \sqrt{x^2 + (y - 4)^2}$. Solving the equation gives $y = 2$. Both of the given points lie on the y-axis. The set of points equidistant from these points is a horizontal line that goes through $(0, 2)$. The equation of this line is $y = 2$.

Question 18

Choice (A) is the correct answer. The sum S of an infinite geometric series is given by $S = \dfrac{a}{1-r}$, where a is the first term and r is the common ratio. In this series, $a = \dfrac{1}{4}$ and $r = \dfrac{1}{2}$. Thus, the sum is $\dfrac{\frac{1}{4}}{1 - \frac{1}{2}} = \dfrac{\frac{1}{4}}{\frac{1}{2}} = \dfrac{1}{2}$.

Choice (D) is incorrect. This results from $\dfrac{1}{1 - \frac{1}{2}} = 2$ (forgetting to include the first term) or from thinking that $S = \dfrac{1-r}{a} = \dfrac{\frac{1}{2}}{\frac{1}{4}} = 2$.

Question 19

Choice (D) is the correct answer. The inequality $p + s > p - s$ is equivalent to $s > -s$, which is equivalent to $2s > 0$. So, $s > 0$.

Question 20

Choice (D) is the correct answer. Since a and b are in the domain of the function f and $f(a) < f(b)$, it must be true that $f(a) \neq f(b)$. This implies that $a \neq b$. Note that a could be less than b if, for example, the function is increasing, and a could be greater than b if the function is decreasing.

Question 21

Choice (C) is the correct answer. You need to recognize that the probability you seek corresponds to a compound event, since the person must live within 10 miles of the largest city *and* live in a single-family house. If P represents the entire state's population, then $0.75P$ residents live within 10 miles of the largest city. Of the $0.75P$ residents, 40% live in single-family houses. This is equal to $(0.40)(0.75P) = (0.30)P$. This tells you that 30% of the state's population live in single-family houses within 10 miles of the largest city. This means that the desired probability is 0.30. Choice (A) is incorrect. This results from taking 40% of the 25% of the population that do not live within ten miles of the largest city (0.40×0.25). Choice (B) is incorrect. This is equal to 0.60×0.25. Choice (D) is incorrect. This is equal to $0.75 - 0.40$.

Question 22

Choice (C) is the correct answer. In the right triangle, the length of the hypotenuse is 5, and the length of the side opposite the smallest angle A in the triangle is 3. Thus, $\sin A = \dfrac{3}{5}$ and $\sin^{-1}\left(\dfrac{3}{5}\right) \approx 36.87°$.

The measure of the smallest angle in the right triangle rounded to the nearest degree is 37°.

Question 23

Choice (C) is the correct answer. The product of the slopes of two perpendicular lines is −1. Since the line $y = -2x + 3$ has a slope of −2, a line perpendicular to that line has a slope of $\dfrac{1}{2}$. Among the choices, only choice (C) gives the equation of a line that has a slope of $\dfrac{1}{2}$.

Question 24

Choice (B) is the correct answer. The range of the function f depends on the range of $\sin(2x + 5\pi)$. Since $-1 \leq \sin(2x + 5\pi) \leq 1$, $-3 \leq 3\sin(2x + 5\pi) \leq 3$ and $-7 \leq -4 + 3\sin(2x + 5\pi) \leq -1$.

Question 25

Choice (E) is the correct answer. The standard deviation of three numbers will be smallest for the numbers that are closest to each other. In choice (E), the three numbers all have the same value, so their standard deviation is 0. If all three numbers are not identical, then the standard deviation of the numbers, regardless of how small the numbers are, will always be greater than 0.

Question 26

Choice (D) is the correct answer. According to the formula, $5,000 = 1,000e^{0.08t}$, which is equivalent to $5 = e^{0.08t}$. Taking the natural logarithm of both sides of the equation gives $\ln 5 = 0.08t$. Thus,
$$t = \frac{\ln 5}{0.08} \approx 20.1.$$

Question 27

Choice (B) is the correct answer. Since $\sin \theta > 0$, the product $\sin \theta \cos \theta$ will be negative only when $\cos \theta$ is negative. Since $\sin \theta$ is positive in the first and second quadrants, and $\cos \theta$ is negative in the second and third quadrants, θ must be in the second quadrant. Choice (A) is incorrect. In quadrant I, the second inequality fails. Choice (C) is incorrect. In quadrant III, $\sin \theta < 0$, so the first inequality fails.

Question 28

Choice (C) is the correct answer. The graph of the function f is the set of points $(x, f(x))$. Since $(3, 8)$ is on the graph, $f(3) = 8$. Since $f(-x) = f(x)$, $f(-3) = f(3) = 8$. This means that the point $(-3, 8)$ is also on the graph of f.

Question 29

Choice (E) is the correct answer. It is given that if $x = y$, then $x^2 = y^2$. You need to examine each choice to see if it can or cannot be inferred. Choice (A) can be inferred. If $x = y$, we know that x^2 must be equal to y^2 from the given statement. Choice (B) can be inferred. If $x^2 \neq y^2$, then it must be true that $x \neq y$. Choice (C) can be inferred. This is another way to state that if $x = y$, then $x^2 = y^2$. Choice (D) can be inferred. If $x^2 \neq y^2$, then it is not possible for x to equal y. Choice (E) cannot be inferred. If $x^2 = y^2$, then $x = y$ or $x = -y$.

Question 30

Choice (D) is the correct answer. There are 9 choices for the first position, 8 choices for the second position, and so on. So, nine students can arrange themselves in a straight line in $9 \cdot 8 \cdot 7 \cdot 6 \cdot 5 \cdot 4 \cdot 3 \cdot 2 \cdot 1$ ways. The product is $9! = 362,880$.

Question 31

Choice (C) is the correct answer. By using a graphing calculator, one can see that the value of the function $\frac{\ln x}{x-1}$ approaches 1 as x approaches 1 from both sides. You can examine the graph of the function or a table of values for the function as x approaches 1 from both sides. Thus, $\lim\limits_{x \to 1} \frac{\ln x}{x-1} = 1$.

Question 32

Choice (D) is the correct answer. $f(2) = |5 - 3 \cdot 2| = |-1| = 1$. Since $|-1| = |1|$, $f(x) = |1|$ when $5 - 3x = 1$ or when $x = \frac{4}{3}$. Thus, $f(2) = f\left(\frac{4}{3}\right)$.

Question 33

Choice (D) is the correct answer. The period of the graph of $y = 2 \tan(3\pi x + 4)$ is the same as the period of the graph of $y = \tan(3\pi x)$. Since the period of the graph of $y = \tan x$ is π, the period of the graph of $y = \tan(3\pi x)$ is $\left(\frac{1}{3\pi}\right)\pi = \frac{1}{3}$.

Question 34

Choice (C) is the correct answer. Let n represent the distance the truck travels along North Road. Then $n^2 + 20^2 = 50^2$, so $n = \sqrt{2,100}$ miles. Thus, the total distance traveled by the truck from point B to point A is $\sqrt{2,100} + 20$ miles. The time it takes the truck to get to the car is equal to $\frac{(\sqrt{2,100} + 20) \text{ miles}}{45 \text{ miles/hour}} \approx 1.46$ hours. The 0.46 hours is converted to minutes by multiplying 0.46 by 60, which gives 27.6 or 28 minutes. Choice (A) is incorrect. This is equal to the time it takes to travel from the intersection to A along East Road. Choice (B) is incorrect. This is equal to the time it takes to drive from B to A directly instead of along North and East Roads. Choice (D) is incorrect. This is obtained by adding the two given values, 50 miles and 20 miles, and computing the time to travel 70 miles. Choice (E) is incorrect. It takes the truck 1.46 hours to get to the car, and 0.46 hour is not the same as 46 minutes.

Question 35

Choice (B) is the correct answer. Since $f(-1) = 0$, $(x + 1)$ is a factor of $f(x)$. Similarly, since $f(2) = 0$, $(x - 2)$ is a factor of $f(x)$. This means that $f(x)$ can be written as $f(x) = (x + 1)(x - 2)(x - a)$ for some real number a. Using $f(0) = 1$ gives $(0 + 1)(0 - 2)(0 - a) = 1$, which simplifies to $a = \frac{1}{2}$. Similarly, using $f(1) = -1$ gives $(1 + 1)(1 - 2)(1 - a) = -1$, which also simplifies to $a = \frac{1}{2}$. Thus, $f(x)$ could be equal to $f(x) = (x + 1)(x - 2)(x - \frac{1}{2})$.

Question 36

Choice (D) is the correct answer. Since the only prime factors of the number n are 2, 5, 7, and 17, the only prime factors of any factor of n are 2, 5, 7, and 17. Hence the numbers $10 = 2 \times 5$, $20 = 2^2 \times 5$, $25 = 5^2$, and $34 = 2 \times 17$ are all possible factors of n, but $30 = 2 \times 3 \times 5$ could <u>not</u> be a factor of n, since 3 is not one of the prime factors of n.

Question 37

Choice (E) is the correct answer. The equation $\sin x = 3 \cos x$ can be rewritten as $\tan x = 3$, when $x \neq \frac{\pi}{2}$. Solving for x yields $x = \tan^{-1}(3) \approx 1.249$.

Question 38

Choice (C) is the correct answer. To find $f^{-1}(10)$, you need to find the value of x for which $10 = 5\sqrt{2x}$. This equation simplifies to $2 = \sqrt{2x}$ and so $x = 2$.

Question 39

Choice (C) is the correct answer. In the sequence, a_n is equal to the sum of the previous two terms for $n \geq 3$. Thus, the first ten terms of the sequence are 1, 1, 2, 3, 5, 8, 13, 21, 34, 55. Choice (A) is incorrect. This is a_8. Choice (B) is incorrect. This is a_9. Choice (D) is incorrect. This is $a_{11} = a_{10} + a_9 = 89$. Choice (E) is incorrect. This is $a_{12} = a_{11} + a_{10} = 144$.

Question 40

Choice (D) is the correct answer. Use a graphing calculator to draw the graph of the function f. The graph shows that f has three x-intercepts; therefore, the equation $f(x) = 0$ has three real solutions. Thus, statement II is false. The graph also shows that f has just two turning points: a local maximum at the point $\left(-\frac{1}{3}, \frac{68}{27}\right)$ and a local minimum at the point $(3, -16)$. Thus, f is increasing for $x \geq 3$ and $f(x) \geq -16$ for all $x \geq 0$. Statements I and III are true.

Question 41

Choice (A) is the correct answer. For $x > 0$, $f(x) > 0$ and $g(x) < 0$, so $(fg)(x) = f(x)g(x) < 0$. For $x < 0$, $f(x) < 0$ and $g(x) > 0$, so $(fg)(x) = f(x)g(x) < 0$. Thus, $(fg)(x) < 0$ for all nonzero x shown and $(fg)(0) = f(0)g(0) = 0 \cdot 0 = 0$. Moreover, since $|(fg)(x)|$ increases as $|x|$ increases, fg is increasing for $x < 0$ and decreasing for $x > 0$.

Question 42

Choice (B) is the correct answer. Every positive number n has two square roots, one positive and the other negative, but $\sqrt{n}$ denotes the positive number whose square is n. The square root of 0 is 0. In this case, this means that $\sqrt{x^2} \geq 0$, therefore $-x$ must be nonnegative and x must be nonpositive. Hence, the set of all real numbers x such that $\sqrt{x^2} = -x$ consists of nonpositive real numbers only.

Question 43

Choice (C) is the correct answer. Using the law of sines, $\dfrac{4}{\sin \alpha} = \dfrac{3}{\sin 30°}$. Since $\sin 30° = \dfrac{1}{2}$ this becomes $\dfrac{4}{\sin \alpha} = 6$. Hence, $\sin \alpha = \dfrac{4}{6} = \dfrac{2}{3}$.

Question 44

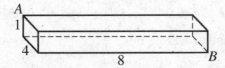

Choice (B) is the correct answer. To answer this question, it is helpful to draw a figure. The longest line segment shown in the figure is the segment between the points labeled A and B. $\overline{AB}$ is the hypotenuse of a right triangle in which one leg is the height of the rectangular solid and the second leg is the diagonal of the face with sides of length 4 and 8. By the Pythagorean theorem, the length of $\overline{AB}$ is $\sqrt{1^2 + \left(\sqrt{4^2 + 8^2}\right)^2} = \sqrt{1 + \left(\sqrt{80}\right)^2} = \sqrt{81} = 9$. Choice (A) is incorrect. This is the length of the longest diagonal of any face of the solid. However, a segment joining opposite vertices is longer than a diagonal of a face.

Question 45

Choice (A) is the correct answer. Since $\log_a 45 = \log_a (9 \cdot 5) = \log_a 9 + \log_a 5 = \log_a 3^2 + \log_a 5 = 2 \log_a 3 + \log_a 5 = 2x + y$, thus, $\log_a 45 = 2x + y$.

Question 46

Choice (B) is the correct answer. Since $\sin^2 \theta + \cos^2 \theta = 1$, $\cos^2 \theta = 1 - \sin^2 \theta$. Thus, $\cos^2 \theta = 1 - t^2$, since $\sin \theta = t$; and $\cos \theta = \sqrt{1 - t^2}$, since $0 < \theta < \dfrac{\pi}{2}$. Hence, $\tan \theta = \dfrac{\sin \theta}{\cos \theta} = \dfrac{t}{\sqrt{1 - t^2}}$.

Question 47

Choice (E) is the correct answer. Completing the square yields $y = (x^2 - 2x + 1) - 1 + k = (x - 1)^2 + (k - 1)$. Hence, shifting the graph of $y = x^2$ right 1 unit and up $k - 1$ units would result in the graph of $y = x^2 - 2x + k$.

Question 48

Choice (A) is the correct answer. You can solve this problem by comparing the volumes of the original and new cones. If you use h and r for the height and radius, respectively, of the original cone, its volume is $V = \frac{1}{3}\pi r^2 h$. In the new cone, the height is $0.92h$ and the volume is $0.85V$.

You need to determine the percent decrease in the radius, so you could represent the new radius length by kr, where $0 < k < 1$ and $(1 - k)(100)$ is the percent you are looking for. This gives you the volume of the new cone as $0.85V = \frac{1}{3}\pi(kr)^2(0.92h)$. By using $V = \frac{1}{3}\pi r^2 h$, we have $0.85\left(\frac{1}{3}\pi r^2 h\right) = \frac{1}{3}\pi(kr)^2(0.92h)$. If you divide each side by common terms, you get $0.85 = k^2 \cdot (0.92)$ so that $k^2 \approx 0.9239$ or $k \approx 0.9612$. The percent decrease in the radius is $100(1 - k)$, so the correct answer is 4%. Choice (C) is incorrect. If V is the volume of the original cone, the volume of the new cone is equal to $0.85V = \frac{1}{3}\pi(kr)^2(0.92h)$. If you use k instead of k^2, your answer will be 8%.

Question 49

Choice (D) is the correct answer. For two matrices M and N, the product MN exists provided the number of columns of M equals the number of rows of N. The product MN has as many rows as M and as many columns as N. Since matrix B has p columns and matrix A has m rows, the product BA does not exist, so statement I is true. Since A has n columns and B has n rows, the product AB exists and has as many rows as A, which is m rows, and as many columns as B, which is p columns. Thus, statement II is true and statement III is false.

Question 50

Choice (A) is the correct answer. The complex number w is equal to $a + bi$, where $a < 0$ and $b > 0$. Multiplying by $-i$ will give $-ai - bi^2 = b - ai$. Thus, $b > 0$ and $-a > 0$. So $-iw$ is in quadrant I. The x-coordinate of $-iw$ equals b, and the y-coordinate equals $-a$. Choice (C) is incorrect. It results from not recognizing that a was originally negative and thus $-a$ is positive, which will give a point in quadrant IV. Choice (D) is incorrect. This corresponds to omitting the minus sign, and concluding that the point iw is in quadrant III. Choices (B) and (E) are incorrect. They both result from ignoring the a term in $a + bi$. This would mean that $w = bi$, so multiplying by i would produce a complex number with only a real part.

Mathematics Level 2 – Practice Test 4

Practice Helps

The test that follows is an actual, previously administered SAT Subject Test in Mathematics Level 2. To get an idea of what it's like to take this test, practice under conditions that are much like those of an actual test administration.

- Set aside an hour when you can take the test uninterrupted.

- Sit at a desk or table with no other books or papers. Dictionaries, other books, or notes are not allowed in the test room.

- Remember to have a scientific or graphing calculator with you.

- Tear out an answer sheet from the back of this book and fill it in just as you would on the day of the test. One answer sheet can be used for up to three Subject Tests.

- Read the instructions that precede the practice test. During the actual administration you will be asked to read them before answering test questions.

- Use a clock or kitchen timer to time yourself.

- After you finish the practice test, read the sections "How to Score the SAT Subject Test in Mathematics Level 2" and "How Did You Do on the Subject Test in Mathematics Level 2?"

- The appearance of the answer sheet in this book may differ from the answer sheet you see on test day.

- The Reference Information at the start of the practice test is slightly different from what appeared on the original test. It has been modified to reflect the language included on tests administered at the time of this book's printing. These changes are minor and will not affect how you answer the questions.

MATHEMATICS LEVEL 2 TEST

The top portion of the page of the answer sheet that you will use to take the Mathematics Level 2 Test must be filled in exactly as illustrated below. When your supervisor tells you to fill in the circle next to the name of the test you are about to take, mark your answer sheet as shown.

○ Literature	○ Mathematics Level 1	○ German	○ Chinese Listening	○ Japanese Listening
○ Biology E	● Mathematics Level 2	○ Italian	○ French Listening	○ Korean Listening
○ Biology M	○ U.S. History	○ Latin	○ German Listening	○ Spanish Listening
○ Chemistry	○ World History	○ Modern Hebrew		
○ Physics	○ French	○ Spanish	Background Questions: ① ② ③ ④ ⑤ ⑥ ⑦ ⑧ ⑨	

After filling in the circle next to the name of the test you are taking, locate the Background Questions section, which also appears at the top of your answer sheet (as shown above). This is where you will answer the following Background Questions on your answer sheet.

BACKGROUND QUESTIONS

Please answer Part I and Part II below by filling in the appropriate circle in the Background Questions box on your answer sheet. The information you provide is for statistical purposes only and will not affect your test score.

Part I.   Which of the following describes a mathematics course you have taken or are currently taking? (FILL IN **ALL** CIRCLES THAT APPLY.)

- Algebra I or Elementary Algebra **OR** Course I of a college preparatory mathematics sequence   —Fill in circle 1.

- Geometry **OR** Course II of a college preparatory mathematics sequence   —Fill in circle 2.

- Algebra II or Intermediate Algebra **OR** Course III of a college preparatory mathematics sequence   —Fill in circle 3.

- Elementary Functions (Precalculus) and/or Trigonometry **OR** beyond Course III of a college preparatory mathematics sequence   —Fill in circle 4.

- Advanced Placement Mathematics (Calculus AB or Calculus BC)   —Fill in circle 5.

Part II.   What type of calculator did you bring to use for this test? (FILL IN THE **ONE** CIRCLE THAT APPLIES. If you did not bring a scientific or graphing calculator, do not fill in any of circles 6-9.)

- Scientific   —Fill in circle 6.

- Graphing (Fill in the circle corresponding to the model you used.)

    Casio 9700, Casio 9750, Casio 9800, Casio 9850, Casio 9860, Casio FX 1.0, Casio CG-10, Sharp 9200, Sharp 9300, Sharp 9600, Sharp 9900, TI-82, TI-83, TI-83 Plus, TI-83 Plus Silver, TI-84 Plus, TI-84 Plus Silver, TI-85, TI-86, TI-Nspire, or TI-Nspire CX   —Fill in circle 7.

    Casio 9970, Casio Algebra FX 2.0, HP 38G, HP 39 series, HP 40 series, HP 48 series, HP 49 series, HP 50 series, TI-89, TI-89 Titanium, TI-Nspire CAS, or TI-Nspire CX CAS   —Fill in circle 8.

    Some other graphing calculator   —Fill in circle 9.

When the supervisor gives the signal, turn the page and begin the Mathematics Level 2 Test. There are 100 numbered circles on the answer sheet and 50 questions in the Mathematics Level 2 Test. Therefore, use only circles 1 to 50 for recording your answers.

MATHEMATICS LEVEL 2 TEST

REFERENCE INFORMATION

THE FOLLOWING INFORMATION IS FOR YOUR REFERENCE IN ANSWERING SOME OF THE QUESTIONS IN THIS TEST.

Volume of a right circular cone with radius r and height h: $V = \frac{1}{3}\pi r^2 h$

Volume of a sphere with radius r: $V = \frac{4}{3}\pi r^3$

Volume of a pyramid with base area B and height h: $V = \frac{1}{3}Bh$

Surface Area of a sphere with radius r: $S = 4\pi r^2$

DO NOT DETACH FROM BOOK.

GO ON TO THE NEXT PAGE

MATHEMATICS LEVEL 2 TEST

For each of the following problems, decide which is the BEST of the choices given. If the exact numerical value is not one of the choices, select the choice that best approximates this value. Then fill in the corresponding circle on the answer sheet.

<u>Notes:</u> (1) A scientific or graphing calculator will be necessary for answering some (but not all) of the questions in this test. For each question you will have to decide whether or not you should use a calculator.

(2) For some questions in this test you may have to decide whether your calculator should be in the radian mode or the degree mode.

(3) Figures that accompany problems in this test are intended to provide information useful in solving the problems. They are drawn as accurately as possible EXCEPT when it is stated in a specific problem that its figure is not drawn to scale. All figures lie in a plane unless otherwise indicated.

(4) Unless otherwise specified, the domain of any function f is assumed to be the set of all real numbers x for which $f(x)$ is a real number. The range of f is assumed to be the set of all real numbers $f(x)$, where x is in the domain of f.

(5) Reference information that may be useful in answering the questions in this test can be found on the page preceding Question 1.

USE THIS SPACE FOR SCRATCH WORK.

1. If $1 - \dfrac{1}{x} = 3 - \dfrac{3}{x}$, then $1 - \dfrac{1}{x} =$

(A) $-\dfrac{1}{2}$ (B) 0 (C) $\dfrac{1}{2}$ (D) $\dfrac{2}{3}$ (E) 3

2. $a\left(\dfrac{1}{b} + \dfrac{1}{c}\right) =$

(A) $\dfrac{a}{bc}$

(B) $\dfrac{a}{b + c}$

(C) $\dfrac{2a}{b + c}$

(D) $\dfrac{ab + ac}{bc}$

(E) $\dfrac{1}{ab + ac}$

GO ON TO THE NEXT PAGE

MATHEMATICS LEVEL 2 TEST—*Continued*

USE THIS SPACE FOR SCRATCHWORK.

3. Figure 1 shows one cycle of the graph of the function $y = \sin x$ for $0 \le x \le 2\pi$. If the minimum value of the function occurs at point P, then the coordinates of P are

(A) $\left(\dfrac{4\pi}{3}, -\pi\right)$

(B) $\left(\dfrac{4\pi}{3}, -1\right)$

(C) $\left(\dfrac{3\pi}{2}, -\pi\right)$

(D) $\left(\dfrac{3\pi}{2}, -1\right)$

(E) $\left(\dfrac{3\pi}{2}, 0\right)$

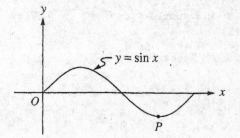

Figure 1
Note: Figure not drawn to scale.

4. If P and Q are different points in a plane, the set of all points in this plane that are closer to P than to Q is

(A) the region of the plane on one side of a line
(B) the interior of a square
(C) a wedge-shaped region of the plane
(D) the region of the plane bounded by a parabola
(E) the interior of a circle

5. If $\sqrt{6y} = 4.73$, then $y =$

(A) 0.62   (B) 1.93   (C) 3.73   (D) 5.33   (E) 11.59

GO ON TO THE NEXT PAGE

USE THIS SPACE FOR SCRATCHWORK.

6. In Figure 2, $r \cos \theta =$

(A) x
(B) y
(C) r
(D) $x + y$
(E) $r + y$

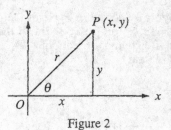

Figure 2

7. If $f(x) = \sqrt{0.3x^2 - x}$ and $g(x) = \dfrac{x + 1}{x - 1}$, then $g(f(10)) =$

(A) 0.2   (B) 1.2   (C) 1.6   (D) 4.5   (E) 5.5

8. If n, p, and t are nonzero real numbers and if
$n^4 p^7 t^9 = \dfrac{4n^3 p^7}{t^{-9}}$, then $n =$

(A) $\dfrac{1}{4}$ (B) $\dfrac{1}{2}$ (C) 4   (D) $4p^2 t^2$ (E) $4p^{18} t^{18}$

9. In the triangle in Figure 3, if $OA = AB$, what is the slope of segment AB?

(A) $\sqrt{2}$

(B) $\dfrac{\sqrt{2}}{2}$

(C) $-\dfrac{\sqrt{2}}{2}$

(D) $-\sqrt{2}$

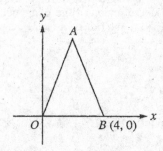

Figure 3

(E) It cannot be determined from the information given.

GO ON TO THE NEXT PAGE

USE THIS SPACE FOR SCRATCHWORK.

10. Where defined, csc(2θ) sin(2θ) =

(A) 1
(B) 0
(C) −1
(D) 2 csc(4θ)
(E) 2 sec(4θ)

11. The graph of $y = f(x)$ is shown in Figure 4. Which
of the following could be the graph of $y = |f(x)|$?

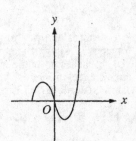

Figure 4

(A)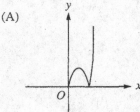

(B)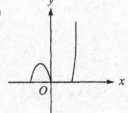

(C)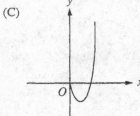

(D)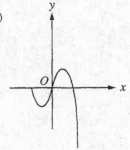

(E)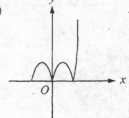

GO ON TO THE NEXT PAGE

USE THIS SPACE FOR SCRATCHWORK.

12. If 3 and −2 are both zeros of the polynomial $p(x)$, then a factor of $p(x)$ is

(A) $x^2 - 6$

(B) $x^2 - x - 6$

(C) $x^2 + 6$

(D) $x^2 + x - 6$

(E) $x^2 + x + 6$

13. A kite string is attached to a peg in the ground. If 100 meters of kite string are played out on the kite and the string makes an angle of 49° with the ground, what is the distance, in meters, from the kite to the ground? (Assume that the string is taut and the ground is level.)

(A) 133   (B) 115   (C) 75   (D) 66   (E) 52

14. If $f(x) = 3x + 5$ and $f(g(1)) = 11$, which of the following could be $g(x)$?

(A) $7x - 5$

(B) $5x + 7$

(C) $5x - 7$

(D) $5x + 3$

(E) $-5x + 3$

GO ON TO THE NEXT PAGE

MATHEMATICS LEVEL 2 TEST—*Continued*

USE THIS SPACE FOR SCRATCHWORK.

15. Figure 5 shows a cube with edge of length 3 centimeters. If points *A* and *C* are midpoints of the edges of the cube, what is the perimeter of region *ABCD* ?

(A) 6.71 cm
(B) 11.25 cm
(C) 13.42 cm
(D) 22.50 cm
(E) 45.00 cm

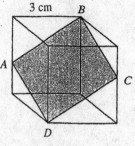

Figure 5

16. An equation of line ℓ in Figure 6 is

(A) $x = 2$
(B) $y = 2$
(C) $x = 0$
(D) $y = x + 2$
(E) $x + y = 2$

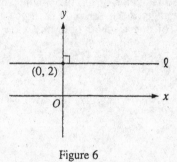

Figure 6

17. The mean weight of the 19 members of an algebra class was 112 pounds. When a new student enrolled, the mean decreased to 111 pounds. What was the weight, in pounds, of the new student?

(A) 91   (B) 92   (C) 93   (D) 101   (E) 110

GO ON TO THE NEXT PAGE

USE THIS SPACE FOR SCRATCHWORK.

18. If $0 < x < \pi$ and $\cos x = 0.875$, what is the value of

$\tan \left(\dfrac{x}{2} \right)$?

(A) 0.008
(B) 0.017
(C) 0.258
(D) 0.277
(E) 0.553

19. Recently 30,744 residents of Lyon County and 20,496 residents of Saline County voted on a referendum. A total of
38,430 residents of the two counties voted yes. If the same
percentage of the voters in each county voted yes, how
many of the residents of Lyon County voted yes?

(A)   7,686
(B) 10,248
(C) 15,372
(D) 17,934
(E) 23,058

20. If $f: (x, y) \rightarrow (x + 2y, y)$ for every pair (x, y)
in the plane, for what points (x, y) is it true that
$(x, y) \rightarrow (x, y)$?

(A) The set of points (x, y) such that $x = 0$
(B) The set of points (x, y) such that $y = 0$
(C) The set of points (x, y) such that $y = 1$
(D) $(0, 0)$ only
(E) $(-1, 1)$ only

GO ON TO THE NEXT PAGE

MATHEMATICS LEVEL 2 TEST—*Continued*

USE THIS SPACE FOR SCRATCHWORK.

21. What number should be added to each of the three numbers 1, 7, and 19 so that the resulting three numbers form a geometric progression?

(A) 2 (B) 3 (C) 4 (D) 5 (E) 6

22. If $f(x) = ax^2 + bx + c$ for all real numbers x and if $f(0) = 1$ and $f(1) = 2$, then $a + b =$

(A) −2 (B) −1 (C) 0 (D) 1 (E) 2

23. What is the degree measure of the largest angle of a triangle that has sides of length 7, 6, and 6 ?

(A) 31.00°
(B) 54.31°
(C) 71.37°
(D) 125.69°
(E) 144.31°

24. What is the domain of $f(x) = \sqrt[3]{-x^2 + 13}$?

(A) $x > 0$
(B) $x > 2.35$
(C) $-2.35 < x < 2.35$
(D) $-3.61 < x < 3.61$
(E) All real numbers

GO ON TO THE NEXT PAGE

USE THIS SPACE FOR SCRATCHWORK.

25. If $\cos x = \tan x$, which of the following is a possible radian value of x ?

(A) -1.00
(B) -0.52
(C) 0.00
(D) 0.52
(E) 0.67

26. Figure 7 shows a portion of the graph of $y = 3^x$. What is the sum of the areas of the three inscribed rectangles shown?

(A) 4,698   (B) 1,638   (C) 819   (D) 182   (E) 91

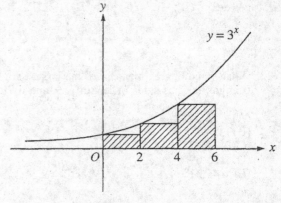

Figure 7

<u>Note:</u> Figure not drawn to scale.

GO ON TO THE NEXT PAGE

USE THIS SPACE FOR SCRATCHWORK.

27. When a certain radioactive element decays, the amount that exists at any time t can be calculated by the function $E(t) = ae^{\frac{-t}{1,000}}$, where a is the initial amount and t is the elapsed time in years. How many years would it take for an initial amount of 600 milligrams of this element to decay to 300 milligrams?

   (A) 0.5
   (B) 500
   (C) 693
   (D) 1,443
   (E) 5,704

28. Which of the following lines are asymptotes of the graph of $y = \dfrac{1 + x}{x}$?

   I. $x = 0$
   II. $y = 0$
   III. $y = 1$

   (A) I only
   (B) II only
   (C) I and II only
   (D) I and III only
   (E) I, II, and III

29. If $f(2x + 1) = 2x - 1$ for all real numbers x, then $f(x) =$

   (A) $-x + 1$

   (B) $x - 1$

   (C) $x - 2$

   (D) $2x - 1$

   (E) $\frac{1}{2}x - 1$

GO ON TO THE NEXT PAGE

MATHEMATICS LEVEL 2 TEST—*Continued*

USE THIS SPACE FOR SCRATCHWORK.

30. Which of the following could be the coordinates of the center of a circle tangent to the x-axis and the y-axis?

    (A) $(-1, 0)$
    (B) $(-1, 2)$
    (C) $(0, 2)$
    (D) $(2, -2)$
    (E) $(2, 1)$

31. What is the range of the function defined by

    $$f(x) = \begin{cases} x^{\frac{1}{3}}, & x > 2 \\ 2x - 1, & x \leq 2 \end{cases} ?$$

    (A) $y > 2^{\frac{1}{3}}$

    (B) $y \leq 3$

    (C) $2^{\frac{1}{3}} < y < 3$

    (D) $y \geq 3$

    (E) All real numbers

32. If $3x - 4y + 7 = 0$ and $2y - x^2 = 0$ for $x \geq 0$, then $x =$

    (A) 1.27
    (B) 2.07
    (C) 2.77
    (D) 4.15
    (E) 5.53

GO ON TO THE NEXT PAGE

USE THIS SPACE FOR SCRATCHWORK.

33. If $f(x) = \log_2 x$ for $x > 0$, then $f^{-1}(x) =$

(A) 2^x

(B) x^2

(C) $\frac{x}{2}$

(D) $\frac{2}{x}$

(E) $\log_x 2$

34. If $x_0 = 0$ and $x_{n+1} = \sqrt{6 + x_n}$, then $x_3 =$

(A) 2.449
(B) 2.907
(C) 2.984
(D) 2.997
(E) 3.162

35. Figure 8 shows a triangle inscribed in a semicircle. What is the area of the triangle in terms of θ ?

(A) $\frac{\theta\pi}{2}$

(B) $\frac{\theta}{2}$

(C) $\tan \theta$

(D) $\sin \theta$

(E) $2 \sin \theta \cos \theta$

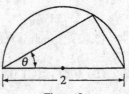

Figure 8

GO ON TO THE NEXT PAGE

USE THIS SPACE FOR SCRATCHWORK.

36. In a certain experiment, there is a 0.2 probability that any thermometer used is in error by more than 1°C. If 4 thermometers are used, what is the probability that all of them are in error by more than 1°C?

(A) 0.0016
(B) 0.0081
(C) 0.16
(D) 0.25
(E) 0.80

37. If the magnitudes of vectors **a** and **b** are 5 and 12, respectively, then the magnitude of vector (**b** − **a**) could NOT be

(A) 5
(B) 7
(C) 10
(D) 12
(E) 17

38. If $(6.31)^m = (3.02)^n$, what is the value of $\dfrac{m}{n}$?

(A) −0.32   (B) 0.32   (C) 0.48   (D) 0.60   (E) 1.67

GO ON TO THE NEXT PAGE

MATHEMATICS LEVEL 2 TEST—*Continued*

39. If $\arccos(\cos x) = 0$ and $0 \le x \le \dfrac{\pi}{2}$, then x could equal

    (A) 0

    (B) $\dfrac{\pi}{6}$

    (C) $\dfrac{\pi}{4}$

    (D) $\dfrac{\pi}{3}$

    (E) $\dfrac{\pi}{2}$

40. If the 20th term of an arithmetic sequence is 100 and the 40th term of the sequence is 250, what is the first term of the sequence?

    (A) -50
    (B) -42.5
    (C) 5
    (D) 42.5
    (E) 50

41. If n distinct planes intersect in a line, and another line ℓ intersects one of these planes in a single point, what is the <u>least</u> number of these n planes that ℓ could intersect?

    (A) n (B) $n-1$ (C) $n-2$ (D) $\dfrac{n}{2}$ (E) $\dfrac{n-1}{2}$

GO ON TO THE NEXT PAGE

MATHEMATICS LEVEL 2 TEST—Continued

USE THIS SPACE FOR SCRATCHWORK.

42. For all θ, $\sin \theta + \sin(-\theta) + \cos \theta + \cos(-\theta) =$

(A) 0   (B) 2   (C) $2 \sin \theta$ (D) $2 \cos \theta$ (E) $2(\sin \theta + \cos \theta)$

43. $\dfrac{[(n-1)!]^2}{[n!]^2} =$

(A) $\dfrac{1}{n}$

(B) $\dfrac{1}{n^2}$

(C) $\dfrac{n-1}{n}$

(D) $\left(\dfrac{n-1}{n}\right)^2$

(E) $(n-1)^2$

44. The radius of the base of a right circular cone is 6 and the radius of a parallel cross section is 4. If the distance between the base and the cross section is 8, what is the height of the cone?

(A) 11

(B) $13\dfrac{1}{3}$

(C) 16

(D) 20

(E) 24

GO ON TO THE NEXT PAGE

USE THIS SPACE FOR SCRATCHWORK.

45. An indirect proof of the statement "If $x = 2$, then $\sqrt{x}$ is <u>not</u> a rational number" could begin with the assumption that

    (A) $x = \sqrt{2}$
    (B) $x^2 = 2$
    (C) $\sqrt{x}$ is rational
    (D) $\sqrt{x}$ is not rational
    (E) x is nonnegative

46. Suppose the graph of $f(x) = -x^2$ is translated 3 units left and 1 unit up. If the resulting graph represents $g(x)$, what is the value of $g(-1.6)$?

    (A) 2.96
    (B) −0.96
    (C) −1.56
    (D) −1.96
    (E) −2.56

47. In how many ways can 10 people be divided into two groups, one with 7 people and the other with 3 people?

    (A) 120   (B) 210   (C) 240   (D) 5,040   (E) 14,400

GO ON TO THE NEXT PAGE

48. Which of the following has an element that is less than any other element in that set?

    I.   The set of positive rational numbers

    II. The set of positive rational numbers r such that $r^2 \geq 2$

    III. The set of positive rational numbers r such that $r^2 > 4$

    (A) None
    (B) I only
    (C) II only
    (D) III only
    (E) I and III

49. What is the length of the major axis of the ellipse whose equation is $60x^2 + 30y^2 = 150$?

    (A) 1.26
    (B) 2.50
    (C) 3.16
    (D) 4.47
    (E) 5.00

50. Under which of the following conditions is $\dfrac{a - b}{ab}$ positive?

    (A) $0 < a < b$
    (B) $a < b < 0$
    (C) $b < a < 0$
    (D) $b < 0 < a$
    (E) None of the above

S T O P

IF YOU FINISH BEFORE TIME IS CALLED, YOU MAY CHECK YOUR WORK ON THIS TEST ONLY.
DO NOT TURN TO ANY OTHER TEST IN THIS BOOK.

How to Score the SAT Subject Test in Mathematics Level 2

When you take the actual SAT Subject Test in Mathematics Level 2, your answer sheet will be "read" by a scanning machine that will record your responses to each question. Then a computer will compare your answers with the correct answers and produce your raw score. You get one point for each correct answer. For each wrong answer, you lose one-quarter of a point. Questions you omit (and any for which you mark more than one answer) are not counted. This raw score is converted to a scaled score that is reported to you and to the colleges you specify.

Worksheet 1. Finding Your Raw Test Score

Step 1: Table A on the following page lists the correct answers for all the questions on the SAT Subject Test in Mathematics Level 2 that is reproduced in this book. It also serves as a worksheet for you to calculate your raw score.

- Compare your answers with those given in the table.

- Put a check in the column marked "Right" if your answer is correct.

- Put a check in the column marked "Wrong" if your answer is incorrect.

- Leave both columns blank if you omitted the question.

Step 2: Count the number of right answers.

Enter the total here: _____

Step 3: Count the number of wrong answers.

Enter the total here: _____

Step 4: Multiply the number of wrong answers by .250.

Enter the product here: _____

Step 5: Subtract the result obtained in Step 4 from the total you obtained in Step 2.

Enter the result here: _____

Step 6: Round the number obtained in Step 5 to the nearest whole number.

Enter the result here: _____

The number you obtained in Step 6 is your raw score.

Answers to Practice Test 4 for Mathematics Level 2

Table A
Answers to the Subject Test in Mathematics Level 2 - Practice Test 4 and Percentage of Students Answering Each Question Correctly

Question Number	Correct Answer	Right	Wrong	Percentage of Students Answering the Question Correctly*	Question Number	Correct Answer	Right	Wrong	Percentage of Students Answering the Question Correctly*
1	B			79	26	D			66
2	D			81	27	C			57
3	D			89	28	D			56
4	A			52	29	C			54
5	C			94	30	D			84
6	A			84	31	E			48
7	C			89	32	C			52
8	C			80	33	A			52
9	E			82	34	C			42
10	A			84	35	E			34
11	E			74	36	A			60
12	B			84	37	A			24
13	C			85	38	D			45
14	A			89	39	A			56
15	C			71	40	B			28
16	B			96	41	B			22
17	B			80	42	D			56
18	C			85	43	B			51
19	E			65	44	E			32
20	B			59	45	C			28
21	D			64	46	B			33
22	D			79	47	A			26
23	C			67	48	A			14
24	E			61	49	D			24
25	E			68	50	C			45

* These percentages are based on an analysis of the answer sheets of a representative sample of 9,983 students who took the original administration of this test and whose mean score was 649. They may be used as an indication of the relative difficulty of a particular question.

Finding Your Scaled Score

When you take SAT Subject Tests, the scores sent to the colleges you specify are reported on the College Board scale, which ranges from 200 to 800. You can convert your practice test raw score to a scaled score by using Table B. To find your scaled score, locate your raw score in the left-hand column of Table B; the corresponding score in the right-hand column is your scaled score. For example, a raw score of 30 on this particular edition of the SAT Subject Test in Mathematics Level 2 corresponds to a scaled score of 670.

Raw scores are converted to scaled scores to ensure that a score earned on any one edition of a particular Subject Test is comparable to the same scaled score earned on any other edition of the same Subject Test. Because some editions of tests may be slightly easier or more difficult than others, scaled scores are adjusted so that they indicate the same level of performance regardless of the edition of the test taken and the ability of the group that takes it. Thus, for example, a score of 400 on one edition of a test taken at a particular administration indicates the same level of achievement as a score of 400 on a different edition of the test taken at a different administration.

When you take the SAT Subject Tests during a national administration, your scores are likely to differ somewhat from the scores you obtain on the tests in this book. People perform at different levels at different times for reasons unrelated to the tests themselves. The precision of any test is also limited because it represents only a sample of all the possible questions that could be asked.

Table B
Scaled Score Conversion Table
Subject Test in Mathematics Level 2 - Practice Test 4

Raw Score	Scaled Score	Raw Score	Scaled Score	Raw Score	Scaled Score
50	800	28	650	6	480
49	800	27	640	5	470
48	800	26	630	4	460
47	800	25	630	3	450
46	800	24	620	2	440
45	800	23	610	1	430
44	800	22	600	0	410
43	800	21	590	−1	390
42	790	20	580	−2	370
41	780	19	570	−3	360
40	770	18	560	−4	340
39	760	17	560	−5	340
38	750	16	550	−6	330
37	740	15	540	−7	320
36	730	14	530	−8	320
35	720	13	530	−9	320
34	710	12	520	−10	320
33	700	11	510	−11	310
32	690	10	500	−12	310
31	680	9	500		
30	670	8	490		
29	660	7	480		

How Did You Do on the Subject Test in Mathematics Level 2?

After you score your test and analyze your performance, think about the following questions:

Did you run out of time before reaching the end of the test?

If so, you may need to pace yourself better. For example, maybe you spent too much time on one or two hard questions. A better approach might be to skip the ones you can't answer right away and try answering all the remaining questions on the test. Then if there's time, go back to the questions you skipped.

Did you take a long time reading the directions?

You will save time when you take the test by learning the directions to the Subject Test in Mathematics Level 2 ahead of time. Each minute you spend reading directions during the test is a minute that you could use to answer questions. Also be familiar with what formulas are given at the front of the test so that you know when to refer to them during the test.

How did you handle questions you were unsure of?

If you were able to eliminate one or more of the answer choices as wrong and guess from the remaining ones, your approach probably worked to your advantage. On the other hand, making haphazard guesses or omitting questions without trying to eliminate choices could cost you valuable points.

How difficult were the questions for you compared with other students who took the test?

Table A shows you how difficult the multiple-choice questions were for the group of students who took this test during its national administration. The right-hand column gives the percentage of students that answered each question correctly.

A question answered correctly by almost everyone in the group is obviously an easier question. For example, 96 percent of the students answered question 16 correctly. However, only 24 percent answered question 49 correctly.

Keep in mind that these percentages are based on just one group of students. They would probably be different with another group of students taking the test.

If you missed several easier questions, go back and try to find out why: Did the questions cover material you haven't reviewed yet? Did you misunderstand the directions?

Answer Explanations

For Practice Test 4

The solutions presented here provide one method for solving each of the problems on this test. Other mathematically correct approaches are possible.

Question 1

Choice (B) is the correct answer. Since $1 - \dfrac{1}{x} = 3 - \dfrac{3}{x}$, then $\dfrac{2}{x} = 2$. Solving for x gives $x = 1$. The value of $1 - \dfrac{1}{x}$ when $x = 1$ is equal to $1 - \dfrac{1}{1} = 0$.

Question 2

Choice (D) is the correct answer. Using the distributive property, $a\left(\dfrac{1}{b} + \dfrac{1}{c}\right) = \dfrac{a}{b} + \dfrac{a}{c}$. To add these fractions, you need to find the least common denominator, which is bc. Thus, $\dfrac{a}{b} + \dfrac{a}{c} = \dfrac{ac}{bc} + \dfrac{ab}{bc}$, which is equivalent to choice (D).

Question 3

Choice (D) is the correct answer. On the closed interval $[0, 2\pi]$, the minimum value of $y = \sin x$ occurs when $x = \dfrac{3\pi}{2} \cdot \sin\left(\dfrac{3\pi}{2}\right)$ is -1. Thus, the coordinates of P are $\left(\dfrac{3\pi}{2}, -1\right)$. Using a graphing calculator to see the graph of $y = \sin x$ may be helpful in solving this problem.

Question 4

Choice (A) is the correct answer. The set of all points in the plane the same distance from P and Q is the line that is perpendicular to $\overline{PQ}$ and bisects $\overline{PQ}$. Thus, the set of all points closer to P than Q is the region in the plane on the side of the line where P lies. The other choices do not include ALL such points that are closer to P than Q.

Question 5

Choice (C) is the correct answer. If $\sqrt{6y} = 4.73$, then $6y = 4.73^2 = 22.3729$ and $y \approx 3.729 \approx 3.73$.

Question 6

Choice (A) is the correct answer. The cosine of an angle is equal to $\dfrac{\text{length of adjacent side}}{\text{length of hypotenuse}}$. Thus, $\cos\theta = \dfrac{x}{r}$, and $r\cos\theta = r\left(\dfrac{x}{r}\right) = x$.

Question 7

Choice (C) is the correct answer. $f(10) = \sqrt{0.3(10)^2 - 10} = \sqrt{20} \approx 4.472$ and

$$g(\sqrt{20}) = \frac{\sqrt{20} + 1}{\sqrt{20} - 1} \approx 1.576 \approx 1.6.$$

Question 8

Choice (C) is the correct answer. The equation given is equivalent to $n^4 \, p^7 \, t^9 = 4n^3 \, p^7 \, t^9$. This simplifies to $n^4 = 4n^3$. Dividing both sides by n^3, you get $n = 4$.

Question 9

Choice (E) is the correct answer because there is not enough information given. If $OA = AB$, then $\triangle OAB$ is an isosceles triangle. The slope of $\overline{AB}$ can be found if the measure of $\angle ABO$ is known or if the coordinates of A can be determined. In this problem, point A is not fixed vertically.

Question 10

Choice (A) is the correct answer. Since $\csc(2\theta) = \dfrac{1}{\sin(2\theta)}$, $\csc(2\theta) \sin(2\theta) = 1$.

Question 11

Choice (E) is the correct answer. Since $|f(x)| \geq 0$, the graph of $y = |f(x)|$ consists of points (x, y), where $y \geq 0$. This eliminates choices (C) and (D). The graphs of $y = f(x)$ and $y = |f(x)|$ are identical where $f(x) \geq 0$. This eliminates choice (A). The portion of the graph of $y = f(x)$ where $f(x) < 0$ must be reflected about the x-axis to produce the graph of $y = |f(x)|$. This eliminates choice (B) because it does not include the reflection of $y = f(x)$ where $f(x) < 0$. Choice (E) is the complete graph of $y = |f(x)|$.

Question 12

Choice (B) is the correct answer. If 3 and –2 are zeros of $p(x)$, then $(x - 3)$ and $(x + 2)$ are factors of $p(x)$. $(x - 3)(x + 2) = x^2 - x - 6$, which is also a factor of $p(x)$. Choices (A), (C), (D), and (E) are incorrect. These choices result from sign errors in determining the factors that give the zeros of $p(x)$ or sign errors in the multiplication of those factors.

Question 13

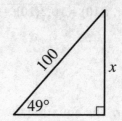

Choice (C) is the correct answer. It is helpful to draw a figure to solve this problem. x represents the distance from the kite to the ground, and $\sin 49° = \dfrac{x}{100}$. Solving for x gives $x \approx 75.471$, which is closest to choice (C). Choice (A) is incorrect. It results from using the incorrect equation $\sin 49° = \dfrac{100}{x}$. Choice (B) is incorrect. It results from using $\tan 49°$ instead of $\sin 49°$. Choice (D) is incorrect. It results from using $\cos 49°$ instead of $\sin 49°$. Choice (E) is incorrect. It results from using the incorrect equation $\cos 49° = \dfrac{100}{x}$ and then subtracting 100 from the solution to the equation.

Question 14

Choice (A) is the correct answer. One way to solve this problem is to first find the value of x for which $f(x) = 11$. Since $3x + 5 = 11$, then $x = 2$. This implies that $g(1) = 2$, and we must determine which of the choices is equal to 2 when $x = 1$. Only choice (A) meets this condition. $7x - 5 = 2$ when $x = 1$.

Question 15

Choice (C) is the correct answer. You can use the Pythagorean theorem to find the length of $\overline{AB}$. $(3)^2 + (1.5)^2 = x^2$ and $x = \sqrt{11.25} \approx 3.35$ cm. All sides of $ABCD$ have the same length, so its perimeter is $4x \approx 13.416 \approx 13.42$ cm. Choice (B) is incorrect. It is the area, in square centimeters, of $ABCD$. Choice (E) is incorrect. It is the perimeter if 11.25 cm is used as the length of a side.

Question 16

Choice (B) is the correct answer. Since line ℓ is perpendicular to the y-axis and intersects the y-axis at $(0, 2)$, each point on line ℓ has the y-coordinate 2, and therefore, the equation of ℓ is $y = 2$.

Question 17

Choice (B) is the correct answer. You can set up an equation to solve this problem. Let x be the weight of the new student, in pounds. The total weight of the 20 students is equal to $19(112) + x$. Since the mean weight is 111, it follows that $\frac{19(112)+x}{20} = 111$. Solving for x gives 92 as the weight of the new student.

Question 18

Choice (C) is the correct answer. For $0 < x < \pi$, you can set your calculator in radian mode to find the value of x, which is equal to $\cos^{-1}(0.875) \approx 0.5054$. Keep this value in your calculator to evaluate $\tan\left(\frac{x}{2}\right)$. $\tan\left(\frac{x}{2}\right) \approx \tan\left(\frac{0.5054}{2}\right) \approx 0.2582$. Choice (D) is incorrect. It is equal to $\frac{\tan(28.955°)}{2}$, where $28.955° \approx \cos^{-1}(0.875)$ with the calculator set in degree mode. Choice (E) is incorrect. It is equal to $\tan(28.955°)$, where $28.955° \approx \cos^{-1}(0.875)$ with the calculator set in degree mode.

Question 19

Choice (E) is the correct answer. You can set up an equation to solve this problem. Let $\frac{x}{100}$ represent the percent of residents that voted "yes." $30{,}744\left(\frac{x}{100}\right) + 20{,}496\left(\frac{x}{100}\right) = 38{,}430$. This simplifies to $307.44x + 204.96x = 38{,}430$. Solving for x gives 75. Thus, 75% of the residents voted "yes," and 75% of 30,744 is 23,058. Choice (A) is incorrect. It is 25% of those who voted from Lyon County. Choice (C) is incorrect. It is 75% of those who voted from Saline County.

Question 20

Choice (B) is the correct answer. In this problem, the function f maps a point (x, y) in the plane to the point $(x + 2y, y)$. You are looking for all points at which the image has the same x-coordinate as the original point. If $x = x + 2y$, then y must equal 0. Thus, you want all points (x, y) such that $y = 0$.

Question 21

Choice (D) is the correct answer. Let x be the number to be added so that $1 + x$, $7 + x$, and $19 + x$ form a geometric progression. Then, $\frac{19 + x}{7 + x} = \frac{7 + x}{1 + x}$. This equation simplifies to $6x = 30$. Therefore, $x = 5$.

Question 22

Choice (D) is the correct answer. Since $f(0) = 1$, $1 = a(0) + b(0) + c$ and $c = 1$. Since $f(1) = 2$, $2 = a(1) + b(1) + 1 = a + b + 1$. Thus, $a + b = 1$.

Question 23

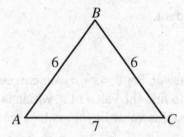

Choice (C) is the correct answer. It is helpful to draw a figure to solve this problem. The largest angle is $\angle B$, since it is opposite the longest side. The measure of $\angle B$ can be found using the law of cosines.

$$(AC)^2 = (AB)^2 + (BC)^2 - 2(AB)(BC) \cos \angle B$$

$$\cos \angle B = \frac{(AC)^2 - (AB)^2 - (BC)^2}{-2(AB)(BC)}$$

$$= \frac{49 - 36 - 36}{-2(6)(6)}$$

Since $\cos \angle B = \frac{23}{72}$, the measure of $\angle B$ is $\cos^{-1}\left(\frac{23}{72}\right) \approx 71.37°$. Choice (B) is incorrect. It is the measure of $\angle A$ and $\angle C$.

Question 24

Choice (E) is the correct answer. The cube root of any real number is a real number. Thus, the domain of f is all real numbers. Choices (B) and (C) are incorrect. They both incorrectly use $\sqrt[3]{13} \approx 2.35$. Choice (D) is incorrect. It incorrectly assumes that $-x^2 + 13 \geq 0$.

Question 25

Choice (E) is the correct answer. Since $\tan x = \frac{\sin x}{\cos x}$, the equation can be rewritten as $\cos x = \frac{\sin x}{\cos x}$, and $\cos^2 x - \sin x = 0$. Using the identity $\sin^2 x + \cos^2 x = 1$, the equation becomes $1 - \sin^2 x - \sin x = 0$. This is a quadratic equation in $\sin x$. Let $y = \sin x$ and use the quadratic formula to solve $y^2 + y - 1 = 0$.

$$y = \frac{-1 \pm \sqrt{1 - 4(1)(-1)}}{2}$$

$$= \frac{-1 \pm \sqrt{5}}{2} \approx 0.6180, -1.6180$$

sin $x = -1.6180$ has no solution. Solving sin $x = 0.6180$ gives $x = \sin^{-1}(0.6180) \approx 0.67$. Alternatively, you can use a graphing calculator to graph $y = \cos x$ and $y = \tan x$ on the interval $\left[0, \dfrac{\pi}{2}\right]$ and find the x-coordinate of the point of intersection.

Question 26

Choice (D) is the correct answer. The width of each rectangle is 2. The heights of the rectangles are 3^0, 3^2, and 3^4, respectively. The sum of the areas is $3^0(2) + 3^2(2) + 3^4(2) = 2 + 18 + 162 = 182$. Choice (B) is incorrect. It results from using the right endpoint instead of the left one for the heights of the rectangles (3^2, 3^4, and 3^6). Choice (C) is incorrect. It results from using the right endpoint for the heights of the rectangles and forgetting to multiply by 2. Choice (E) is incorrect. It results from forgetting to multiply by 2.

Question 27

Choice (C) is the correct answer. For the function given, let $a = 600$ and $E(t) = 300$. Thus, $300 = 600e^{-t/1000}$, which simplifies to $\dfrac{1}{2} = e^{-t/1000}$. Taking the natural logarithm of both sides of the equation gives $\ln\left(\dfrac{1}{2}\right) = \dfrac{-t}{1{,}000}$. Solving for t yields $t \approx 693.147 \approx 693$. Alternatively, you can use a graphing calculator to graph $y = 300$ and $y = 600e^{-t/1000}$ and find the x-coordinate of the point of intersection.

Question 28

Choice (D) is the correct answer. The lines $x = 0$ and $y = 1$ are asymptotes of the graph of $y = \dfrac{1+x}{x}$. The correct answer is I and III only. The line $y = 1$ is a horizontal asymptote, because as the value of x increases without bound, the value of y approaches 1. The line $x = 0$ is a vertical asymptote, because the value of y is undefined when $x = 0$.

Question 29

Choice (C) is the correct answer. To find an expression for $f(x)$, you must understand what $f(2x + 1)$ means. If f is evaluated at $2x + 1$, the value is $2x - 1$, which is equal to $(2x + 1) - 2$. So, the "input" value for f has 2 subtracted from it to produce the "output" value of the function. Thus, if the original "input" value is x, the "output" value is $x - 2$. Therefore, $f(x) = x - 2$.

Question 30

Choice (D) is the correct answer. In order for the circle to be tangent to both the x-axis and y-axis, the center of the circle must be the same distance from both axes. Choices (A) and (C) are incorrect. They can be eliminated because they are each on a coordinate axis. Choices (B) and (E) are incorrect. They can be eliminated because each of these points is closer to one of the coordinate axes than the other. $(2, -2)$ is the answer because it is 2 units from both coordinate axes.

Question 31

Choice (E) is the correct answer. To find the range of this piecewise-defined function, you must consider both parts. For $x > 2$, $f(x) = x^{\frac{1}{3}}$. The range of the function is $y > 2^{\frac{1}{3}}$, since the function is increasing for all $x > 2$. For $x \le 2$, $f(x) = 2x - 1$. The range of this function is $y \le 3$, since the function is decreasing as x is decreasing for $x \le 2$. Combining $y > 2^{\frac{1}{3}}$ and $y \le 3$ gives all real numbers for the range. Choices (A) and (B) are incorrect. They result from considering only one part of the function. Choice (C) is incorrect. It results from incorrectly looking at the interval between the endpoints of the ranges of the respective parts.

Question 32

Choice (C) is the correct answer. Since $2y - x^2 = 0$, $y = \dfrac{x^2}{2}$ for $x \ge 0$.

Substituting that into the first equation yields $3x - 4\left(\dfrac{x^2}{2}\right) + 7 = 0$. This simplifies to $3x - 2x^2 + 7 = 0$ or $2x^2 - 3x - 7 = 0$. Using the quadratic formula,

$$x = \frac{3 \pm \sqrt{9 - 4(2)(-7)}}{4}$$

$$= \frac{3 \pm \sqrt{65}}{4}$$

$$\approx 2.77, -1.27.$$

Since $x \ge 0$, the answer is 2.77. Choice (A) is incorrect. It results from a sign error in solving for x.

Question 33

Choice (A) is the correct answer. The inverse of a logarithmic function with base a ($f(x) = \log_a x$, where $x > 0$) is an exponential function with base a ($f^{-1}(x) = a^x$). In this case, the inverse of $f(x) = \log_2 x$ for $x > 0$ is $f^{-1}(x) = 2^x$.

Question 34

Choice (C) is the correct answer. Since $x_0 = 0$, $x_1 = \sqrt{6 + x_0} = \sqrt{6} \approx 2.449$, which is choice (A). Choice (A) is incorrect. $x_2 = \sqrt{6 + x_1} = \sqrt{6 + \sqrt{6}} \approx 2.907$, which is choice (B). Choice (B) is incorrect. $x_3 = \sqrt{6 + x_2} = \sqrt{6 + \sqrt{6 + \sqrt{6}}} \approx 2.984$. Choice (D) is incorrect. It is x_4.

Question 35

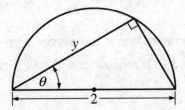

Choice (E) is the correct answer. Since the triangle is inscribed in a semicircle, it is a right triangle. The area of the triangle is equal to $\frac{1}{2}ab \sin \theta$, where a and b represent adjacent sides and θ is the included angle. In the figure, $\cos \theta = \frac{y}{2}$ and $y = 2 \cos \theta$. Thus, the area of the triangle is equal to $\frac{1}{2}(2)(2 \cos \theta) \sin \theta = 2 \cos \theta \sin \theta$ which is equivalent to choice (E).

Question 36

Choice (A) is the correct answer. Since the use of each thermometer is an independent event, the probability is equal to $(0.2)^4 = 0.0016$.

Question 37

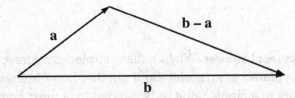

Choice (A) is the correct answer. Vectors **a**, **b**, and **b** − **a** can be represented as shown in the figure. Using the triangle inequality, $7 \le$ magnitude of **b** − **a** ≤ 17. Thus, the magnitude of **b** − **a** cannot be 5. The other choices are all possible magnitudes.

Question 38

Choice (D) is the correct answer. Since $(6.31)^m = (3.02)^n$, $\log (6.31)^m = \log (3.02)^n$ and $m \log 6.31 = n \log 3.02$. $\frac{m}{n} = \frac{\log 3.02}{\log 6.31} \approx 0.60$. Choice (A) is incorrect. It is equal to $\log \left(\frac{3.02}{6.31} \right)$. Choice (C) is incorrect. It is equal to $\frac{3.02}{6.31}$. Choice (E) is incorrect. It is equal to $\frac{\log 6.31}{\log 3.02}$.

Question 39

Choice (A) is the correct answer. $\cos x$ and $\arccos x$ are inverses of each other on the interval $0 \leq x \leq \frac{\pi}{2}$. If $\arccos (\cos x) = 0$, x could equal 0.

Question 40

Choice (B) is the correct answer. You can use the given information to set up two equations. Let a_1 represent the first term of the arithmetic sequence, and let d represent the common difference.

$$100 = a_{20} = a_1 + (20 - 1) d$$
$$250 = a_{40} = a_1 + (40 - 1) d$$

Solving both of these for a_1 yields $a_1 = 100 - 19d$ and $a_1 = 250 - 39d$.

$$100 - 19d = 250 - 39d$$
$$d = \frac{15}{2} = 7.5$$
$$a_1 = 100 - 19(7.5) = -42.5$$

Choice (A) is incorrect. It results from using $a_{20} = a_1 + 20d$ and $a_{40} = a_1 + 40d$. Choice (C) is incorrect. It results from thinking that the first term is $\frac{100}{20}$. Choice (D) is incorrect. It results from a sign error.

Question 41

Choice (B) is the correct answer. When n distinct planes intersect in a line, no two of the planes are parallel. So if another line ℓ intersects one of these planes in a single point, it is parallel to at most one of the planes. Therefore, line ℓ would intersect at least $n - 1$ planes. Thus, the least number of these n planes that line ℓ intersects is $n - 1$.

Question 42

Choice (D) is the correct answer. Since $\sin \theta$ is odd,
$\sin(-\theta) = -\sin(\theta)$. Since $\cos \theta$ is even, $\cos(-\theta) = \cos(\theta)$. Thus,
$\sin \theta + \sin(-\theta) + \cos \theta + \cos(-\theta) = \sin \theta - \sin(\theta) + \cos \theta + \cos \theta = 2\cos \theta$.

Question 43

Choice (B) is the correct answer. Since $n! = (n-1)!n$, then $\dfrac{((n-1)!)^2}{(n!)^2} =$
$\dfrac{(n-1)!(n-1)!}{(n-1)!n(n-1)!n} = \dfrac{1}{n^2}$.

Question 44

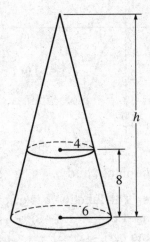

Choice (E) is the correct answer. It is helpful to draw a figure. This problem can be solved using similar triangles. Setting up the proportion $\dfrac{4}{6} = \dfrac{h-8}{h}$ results in

$$4h = 6(h-8)$$
$$4h = 6h - 48$$
$$48 = 2h$$
$$h = 24$$

Choice (C) is incorrect. It is the height of the smaller cone whose base is the parallel cross section.

Question 45

Choice (C) is the correct answer. An indirect proof begins with assuming the negative of the conclusion. The conclusion is "$\sqrt{x}$ is NOT a rational number." The negative of this statement is "$\sqrt{x}$ is a rational number."

Question 46

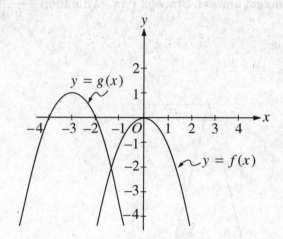

It may be helpful to draw a graph of f and g.

Choice (B) is the correct answer. The function g is given by $g(x) = -(x + 3)^2 + 1$. Therefore, $g(-1.6) = -(-1.6 + 3)^2 + 1 = -0.96$. Choice (A) is incorrect. It results from using $g(x) = (x + 3)^2 + 1$. Choice (C) is incorrect. It is $f(-1.6) + 1$. Choice (D) is incorrect. It results from using $g(x) = -(x + 3)^2$. Choice (E) is incorrect. It is $f(-1.6)$.

Question 47

Choice (A) is the correct answer. To determine the number of ways that 10 people can be divided into the two groups, find either $\binom{10}{7}$ or $\binom{10}{3}$, which are equivalent. Once the number of ways to form one of the groups is determined, there is only one way to form the other group. So, $\binom{10}{7} = \dfrac{10!}{3!7!} = \dfrac{10 \cdot 9 \cdot 8 \cdot 7!}{3 \cdot 2 \cdot 7!} = 120$.

Question 48

Choice (A) is the correct answer. You need to examine each set separately. Consider I. There is no least positive rational number, so "the set of positive rational numbers" does not satisfy the desired condition. Consider II. $\sqrt{2}$ is the smallest positive real number that satisfies $r^2 \geq 2$, but $\sqrt{2}$ is irrational. Thus, there is no smallest positive rational number that satisfies the desired condition. Consider III. $r > 2$, but there is no smallest rational number that satisfies this condition. None of the three sets has an element that is less than any other element in the set.

Question 49

Choice (D) is the correct answer. The standard form for the equation of an ellipse centered at the origin is $\frac{x^2}{a^2} + \frac{y^2}{b^2} = 1$. $60x^2 + 30y^2 = 150$ can be rewritten as $\frac{60x^2}{150} + \frac{30y^2}{150} = \frac{150}{150}$, which is equivalent to $\frac{x^2}{2.5} + \frac{y^2}{5} = 1$. Because the denominator of the y^2 term is larger than the denominator of the x^2 term, the major axis of this ellipse is vertical. Since $b^2 = 5$, the vertices are $(0, \sqrt{5})$ and $(0, -\sqrt{5})$. The length of the major axis is $2b = 2\sqrt{5} \approx 4.47$. Choice (B) is incorrect. It is a^2. Choice (C) is incorrect. It is $2a = 2\sqrt{2.5} \approx 3.16$, which is the length of the minor axis of this ellipse. Choice (E) is incorrect. It is b^2.

Question 50

Choice (C) is the correct answer. You need to determine for which of the conditions $\frac{a-b}{ab} > 0$. It is helpful to examine each of the answer choices. Choice (A) is incorrect. $0 < a < b$. In this case, $a - b < 0$ and $ab > 0$, so the expression is NEGATIVE. Choice (B) is incorrect. $a < b < 0$. In this case, $a - b < 0$ and $ab > 0$, so the expression is NEGATIVE. In choice (C), $a - b > 0$ and $ab > 0$, so the expression is POSITIVE. You are looking for a positive result. Choice (D) is incorrect. $b < 0 < a$. In this case, $a - b > 0$ and $ab < 0$, so the expression is NEGATIVE.

 **CollegeBoard**

SAT Subject Tests™

| COMPLETE MARK ● | EXAMPLES OF INCOMPLETE MARKS | **You must use a No. 2 pencil and marks must be complete. Do not use a mechanical pencil.** *It is very important that you fill in the entire circle darkly and completely. If you change your response, erase as completely as possible. Incomplete marks or erasures may affect your score.* |

1 **Your Name:**
(Print)

_____ Last _____ First _____ M.I.

I agree to the conditions on the front and back of the SAT Subject Tests™ book. I also agree with the SAT Test Security and Fairness policies and understand that any violation of these policies will result in score cancellation and may result in reporting of certain violations to law enforcement.

Signature: _____

Today's Date: ___ / ___ / ___
　　　　　　　　 MM　DD　YY

Home Address: _____
(Print)　　　Number and Street　　City　　State/Country　Zip Code

Phone: (___) _____　**Test Center:** _____
　　　　　　　　　　　　　　(Print)　　City　　State/Country

2 **YOUR NAME**
Last Name (First 6 Letters)　First Name (First 4 Letters)　Mid. Init.

3 **DATE OF BIRTH**
MONTH　DAY　YEAR
Jan, Feb, Mar, Apr, May, Jun, Jul, Aug, Sep, Oct, Nov, Dec

4 **REGISTRATION NUMBER**
(Copy from Admission Ticket.)

Important: Fill in items 8 and 9 exactly as shown on the back of test book.

7 **TEST BOOK SERIAL NUMBER**
(Copy from front of test book.)

8 **BOOK CODE**
(Copy and grid as on back of test book.)

9 **BOOK ID**
(Copy from back of test book.)

PLEASE MAKE SURE to fill in these fields completely and correctly. If they are not correct, we won't be able to score your test(s)!

5 **ZIP CODE**

6 **TEST CENTER**
(Supplied by Test Center Supervisor.)

FOR OFFICIAL USE ONLY

103648-77191 • NS1114C1085 • Printed in U.S.A.

194415-001　1 2 3 4 5 A B C D E　Printed in the USA　ISD11312　783175

PLEASE DO NOT WRITE IN THIS AREA　CollegeBoard　**SERIAL #**

○ Literature
○ Biology E
○ Biology M
○ Chemistry
○ Physics

○ Mathematics Level 1
○ Mathematics Level 2
○ U.S. History
○ World History
○ French

○ German
○ Italian
○ Latin
○ Modern Hebrew
○ Spanish

○ Chinese Listening
○ French Listening
○ German Listening

○ Japanese Listening
○ Korean Listening
○ Spanish Listening

Background Questions: ① ② ③ ④ ⑤ ⑥ ⑦ ⑧ ⑨

1 Ⓐ Ⓑ Ⓒ Ⓓ Ⓔ 26 Ⓐ Ⓑ Ⓒ Ⓓ Ⓔ 51 Ⓐ Ⓑ Ⓒ Ⓓ Ⓔ 76 Ⓐ Ⓑ Ⓒ Ⓓ Ⓔ
2 Ⓐ Ⓑ Ⓒ Ⓓ Ⓔ 27 Ⓐ Ⓑ Ⓒ Ⓓ Ⓔ 52 Ⓐ Ⓑ Ⓒ Ⓓ Ⓔ 77 Ⓐ Ⓑ Ⓒ Ⓓ Ⓔ
3 Ⓐ Ⓑ Ⓒ Ⓓ Ⓔ 28 Ⓐ Ⓑ Ⓒ Ⓓ Ⓔ 53 Ⓐ Ⓑ Ⓒ Ⓓ Ⓔ 78 Ⓐ Ⓑ Ⓒ Ⓓ Ⓔ
4 Ⓐ Ⓑ Ⓒ Ⓓ Ⓔ 29 Ⓐ Ⓑ Ⓒ Ⓓ Ⓔ 54 Ⓐ Ⓑ Ⓒ Ⓓ Ⓔ 79 Ⓐ Ⓑ Ⓒ Ⓓ Ⓔ
5 Ⓐ Ⓑ Ⓒ Ⓓ Ⓔ 30 Ⓐ Ⓑ Ⓒ Ⓓ Ⓔ 55 Ⓐ Ⓑ Ⓒ Ⓓ Ⓔ 80 Ⓐ Ⓑ Ⓒ Ⓓ Ⓔ
6 Ⓐ Ⓑ Ⓒ Ⓓ Ⓔ 31 Ⓐ Ⓑ Ⓒ Ⓓ Ⓔ 56 Ⓐ Ⓑ Ⓒ Ⓓ Ⓔ 81 Ⓐ Ⓑ Ⓒ Ⓓ Ⓔ
7 Ⓐ Ⓑ Ⓒ Ⓓ Ⓔ 32 Ⓐ Ⓑ Ⓒ Ⓓ Ⓔ 57 Ⓐ Ⓑ Ⓒ Ⓓ Ⓔ 82 Ⓐ Ⓑ Ⓒ Ⓓ Ⓔ
8 Ⓐ Ⓑ Ⓒ Ⓓ Ⓔ 33 Ⓐ Ⓑ Ⓒ Ⓓ Ⓔ 58 Ⓐ Ⓑ Ⓒ Ⓓ Ⓔ 83 Ⓐ Ⓑ Ⓒ Ⓓ Ⓔ
9 Ⓐ Ⓑ Ⓒ Ⓓ Ⓔ 34 Ⓐ Ⓑ Ⓒ Ⓓ Ⓔ 59 Ⓐ Ⓑ Ⓒ Ⓓ Ⓔ 84 Ⓐ Ⓑ Ⓒ Ⓓ Ⓔ
10 Ⓐ Ⓑ Ⓒ Ⓓ Ⓔ 35 Ⓐ Ⓑ Ⓒ Ⓓ Ⓔ 60 Ⓐ Ⓑ Ⓒ Ⓓ Ⓔ 85 Ⓐ Ⓑ Ⓒ Ⓓ Ⓔ
11 Ⓐ Ⓑ Ⓒ Ⓓ Ⓔ 36 Ⓐ Ⓑ Ⓒ Ⓓ Ⓔ 61 Ⓐ Ⓑ Ⓒ Ⓓ Ⓔ 86 Ⓐ Ⓑ Ⓒ Ⓓ Ⓔ
12 Ⓐ Ⓑ Ⓒ Ⓓ Ⓔ 37 Ⓐ Ⓑ Ⓒ Ⓓ Ⓔ 62 Ⓐ Ⓑ Ⓒ Ⓓ Ⓔ 87 Ⓐ Ⓑ Ⓒ Ⓓ Ⓔ
13 Ⓐ Ⓑ Ⓒ Ⓓ Ⓔ 38 Ⓐ Ⓑ Ⓒ Ⓓ Ⓔ 63 Ⓐ Ⓑ Ⓒ Ⓓ Ⓔ 88 Ⓐ Ⓑ Ⓒ Ⓓ Ⓔ
14 Ⓐ Ⓑ Ⓒ Ⓓ Ⓔ 39 Ⓐ Ⓑ Ⓒ Ⓓ Ⓔ 64 Ⓐ Ⓑ Ⓒ Ⓓ Ⓔ 89 Ⓐ Ⓑ Ⓒ Ⓓ Ⓔ
15 Ⓐ Ⓑ Ⓒ Ⓓ Ⓔ 40 Ⓐ Ⓑ Ⓒ Ⓓ Ⓔ 65 Ⓐ Ⓑ Ⓒ Ⓓ Ⓔ 90 Ⓐ Ⓑ Ⓒ Ⓓ Ⓔ
16 Ⓐ Ⓑ Ⓒ Ⓓ Ⓔ 41 Ⓐ Ⓑ Ⓒ Ⓓ Ⓔ 66 Ⓐ Ⓑ Ⓒ Ⓓ Ⓔ 91 Ⓐ Ⓑ Ⓒ Ⓓ Ⓔ
17 Ⓐ Ⓑ Ⓒ Ⓓ Ⓔ 42 Ⓐ Ⓑ Ⓒ Ⓓ Ⓔ 67 Ⓐ Ⓑ Ⓒ Ⓓ Ⓔ 92 Ⓐ Ⓑ Ⓒ Ⓓ Ⓔ
18 Ⓐ Ⓑ Ⓒ Ⓓ Ⓔ 43 Ⓐ Ⓑ Ⓒ Ⓓ Ⓔ 68 Ⓐ Ⓑ Ⓒ Ⓓ Ⓔ 93 Ⓐ Ⓑ Ⓒ Ⓓ Ⓔ
19 Ⓐ Ⓑ Ⓒ Ⓓ Ⓔ 44 Ⓐ Ⓑ Ⓒ Ⓓ Ⓔ 69 Ⓐ Ⓑ Ⓒ Ⓓ Ⓔ 94 Ⓐ Ⓑ Ⓒ Ⓓ Ⓔ
20 Ⓐ Ⓑ Ⓒ Ⓓ Ⓔ 45 Ⓐ Ⓑ Ⓒ Ⓓ Ⓔ 70 Ⓐ Ⓑ Ⓒ Ⓓ Ⓔ 95 Ⓐ Ⓑ Ⓒ Ⓓ Ⓔ
21 Ⓐ Ⓑ Ⓒ Ⓓ Ⓔ 46 Ⓐ Ⓑ Ⓒ Ⓓ Ⓔ 71 Ⓐ Ⓑ Ⓒ Ⓓ Ⓔ 96 Ⓐ Ⓑ Ⓒ Ⓓ Ⓔ
22 Ⓐ Ⓑ Ⓒ Ⓓ Ⓔ 47 Ⓐ Ⓑ Ⓒ Ⓓ Ⓔ 72 Ⓐ Ⓑ Ⓒ Ⓓ Ⓔ 97 Ⓐ Ⓑ Ⓒ Ⓓ Ⓔ
23 Ⓐ Ⓑ Ⓒ Ⓓ Ⓔ 48 Ⓐ Ⓑ Ⓒ Ⓓ Ⓔ 73 Ⓐ Ⓑ Ⓒ Ⓓ Ⓔ 98 Ⓐ Ⓑ Ⓒ Ⓓ Ⓔ
24 Ⓐ Ⓑ Ⓒ Ⓓ Ⓔ 49 Ⓐ Ⓑ Ⓒ Ⓓ Ⓔ 74 Ⓐ Ⓑ Ⓒ Ⓓ Ⓔ 99 Ⓐ Ⓑ Ⓒ Ⓓ Ⓔ
25 Ⓐ Ⓑ Ⓒ Ⓓ Ⓔ 50 Ⓐ Ⓑ Ⓒ Ⓓ Ⓔ 75 Ⓐ Ⓑ Ⓒ Ⓓ Ⓔ 100 Ⓐ Ⓑ Ⓒ Ⓓ Ⓔ

PLEASE MAKE SURE to fill in these fields completely and correctly. If they are not correct, we won't be able to score your test(s)!

7 TEST BOOK SERIAL NUMBER (Copy from front of test book.)

0 0 0 0 0 0
1 1 1 1 1 1
2 2 2 2 2 2
3 3 3 3 3 3
4 4 4 4 4 4
5 5 5 5 5 5
6 6 6 6 6 6
7 7 7 7 7 7
8 8 8 8 8 8
9 9 9 9 9 9

8 BOOK CODE (Copy and grid as on back of test book.)

0 A 0
1 B 1
2 C 2
3 D 3
4 E 4
5 F 5
6 G 6
7 H 7
8 I 8
9 J 9
K
L
M
N
O
P
Q
R
S
T
U
V
W
X
Y
Z

9 BOOK ID (Copy from back of test book.)

Quality Assurance Mark ●

Chemistry *Fill in circle CE only if II is correct explanation of I.

	I	II	CE*		I	II	CE*
101	Ⓣ Ⓕ	Ⓣ Ⓕ	○	109	Ⓣ Ⓕ	Ⓣ Ⓕ	○
102	Ⓣ Ⓕ	Ⓣ Ⓕ	○	110	Ⓣ Ⓕ	Ⓣ Ⓕ	○
103	Ⓣ Ⓕ	Ⓣ Ⓕ	○	111	Ⓣ Ⓕ	Ⓣ Ⓕ	○
104	Ⓣ Ⓕ	Ⓣ Ⓕ	○	112	Ⓣ Ⓕ	Ⓣ Ⓕ	○
105	Ⓣ Ⓕ	Ⓣ Ⓕ	○	113	Ⓣ Ⓕ	Ⓣ Ⓕ	○
106	Ⓣ Ⓕ	Ⓣ Ⓕ	○	114	Ⓣ Ⓕ	Ⓣ Ⓕ	○
107	Ⓣ Ⓕ	Ⓣ Ⓕ	○	115	Ⓣ Ⓕ	Ⓣ Ⓕ	○
108	Ⓣ Ⓕ	Ⓣ Ⓕ	○				

FOR OFFICIAL USE ONLY				
R/C	W/S1	FS/S2	CS/S3	WS

CERTIFICATION STATEMENT
Copy the statement below and sign your name as you would an official document.

I hereby agree to the conditions set forth online at sat.collegeboard.org and in any paper registration materials given to me and certify that I am the person whose name, address and signature appear on this answer sheet.

_____

_____

_____

_____

Signature _____ Date _____

○ Literature
○ Biology E
○ Biology M
○ Chemistry
○ Physics

○ Mathematics Level 1
○ Mathematics Level 2
○ U.S. History
○ World History
○ French

○ German
○ Italian
○ Latin
○ Modern Hebrew
○ Spanish

○ Chinese Listening
○ French Listening
○ German Listening

○ Japanese Listening
○ Korean Listening
○ Spanish Listening

Background Questions: ① ② ③ ④ ⑤ ⑥ ⑦ ⑧ ⑨

PLEASE MAKE SURE to fill in these fields completely and correctly. If they are not correct, we won't be able to score your test(s)!

1–100: each question A B C D E

Quality Assurance Mark ●

7 TEST BOOK SERIAL NUMBER (Copy from front of test book.)
Grid digits 0–9

8 BOOK CODE (Copy and grid as on back of test book.)
Digit column 0–9; Letter column A–Z

9 BOOK ID (Copy from back of test book.)

Chemistry *Fill in circle CE only if II is correct explanation of I.

	I	II	CE*		I	II	CE*
101	T F	T F	○	109	T F	T F	○
102	T F	T F	○	110	T F	T F	○
103	T F	T F	○	111	T F	T F	○
104	T F	T F	○	112	T F	T F	○
105	T F	T F	○	113	T F	T F	○
106	T F	T F	○	114	T F	T F	○
107	T F	T F	○	115	T F	T F	○
108	T F	T F	○				

FOR OFFICIAL USE ONLY

R/C	W/S1	FS/S2	CS/S3	WS

Page 3

○ Literature
○ Biology E
○ Biology M
○ Chemistry
○ Physics

○ Mathematics Level 1
○ Mathematics Level 2
○ U.S. History
○ World History
○ French

○ German
○ Italian
○ Latin
○ Modern Hebrew
○ Spanish

○ Chinese Listening
○ French Listening
○ German Listening

○ Japanese Listening
○ Korean Listening
○ Spanish Listening

Background Questions: ① ② ③ ④ ⑤ ⑥ ⑦ ⑧ ⑨

PLEASE MAKE SURE to fill in these fields completely and correctly. If they are not correct, we won't be able to score your test(s)!

1–100: (A) (B) (C) (D) (E) answer grid

Chemistry *Fill in circle CE only if II is correct explanation of I.

	I	II	CE*		I	II	CE*
101	T F	T F	○	109	T F	T F	○
102	T F	T F	○	110	T F	T F	○
103	T F	T F	○	111	T F	T F	○
104	T F	T F	○	112	T F	T F	○
105	T F	T F	○	113	T F	T F	○
106	T F	T F	○	114	T F	T F	○
107	T F	T F	○	115	T F	T F	○
108	T F	T F	○				

FOR OFFICIAL USE ONLY				
R/C	W/S1	FS/S2	CS/S3	WS

8 BOOK CODE (Copy and grid as on back of test book.)

0 A 0
1 B 1
2 C 2
3 D 3
4 E 4
5 F 5
6 G 6
7 H 7
8 I 8
9 J 9
K
L
M
N
O
P
Q
R
S
T
U
V
W
X
Y
Z

7 TEST BOOK SERIAL NUMBER (Copy from front of test book.)

0 0 0 0 0 0
1 1 1 1 1 1
2 2 2 2 2 2
3 3 3 3 3 3
4 4 4 4 4 4
5 5 5 5 5 5
6 6 6 6 6 6
7 7 7 7 7 7
8 8 8 8 8 8
9 9 9 9 9 9

9 BOOK ID (Copy from back of test book.)

● Quality Assurance Mark

Page 4

SAT Subject Tests™

COMPLETE MARK ● **EXAMPLES OF INCOMPLETE MARKS** Ⓐ ⊗ ⊖ Ⓒ / Ⓑ ⊘ ⊜

You must use a No. 2 pencil and marks must be complete. Do not use a mechanical pencil. It is very important that you fill in the entire circle darkly and completely. If you change your response, erase as completely as possible. Incomplete marks or erasures may affect your score.

1 Your Name:
(Print)

Last   First   M.I.

I agree to the conditions on the front and back of the SAT Subject Tests™ book. I also agree with the SAT Test Security and Fairness policies and understand that any violation of these policies will result in score cancellation and may result in reporting of certain violations to law enforcement.

Signature: _____

Today's Date: ___/___/___
MM   DD   YY

Home Address: _____
(Print)   Number and Street   City   State/Country   Zip Code

Phone: (___) _____   **Test Center:** _____
(Print)   City   State/Country

2 YOUR NAME

Last Name (First 6 Letters)   First Name (First 4 Letters)   Mid. Init.

3 DATE OF BIRTH

MONTH | DAY | YEAR
Jan, Feb, Mar, Apr, May, Jun, Jul, Aug, Sep, Oct, Nov, Dec

4 REGISTRATION NUMBER
(Copy from Admission Ticket.)

Important: Fill in items 8 and 9 exactly as shown on the back of test book.

7 TEST BOOK SERIAL NUMBER
(Copy from front of test book.)

8 BOOK CODE
(Copy and grid as on back of test book.)

9 BOOK ID
(Copy from back of test book.)

PLEASE MAKE SURE to fill in these fields completely and correctly. If they are not correct, we won't be able to score your test(s)!

5 ZIP CODE

6 TEST CENTER
(Supplied by Test Center Supervisor.)

FOR OFFICIAL USE ONLY
0 1 2 3 4 5 6
0 1 2 3 4 5 6
0 1 2 3 4 5 6

103648-77191 · NS1114C1085 · Printed in U.S.A.

194415-001   1 2 3 4 5 A B C D E   Printed in the USA   ISD11312   783175

PLEASE DO NOT WRITE IN THIS AREA

SERIAL #

○ Literature
○ Biology E
○ Biology M
○ Chemistry
○ Physics

○ Mathematics Level 1
○ Mathematics Level 2
○ U.S. History
○ World History
○ French

○ German
○ Italian
○ Latin
○ Modern Hebrew
○ Spanish

○ Chinese Listening
○ French Listening
○ German Listening

○ Japanese Listening
○ Korean Listening
○ Spanish Listening

Background Questions: ① ② ③ ④ ⑤ ⑥ ⑦ ⑧ ⑨

1–100 answer grid, each item A B C D E

PLEASE MAKE SURE to fill in these fields completely and correctly. If they are not correct, we won't be able to score your test(s)!

8 BOOK CODE (Copy and grid as on back of test book.)

0 A 0
1 B 1
2 C 2
3 D 3
4 E 4
5 F 5
6 G 6
7 H 7
8 I 8
9 J 9
K
L
M
N
O
P
Q
R
S
T
U
V
W
X
Y
Z

7 TEST BOOK SERIAL NUMBER (Copy from front of test book.)

0 0 0 0 0 0
1 1 1 1 1 1
2 2 2 2 2 2
3 3 3 3 3 3
4 4 4 4 4 4
5 5 5 5 5 5
6 6 6 6 6 6
7 7 7 7 7 7
8 8 8 8 8 8
9 9 9 9 9 9

9 BOOK ID (Copy from back of test book.)

Quality Assurance Mark ●

Chemistry *Fill in circle CE only if II is correct explanation of I.

	I	II	CE*		I	II	CE*
101	T F	T F	○	109	T F	T F	○
102	T F	T F	○	110	T F	T F	○
103	T F	T F	○	111	T F	T F	○
104	T F	T F	○	112	T F	T F	○
105	T F	T F	○	113	T F	T F	○
106	T F	T F	○	114	T F	T F	○
107	T F	T F	○	115	T F	T F	○
108	T F	T F	○				

FOR OFFICIAL USE ONLY				
R/C	W/S1	FS/S2	CS/S3	WS

CERTIFICATION STATEMENT Copy the statement below and sign your name as you would an official document.

I hereby agree to the conditions set forth online at sat.collegeboard.org and in any paper registration materials given to me and certify that I am the person whose name, address and signature appear on this answer sheet.

Signature _____   Date _____

- ○ Literature
- ○ Biology E
- ○ Biology M
- ○ Chemistry
- ○ Physics
- ○ Mathematics Level 1
- ○ Mathematics Level 2
- ○ U.S. History
- ○ World History
- ○ French
- ○ German
- ○ Italian
- ○ Latin
- ○ Modern Hebrew
- ○ Spanish
- ○ Chinese Listening
- ○ French Listening
- ○ German Listening
- ○ Japanese Listening
- ○ Korean Listening
- ○ Spanish Listening

Background Questions: ① ② ③ ④ ⑤ ⑥ ⑦ ⑧ ⑨

PLEASE MAKE SURE to fill in these fields completely and correctly. If they are not correct, we won't be able to score your test(s)!

Quality Assurance Mark ●

Answer grid: questions 1–100, each with options A B C D E

7 TEST BOOK SERIAL NUMBER (Copy from front of test book.) — digits 0–9

8 BOOK CODE (Copy and grid as on back of test book.) — 0–9, A–Z

9 BOOK ID (Copy from back of test book.)

Chemistry *Fill in circle CE only if II is correct explanation of I.

	I	II	CE*		I	II	CE*
101	T F	T F	○	109	T F	T F	○
102	T F	T F	○	110	T F	T F	○
103	T F	T F	○	111	T F	T F	○
104	T F	T F	○	112	T F	T F	○
105	T F	T F	○	113	T F	T F	○
106	T F	T F	○	114	T F	T F	○
107	T F	T F	○	115	T F	T F	○
108	T F	T F	○				

FOR OFFICIAL USE ONLY				
R/C	W/S1	FS/S2	CS/S3	WS

○ Literature   ○ Mathematics Level 1   ○ German   ○ Chinese Listening   ○ Japanese Listening
○ Biology E   ○ Mathematics Level 2   ○ Italian   ○ French Listening   ○ Korean Listening
○ Biology M   ○ U.S. History   ○ Latin   ○ German Listening   ○ Spanish Listening
○ Chemistry   ○ World History   ○ Modern Hebrew
○ Physics   ○ French   ○ Spanish

Background Questions: ① ② ③ ④ ⑤ ⑥ ⑦ ⑧ ⑨

PLEASE MAKE SURE to fill in these fields completely and correctly. If they are not correct, we won't be able to score your test(s)!

7 TEST BOOK SERIAL NUMBER
(Copy from front of test book.)

8 BOOK CODE
(Copy and grid as on back of test book.)

9 BOOK ID
(Copy from back of test book.)

Quality Assurance Mark

Chemistry *Fill in circle CE only if II is correct explanation of I.

	I	II	CE*		I	II	CE*
101	T F	T F	○	109	T F	T F	○
102	T F	T F	○	110	T F	T F	○
103	T F	T F	○	111	T F	T F	○
104	T F	T F	○	112	T F	T F	○
105	T F	T F	○	113	T F	T F	○
106	T F	T F	○	114	T F	T F	○
107	T F	T F	○	115	T F	T F	○
108	T F	T F	○				

FOR OFFICIAL USE ONLY				
R/C	W/S1	FS/S2	CS/S3	WS

Page 4

PLEASE DO NOT WRITE IN THIS AREA

SERIAL #

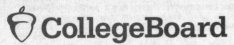

SAT Subject Tests™

COMPLETE MARK ●   **EXAMPLES OF INCOMPLETE MARKS** Ⓐ ⊗ ⊜ Ⓒ / Ⓑ ⊘ ⊘ ⊘

You must use a No. 2 pencil and marks must be complete. Do not use a mechanical pencil. *It is very important that you fill in the entire circle darkly and completely. If you change your response, erase as completely as possible. Incomplete marks or erasures may affect your score.*

1   **Your Name:**
(Print)

Last   First   M.I.

I agree to the conditions on the front and back of the SAT Subject Tests™ book. I also agree with the SAT Test Security and Fairness policies and understand that any violation of these policies will result in score cancellation and may result in reporting of certain violations to law enforcement.

Signature: _____   Today's Date: __ / __ / __
                                             MM   DD   YY

Home Address: _____
(Print)   Number and Street   City   State/Country   Zip Code

Phone: (___) _____   Test Center: _____
                                     (Print)   City   State/Country

2   **YOUR NAME**

Last Name (First 6 Letters)   First Name (First 4 Letters)   Mid. Init.

3   **DATE OF BIRTH**

MONTH	DAY	YEAR
○ Jan		
○ Feb		
○ Mar		
○ Apr		
○ May		
○ Jun		
○ Jul		
○ Aug		
○ Sep		
○ Oct		
○ Nov		
○ Dec		

4   **REGISTRATION NUMBER**
(Copy from Admission Ticket.)

Important: Fill in items 8 and 9 exactly as shown on the back of test book.

7   **TEST BOOK SERIAL NUMBER**
(Copy from front of test book.)

8   **BOOK CODE**
(Copy and grid as on back of test book.)

5   **ZIP CODE**

6   **TEST CENTER**
(Supplied by Test Center Supervisor.)

9   **BOOK ID**
(Copy from back of test book.)

PLEASE MAKE SURE to fill in these fields completely and correctly. If they are not correct, we won't be able to score your test(s)!

FOR OFFICIAL USE ONLY
0 1 2 3 4 5 6
0 1 2 3 4 5 6
0 1 2 3 4 5 6

103648-77191 · NS1114C1085 · Printed in U.S.A.

194415-001   1 2 3 4 5 A B C D E   Printed in the USA   ISD11312

783175

PLEASE DO NOT WRITE IN THIS AREA   **SAT Subject**

CollegeBoard   **SERIAL #**

COMPLETE MARK ● **EXAMPLES OF INCOMPLETE MARKS** Ⓐ ⊗ ⊖ Ⓕ ⊘ ⊘ ⊚ ⊛

You must use a No. 2 pencil and marks must be complete. Do not use a mechanical pencil. It is very important that you fill in the entire circle darkly and completely. If you change your response, erase as completely as possible. Incomplete marks or erasures may affect your score.

- ○ Literature
- ○ Biology E
- ○ Biology M
- ○ Chemistry
- ○ Physics
- ○ Mathematics Level 1
- ○ Mathematics Level 2
- ○ U.S. History
- ○ World History
- ○ French
- ○ German
- ○ Italian
- ○ Latin
- ○ Modern Hebrew
- ○ Spanish
- ○ Chinese Listening
- ○ French Listening
- ○ German Listening
- ○ Japanese Listening
- ○ Korean Listening
- ○ Spanish Listening

Background Questions: ① ② ③ ④ ⑤ ⑥ ⑦ ⑧ ⑨

1–100: Ⓐ Ⓑ Ⓒ Ⓓ Ⓔ (answer grid, questions 1 through 100)

PLEASE MAKE SURE to fill in these fields completely and correctly. If they are not correct, we won't be able to score your test(s)!

8 BOOK CODE (Copy and grid as on back of test book.)
0 A 0 / 1 B 1 / 2 C 2 / 3 D 3 / 4 E 4 / 5 F 5 / 6 G 6 / 7 H 7 / 8 I 8 / 9 J 9 / K / L / M / N / O / P / Q / R / S / T / U / V / W / X / Y / Z

7 TEST BOOK SERIAL NUMBER (Copy from front of test book.)
0 1 2 3 4 5 6 7 8 9 (six columns)

9 BOOK ID (Copy from back of test book.)

Quality Assurance Mark ●

Chemistry *Fill in circle CE only if II is correct explanation of I.

	I	II	CE*		I	II	CE*
101	Ⓣ Ⓕ	Ⓣ Ⓕ	○	109	Ⓣ Ⓕ	Ⓣ Ⓕ	○
102	Ⓣ Ⓕ	Ⓣ Ⓕ	○	110	Ⓣ Ⓕ	Ⓣ Ⓕ	○
103	Ⓣ Ⓕ	Ⓣ Ⓕ	○	111	Ⓣ Ⓕ	Ⓣ Ⓕ	○
104	Ⓣ Ⓕ	Ⓣ Ⓕ	○	112	Ⓣ Ⓕ	Ⓣ Ⓕ	○
105	Ⓣ Ⓕ	Ⓣ Ⓕ	○	113	Ⓣ Ⓕ	Ⓣ Ⓕ	○
106	Ⓣ Ⓕ	Ⓣ Ⓕ	○	114	Ⓣ Ⓕ	Ⓣ Ⓕ	○
107	Ⓣ Ⓕ	Ⓣ Ⓕ	○	115	Ⓣ Ⓕ	Ⓣ Ⓕ	○
108	Ⓣ Ⓕ	Ⓣ Ⓕ	○				

FOR OFFICIAL USE ONLY				
R/C	W/S1	FS/S2	CS/S3	WS

CERTIFICATION STATEMENT

Copy the statement below and sign your name as you would an official document.

I hereby agree to the conditions set forth online at sat.collegeboard.org and in any paper registration materials given to me and certify that I am the person whose name, address and signature appear on this answer sheet.

_____

_____

_____

_____

Signature _____   Date _____

○ Literature
○ Biology E
○ Biology M
○ Chemistry
○ Physics

○ Mathematics Level 1
○ Mathematics Level 2
○ U.S. History
○ World History
○ French

○ German
○ Italian
○ Latin
○ Modern Hebrew
○ Spanish

○ Chinese Listening
○ French Listening
○ German Listening

○ Japanese Listening
○ Korean Listening
○ Spanish Listening

Background Questions: ① ② ③ ④ ⑤ ⑥ ⑦ ⑧ ⑨

PLEASE MAKE SURE to fill in these fields completely and correctly. If they are not correct, we won't be able to score your test(s)!

Questions 1–100: each with answer choices A B C D E

Quality Assurance Mark

7 TEST BOOK SERIAL NUMBER
(Copy from front of test book.)
0 0 0 0 0 0
1 1 1 1 1 1
2 2 2 2 2 2
3 3 3 3 3 3
4 4 4 4 4 4
5 5 5 5 5 5
6 6 6 6 6 6
7 7 7 7 7 7
8 8 8 8 8 8
9 9 9 9 9 9

8 BOOK CODE
(Copy and grid as on back of test book.)
0 A 0
1 B 1
2 C 2
3 D 3
4 E 4
5 F 5
6 G 6
7 H 7
8 I 8
9 J 9
K
L
M
N
O
P
Q
R
S
T
U
V
W
X
Y
Z

9 BOOK ID
(Copy from back of test book.)

Chemistry *Fill in circle CE only if II is correct explanation of I.

	I	II	CE*		I	II	CE*
101	T F	T F	○	109	T F	T F	○
102	T F	T F	○	110	T F	T F	○
103	T F	T F	○	111	T F	T F	○
104	T F	T F	○	112	T F	T F	○
105	T F	T F	○	113	T F	T F	○
106	T F	T F	○	114	T F	T F	○
107	T F	T F	○	115	T F	T F	○
108	T F	T F	○				

FOR OFFICIAL USE ONLY				
R/C	W/S1	FS/S2	CS/S3	WS

Page 3

○ Literature
○ Biology E
○ Biology M
○ Chemistry
○ Physics

○ Mathematics Level 1
○ Mathematics Level 2
○ U.S. History
○ World History
○ French

○ German
○ Italian
○ Latin
○ Modern Hebrew
○ Spanish

○ Chinese Listening
○ French Listening
○ German Listening

○ Japanese Listening
○ Korean Listening
○ Spanish Listening

Background Questions: ① ② ③ ④ ⑤ ⑥ ⑦ ⑧ ⑨

1 (A)(B)(C)(D)(E)	26 (A)(B)(C)(D)(E)	51 (A)(B)(C)(D)(E)	76 (A)(B)(C)(D)(E)
2 (A)(B)(C)(D)(E)	27 (A)(B)(C)(D)(E)	52 (A)(B)(C)(D)(E)	77 (A)(B)(C)(D)(E)
3 (A)(B)(C)(D)(E)	28 (A)(B)(C)(D)(E)	53 (A)(B)(C)(D)(E)	78 (A)(B)(C)(D)(E)
4 (A)(B)(C)(D)(E)	29 (A)(B)(C)(D)(E)	54 (A)(B)(C)(D)(E)	79 (A)(B)(C)(D)(E)
5 (A)(B)(C)(D)(E)	30 (A)(B)(C)(D)(E)	55 (A)(B)(C)(D)(E)	80 (A)(B)(C)(D)(E)
6 (A)(B)(C)(D)(E)	31 (A)(B)(C)(D)(E)	56 (A)(B)(C)(D)(E)	81 (A)(B)(C)(D)(E)
7 (A)(B)(C)(D)(E)	32 (A)(B)(C)(D)(E)	57 (A)(B)(C)(D)(E)	82 (A)(B)(C)(D)(E)
8 (A)(B)(C)(D)(E)	33 (A)(B)(C)(D)(E)	58 (A)(B)(C)(D)(E)	83 (A)(B)(C)(D)(E)
9 (A)(B)(C)(D)(E)	34 (A)(B)(C)(D)(E)	59 (A)(B)(C)(D)(E)	84 (A)(B)(C)(D)(E)
10 (A)(B)(C)(D)(E)	35 (A)(B)(C)(D)(E)	60 (A)(B)(C)(D)(E)	85 (A)(B)(C)(D)(E)
11 (A)(B)(C)(D)(E)	36 (A)(B)(C)(D)(E)	61 (A)(B)(C)(D)(E)	86 (A)(B)(C)(D)(E)
12 (A)(B)(C)(D)(E)	37 (A)(B)(C)(D)(E)	62 (A)(B)(C)(D)(E)	87 (A)(B)(C)(D)(E)
13 (A)(B)(C)(D)(E)	38 (A)(B)(C)(D)(E)	63 (A)(B)(C)(D)(E)	88 (A)(B)(C)(D)(E)
14 (A)(B)(C)(D)(E)	39 (A)(B)(C)(D)(E)	64 (A)(B)(C)(D)(E)	89 (A)(B)(C)(D)(E)
15 (A)(B)(C)(D)(E)	40 (A)(B)(C)(D)(E)	65 (A)(B)(C)(D)(E)	90 (A)(B)(C)(D)(E)
16 (A)(B)(C)(D)(E)	41 (A)(B)(C)(D)(E)	66 (A)(B)(C)(D)(E)	91 (A)(B)(C)(D)(E)
17 (A)(B)(C)(D)(E)	42 (A)(B)(C)(D)(E)	67 (A)(B)(C)(D)(E)	92 (A)(B)(C)(D)(E)
18 (A)(B)(C)(D)(E)	43 (A)(B)(C)(D)(E)	68 (A)(B)(C)(D)(E)	93 (A)(B)(C)(D)(E)
19 (A)(B)(C)(D)(E)	44 (A)(B)(C)(D)(E)	69 (A)(B)(C)(D)(E)	94 (A)(B)(C)(D)(E)
20 (A)(B)(C)(D)(E)	45 (A)(B)(C)(D)(E)	70 (A)(B)(C)(D)(E)	95 (A)(B)(C)(D)(E)
21 (A)(B)(C)(D)(E)	46 (A)(B)(C)(D)(E)	71 (A)(B)(C)(D)(E)	96 (A)(B)(C)(D)(E)
22 (A)(B)(C)(D)(E)	47 (A)(B)(C)(D)(E)	72 (A)(B)(C)(D)(E)	97 (A)(B)(C)(D)(E)
23 (A)(B)(C)(D)(E)	48 (A)(B)(C)(D)(E)	73 (A)(B)(C)(D)(E)	98 (A)(B)(C)(D)(E)
24 (A)(B)(C)(D)(E)	49 (A)(B)(C)(D)(E)	74 (A)(B)(C)(D)(E)	99 (A)(B)(C)(D)(E)
25 (A)(B)(C)(D)(E)	50 (A)(B)(C)(D)(E)	75 (A)(B)(C)(D)(E)	100 (A)(B)(C)(D)(E)

PLEASE MAKE SURE to fill in these fields completely and correctly. If they are not correct, we won't be able to score your test(s)!

7 TEST BOOK SERIAL NUMBER
(Copy from front of test book.)

0 0 0 0 0 0
1 1 1 1 1 1
2 2 2 2 2 2
3 3 3 3 3 3
4 4 4 4 4 4
5 5 5 5 5 5
6 6 6 6 6 6
7 7 7 7 7 7
8 8 8 8 8 8
9 9 9 9 9 9

8 BOOK CODE
(Copy and grid as on back of test book.)

0 (A) 0
1 (B) 1
2 (C) 2
3 (D) 3
4 (E) 4
5 (F) 5
6 (G) 6
7 (H) 7
8 (I) 8
9 (J) 9
(K)
(L)
(M)
(N)
(O)
(P)
(Q)
(R)
(S)
(T)
(U)
(V)
(W)
(X)
(Y)
(Z)

9 BOOK ID
(Copy from back of test book.)

Quality Assurance Mark

Chemistry *Fill in circle CE only if II is correct explanation of I.*

	I	II	CE*		I	II	CE*
101	(T)(F)	(T)(F)	○	109	(T)(F)	(T)(F)	○
102	(T)(F)	(T)(F)	○	110	(T)(F)	(T)(F)	○
103	(T)(F)	(T)(F)	○	111	(T)(F)	(T)(F)	○
104	(T)(F)	(T)(F)	○	112	(T)(F)	(T)(F)	○
105	(T)(F)	(T)(F)	○	113	(T)(F)	(T)(F)	○
106	(T)(F)	(T)(F)	○	114	(T)(F)	(T)(F)	○
107	(T)(F)	(T)(F)	○	115	(T)(F)	(T)(F)	○
108	(T)(F)	(T)(F)	○				

FOR OFFICIAL USE ONLY

R/C	W/S1	FS/S2	CS/S3	WS

SAT Subject Tests™

COMPLETE MARK ● **EXAMPLES OF INCOMPLETE MARKS** Ⓐ ⊗ ⊗ ⊖ ⓒ ● ∅ ⊘ ⊛

You must use a No. 2 pencil and marks must be complete. Do not use a mechanical pencil. It is very important that you fill in the entire circle darkly and completely. If you change your response, erase as completely as possible. Incomplete marks or erasures may affect your score.

1 Your Name:
(Print)

Last _____ First _____ M.I. ____

I agree to the conditions on the front and back of the SAT Subject Tests™ book. I also agree with the SAT Test Security and Fairness policies and understand that any violation of these policies will result in score cancellation and may result in reporting of certain violations to law enforcement.

Signature: _____ Today's Date: ___/___/___
MM DD YY

Home Address:
(Print) _____
Number and Street ____ City ____ State/Country ____ Zip Code

Phone: ( ) ____ **Test Center:** _____
(Print) ____ City ____ State/Country

2 YOUR NAME

Last Name (First 6 Letters) First Name (First 4 Letters) Mid. Init.

3 DATE OF BIRTH

MONTH	DAY	YEAR
Jan		
Feb		
Mar		
Apr		
May		
Jun		
Jul		
Aug		
Sep		
Oct		
Nov		
Dec		

4 REGISTRATION NUMBER
(Copy from Admission Ticket.)

Important: Fill in items 8 and 9 exactly as shown on the back of test book.

7 TEST BOOK SERIAL NUMBER
(Copy from front of test book.)

8 BOOK CODE
(Copy and grid as on back of test book.)

9 BOOK ID
(Copy from back of test book.)

PLEASE MAKE SURE to fill in these fields completely and correctly. If they are not correct, we won't be able to score your test(s)!

5 ZIP CODE

6 TEST CENTER
(Supplied by Test Center Supervisor.)

FOR OFFICIAL USE ONLY

103648-77191 • NS1114C1085 • Printed in U.S.A.

194415-001 1 2 3 4 5 A B C D E Printed in the USA ISD11312

783175

PLEASE DO NOT WRITE IN THIS AREA

SERIAL #

○ Literature
○ Biology E
○ Biology M
○ Chemistry
○ Physics

○ Mathematics Level 1
○ Mathematics Level 2
○ U.S. History
○ World History
○ French

○ German
○ Italian
○ Latin
○ Modern Hebrew
○ Spanish

○ Chinese Listening
○ French Listening
○ German Listening

○ Japanese Listening
○ Korean Listening
○ Spanish Listening

Background Questions: ① ② ③ ④ ⑤ ⑥ ⑦ ⑧ ⑨

1–100 answer grid, each with options A B C D E

PLEASE MAKE SURE to fill in these fields completely and correctly. If they are not correct, we won't be able to score your test(s)!

8 BOOK CODE (Copy and grid as on back of test book.)

7 TEST BOOK SERIAL NUMBER (Copy from front of test book.)

9 BOOK ID (Copy from back of test book.)

Quality Assurance Mark

Chemistry *Fill in circle CE only if II is correct explanation of I.

	I	II	CE*		I	II	CE*
101	T F	T F	○	109	T F	T F	○
102	T F	T F	○	110	T F	T F	○
103	T F	T F	○	111	T F	T F	○
104	T F	T F	○	112	T F	T F	○
105	T F	T F	○	113	T F	T F	○
106	T F	T F	○	114	T F	T F	○
107	T F	T F	○	115	T F	T F	○
108	T F	T F	○				

FOR OFFICIAL USE ONLY				
R/C	W/S1	FS/S2	CS/S3	WS

CERTIFICATION STATEMENT Copy the statement below and sign your name as you would an official document.

I hereby agree to the conditions set forth online at sat.collegeboard.org and in any paper registration materials given to me and certify that I am the person whose name, address and signature appear on this answer sheet.

Signature _____ Date _____

○ Literature
○ Biology E
○ Biology M
○ Chemistry
○ Physics

○ Mathematics Level 1
○ Mathematics Level 2
○ U.S. History
○ World History
○ French

○ German
○ Italian
○ Latin
○ Modern Hebrew
○ Spanish

○ Chinese Listening
○ French Listening
○ German Listening

○ Japanese Listening
○ Korean Listening
○ Spanish Listening

Background Questions: ① ② ③ ④ ⑤ ⑥ ⑦ ⑧ ⑨

PLEASE MAKE SURE to fill in these fields completely and correctly. If they are not correct, we won't be able to score your test(s)!

(Answer grid, questions 1–100, options A B C D E)

Quality Assurance Mark ●

7 TEST BOOK SERIAL NUMBER (Copy from front of test book.)

8 BOOK CODE (Copy and grid as on back of test book.)

9 BOOK ID (Copy from back of test book.)

Chemistry *Fill in circle CE only if II is correct explanation of I.

	I	II	CE*		I	II	CE*
101	T F	T F	○	109	T F	T F	○
102	T F	T F	○	110	T F	T F	○
103	T F	T F	○	111	T F	T F	○
104	T F	T F	○	112	T F	T F	○
105	T F	T F	○	113	T F	T F	○
106	T F	T F	○	114	T F	T F	○
107	T F	T F	○	115	T F	T F	○
108	T F	T F	○				

FOR OFFICIAL USE ONLY				
R/C	W/S1	FS/S2	CS/S3	WS

○ Literature ○ Mathematics Level 1 ○ German ○ Chinese Listening ○ Japanese Listening
○ Biology E ○ Mathematics Level 2 ○ Italian ○ French Listening ○ Korean Listening
○ Biology M ○ U.S. History ○ Latin ○ German Listening ○ Spanish Listening
○ Chemistry ○ World History ○ Modern Hebrew
○ Physics ○ French ○ Spanish

Background Questions: ① ② ③ ④ ⑤ ⑥ ⑦ ⑧ ⑨

PLEASE MAKE SURE to fill in these fields completely and correctly. If they are not correct, we won't be able to score your test(s)!

1 Ⓐ Ⓑ Ⓒ Ⓓ Ⓔ   26 Ⓐ Ⓑ Ⓒ Ⓓ Ⓔ   51 Ⓐ Ⓑ Ⓒ Ⓓ Ⓔ   76 Ⓐ Ⓑ Ⓒ Ⓓ Ⓔ
2 Ⓐ Ⓑ Ⓒ Ⓓ Ⓔ   27 Ⓐ Ⓑ Ⓒ Ⓓ Ⓔ   52 Ⓐ Ⓑ Ⓒ Ⓓ Ⓔ   77 Ⓐ Ⓑ Ⓒ Ⓓ Ⓔ
3 Ⓐ Ⓑ Ⓒ Ⓓ Ⓔ   28 Ⓐ Ⓑ Ⓒ Ⓓ Ⓔ   53 Ⓐ Ⓑ Ⓒ Ⓓ Ⓔ   78 Ⓐ Ⓑ Ⓒ Ⓓ Ⓔ
4 Ⓐ Ⓑ Ⓒ Ⓓ Ⓔ   29 Ⓐ Ⓑ Ⓒ Ⓓ Ⓔ   54 Ⓐ Ⓑ Ⓒ Ⓓ Ⓔ   79 Ⓐ Ⓑ Ⓒ Ⓓ Ⓔ
5 Ⓐ Ⓑ Ⓒ Ⓓ Ⓔ   30 Ⓐ Ⓑ Ⓒ Ⓓ Ⓔ   55 Ⓐ Ⓑ Ⓒ Ⓓ Ⓔ   80 Ⓐ Ⓑ Ⓒ Ⓓ Ⓔ
6 Ⓐ Ⓑ Ⓒ Ⓓ Ⓔ   31 Ⓐ Ⓑ Ⓒ Ⓓ Ⓔ   56 Ⓐ Ⓑ Ⓒ Ⓓ Ⓔ   81 Ⓐ Ⓑ Ⓒ Ⓓ Ⓔ
7 Ⓐ Ⓑ Ⓒ Ⓓ Ⓔ   32 Ⓐ Ⓑ Ⓒ Ⓓ Ⓔ   57 Ⓐ Ⓑ Ⓒ Ⓓ Ⓔ   82 Ⓐ Ⓑ Ⓒ Ⓓ Ⓔ
8 Ⓐ Ⓑ Ⓒ Ⓓ Ⓔ   33 Ⓐ Ⓑ Ⓒ Ⓓ Ⓔ   58 Ⓐ Ⓑ Ⓒ Ⓓ Ⓔ   83 Ⓐ Ⓑ Ⓒ Ⓓ Ⓔ
9 Ⓐ Ⓑ Ⓒ Ⓓ Ⓔ   34 Ⓐ Ⓑ Ⓒ Ⓓ Ⓔ   59 Ⓐ Ⓑ Ⓒ Ⓓ Ⓔ   84 Ⓐ Ⓑ Ⓒ Ⓓ Ⓔ
10 Ⓐ Ⓑ Ⓒ Ⓓ Ⓔ   35 Ⓐ Ⓑ Ⓒ Ⓓ Ⓔ   60 Ⓐ Ⓑ Ⓒ Ⓓ Ⓔ   85 Ⓐ Ⓑ Ⓒ Ⓓ Ⓔ
11 Ⓐ Ⓑ Ⓒ Ⓓ Ⓔ   36 Ⓐ Ⓑ Ⓒ Ⓓ Ⓔ   61 Ⓐ Ⓑ Ⓒ Ⓓ Ⓔ   86 Ⓐ Ⓑ Ⓒ Ⓓ Ⓔ
12 Ⓐ Ⓑ Ⓒ Ⓓ Ⓔ   37 Ⓐ Ⓑ Ⓒ Ⓓ Ⓔ   62 Ⓐ Ⓑ Ⓒ Ⓓ Ⓔ   87 Ⓐ Ⓑ Ⓒ Ⓓ Ⓔ
13 Ⓐ Ⓑ Ⓒ Ⓓ Ⓔ   38 Ⓐ Ⓑ Ⓒ Ⓓ Ⓔ   63 Ⓐ Ⓑ Ⓒ Ⓓ Ⓔ   88 Ⓐ Ⓑ Ⓒ Ⓓ Ⓔ
14 Ⓐ Ⓑ Ⓒ Ⓓ Ⓔ   39 Ⓐ Ⓑ Ⓒ Ⓓ Ⓔ   64 Ⓐ Ⓑ Ⓒ Ⓓ Ⓔ   89 Ⓐ Ⓑ Ⓒ Ⓓ Ⓔ
15 Ⓐ Ⓑ Ⓒ Ⓓ Ⓔ   40 Ⓐ Ⓑ Ⓒ Ⓓ Ⓔ   65 Ⓐ Ⓑ Ⓒ Ⓓ Ⓔ   90 Ⓐ Ⓑ Ⓒ Ⓓ Ⓔ
16 Ⓐ Ⓑ Ⓒ Ⓓ Ⓔ   41 Ⓐ Ⓑ Ⓒ Ⓓ Ⓔ   66 Ⓐ Ⓑ Ⓒ Ⓓ Ⓔ   91 Ⓐ Ⓑ Ⓒ Ⓓ Ⓔ
17 Ⓐ Ⓑ Ⓒ Ⓓ Ⓔ   42 Ⓐ Ⓑ Ⓒ Ⓓ Ⓔ   67 Ⓐ Ⓑ Ⓒ Ⓓ Ⓔ   92 Ⓐ Ⓑ Ⓒ Ⓓ Ⓔ
18 Ⓐ Ⓑ Ⓒ Ⓓ Ⓔ   43 Ⓐ Ⓑ Ⓒ Ⓓ Ⓔ   68 Ⓐ Ⓑ Ⓒ Ⓓ Ⓔ   93 Ⓐ Ⓑ Ⓒ Ⓓ Ⓔ
19 Ⓐ Ⓑ Ⓒ Ⓓ Ⓔ   44 Ⓐ Ⓑ Ⓒ Ⓓ Ⓔ   69 Ⓐ Ⓑ Ⓒ Ⓓ Ⓔ   94 Ⓐ Ⓑ Ⓒ Ⓓ Ⓔ
20 Ⓐ Ⓑ Ⓒ Ⓓ Ⓔ   45 Ⓐ Ⓑ Ⓒ Ⓓ Ⓔ   70 Ⓐ Ⓑ Ⓒ Ⓓ Ⓔ   95 Ⓐ Ⓑ Ⓒ Ⓓ Ⓔ
21 Ⓐ Ⓑ Ⓒ Ⓓ Ⓔ   46 Ⓐ Ⓑ Ⓒ Ⓓ Ⓔ   71 Ⓐ Ⓑ Ⓒ Ⓓ Ⓔ   96 Ⓐ Ⓑ Ⓒ Ⓓ Ⓔ
22 Ⓐ Ⓑ Ⓒ Ⓓ Ⓔ   47 Ⓐ Ⓑ Ⓒ Ⓓ Ⓔ   72 Ⓐ Ⓑ Ⓒ Ⓓ Ⓔ   97 Ⓐ Ⓑ Ⓒ Ⓓ Ⓔ
23 Ⓐ Ⓑ Ⓒ Ⓓ Ⓔ   48 Ⓐ Ⓑ Ⓒ Ⓓ Ⓔ   73 Ⓐ Ⓑ Ⓒ Ⓓ Ⓔ   98 Ⓐ Ⓑ Ⓒ Ⓓ Ⓔ
24 Ⓐ Ⓑ Ⓒ Ⓓ Ⓔ   49 Ⓐ Ⓑ Ⓒ Ⓓ Ⓔ   74 Ⓐ Ⓑ Ⓒ Ⓓ Ⓔ   99 Ⓐ Ⓑ Ⓒ Ⓓ Ⓔ
25 Ⓐ Ⓑ Ⓒ Ⓓ Ⓔ   50 Ⓐ Ⓑ Ⓒ Ⓓ Ⓔ   75 Ⓐ Ⓑ Ⓒ Ⓓ Ⓔ   100 Ⓐ Ⓑ Ⓒ Ⓓ Ⓔ

8 BOOK CODE (Copy and grid as on back of test book.)

0 Ⓐ 0
1 Ⓑ 1
2 Ⓒ 2
3 Ⓓ 3
4 Ⓔ 4
5 Ⓕ 5
6 Ⓖ 6
7 Ⓗ 7
8 Ⓘ 8
9 Ⓙ 9
Ⓚ
Ⓛ
Ⓜ
Ⓝ
Ⓞ
Ⓟ
Ⓠ
Ⓡ
Ⓢ
Ⓣ
Ⓤ
Ⓥ
Ⓦ
Ⓧ
Ⓨ
Ⓩ

7 TEST BOOK SERIAL NUMBER (Copy from front of test book.)

0 0 0 0 0 0
1 1 1 1 1 1
2 2 2 2 2 2
3 3 3 3 3 3
4 4 4 4 4 4
5 5 5 5 5 5
6 6 6 6 6 6
7 7 7 7 7 7
8 8 8 8 8 8
9 9 9 9 9 9

9 BOOK ID (Copy from back of test book.)

Quality Assurance Mark ●

Chemistry *Fill in circle CE only if II is correct explanation of I.

	I	II	CE*		I	II	CE*
101	Ⓣ Ⓕ	Ⓣ Ⓕ	○	109	Ⓣ Ⓕ	Ⓣ Ⓕ	○
102	Ⓣ Ⓕ	Ⓣ Ⓕ	○	110	Ⓣ Ⓕ	Ⓣ Ⓕ	○
103	Ⓣ Ⓕ	Ⓣ Ⓕ	○	111	Ⓣ Ⓕ	Ⓣ Ⓕ	○
104	Ⓣ Ⓕ	Ⓣ Ⓕ	○	112	Ⓣ Ⓕ	Ⓣ Ⓕ	○
105	Ⓣ Ⓕ	Ⓣ Ⓕ	○	113	Ⓣ Ⓕ	Ⓣ Ⓕ	○
106	Ⓣ Ⓕ	Ⓣ Ⓕ	○	114	Ⓣ Ⓕ	Ⓣ Ⓕ	○
107	Ⓣ Ⓕ	Ⓣ Ⓕ	○	115	Ⓣ Ⓕ	Ⓣ Ⓕ	○
108	Ⓣ Ⓕ	Ⓣ Ⓕ	○				

FOR OFFICIAL USE ONLY				
R/C	W/S1	FS/S2	CS/S3	WS

PLEASE DO NOT WRITE IN THIS AREA   ○   **SERIAL #**

Show up ready on test day.

Watch **free** online lessons
for science from Khan Academy®.

satsubjecttests.org/biology
satsubjecttests.org/chemistry
satsubjecttests.org/physics

There are over 100 videos to watch covering
a variety of science topics. These lessons are
great refreshers to help you get ready for the
science Subject Tests in Biology, Chemistry,
and Physics.

Disclaimer: Playlists were created based on videos available on Khan Academy.
Content is subject to change in the future.

 |